# PSYCHEDELIC MYSTERIES OF THE FEMININE

"Words like 'essential knowledge' and 'provocative' somehow fail to do justice to the content between these covers. These are contemporary, controversial issues in psychedelics that aren't adequately being addressed elsewhere: abuses of power and the ethical behavior of psychedelic guides and shamans and the role of psychedelics not only in women reclaiming their power but in deconstructing the gender binary. There is mystery and potential in the feminine, the yin shadow. That darkness is an important piece of the power and glory that is woman. I applaud this project and recommend it heartfully. It is crucial information that needs to be integrated into the psychedelic community and the larger tribe of humanity. Also, the artwork is gorgeous and inspiring."

JULIE HOLLAND, M.D., EDITOR OF *ECSTASY: THE COMPLETE GUIDE* AND *THE POT BOOK*

"This edited volume presents a wide-ranging history of the roots of the current psychedelic renaissance. From the ancient rites of Dionysus, scholars and practitioners explore how the Sacred Feminine opens a doorway into the Divine via both ecstatic trance and an embodied connection to nature. *Psychedelic Mysteries of the Feminine* is a valuable addition to all collections of psychedelic mysticism."

RACHEL HARRIS, PH.D., AUTHOR OF *LISTENING TO AYAHUASCA*

"This impressive volume weaves together an evolving understanding of the psychedelic feminine through essays and art. The call for all people to embrace the Divine Feminine in its many forms is loud and clear in this celebration of the feminine voice and historical perspective. We have the power to transform our culture and our world. This anthology is a wonderful aid in discovering a path toward love, healing, and balance."

RICK DOBLIN, PH.D., FOUNDER AND EXECUTIVE DIRECTOR OF THE
MULTIDISCIPLINARY ASSOCIATION FOR PSYCHEDELIC STUDIES

"This book is packed with ideas, information, and analysis on the importance of the feminine in psychedelic, ecstatic, and shamanic practice—topics I find utterly fascinating and sorely needed in this time of crisis, with our longing for transition and with our need for inspiration and magic beyond our current paradigm."

GAIL BRADBROOK, PH.D., COFOUNDER OF EXTINCTION REBELLION

"From this groundbreaking collection there emerges a specific feminine approach to mind-altering substances, a phenomenon that has been breaking through and doing its part in driving the psychedelic renaissance. The multicultural contributors speak from their personal experiences with entheogens. The female perspective amplifies the yin component at the heart of the visionary plant experience. There is authenticity and activism here, along with a wide-ranging body of tremendously useful information enhanced with mind-bending shamanic art."

MICHAEL HOROWITZ, COEDITOR OF *SISTERS OF THE EXTREME:
WOMEN WRITING ON THE DRUG EXPERIENCE*

"*Psychedelic Mysteries of the Feminine* is an essential addition to the world's psychedelic library. A superbly conceived, edited, and visually stimulating anthology in which a chorus of activists, researchers, visionaries, and fourth-wave feminist voices offer remedies to the challenges of our time."

GRAHAM ST JOHN, AUTHOR OF *MYSTERY SCHOOL IN
HYPERSPACE: A CULTURAL HISTORY OF DMT*

# PSYCHEDELIC MYSTERIES OF THE FEMININE

## FEMININE

### CREATIVITY • ECSTASY • HEALING

Edited by Maria Papaspyrou,
Chiara Baldini & David Luke

Park Street Press
Rochester, Vermont

Park Street Press
One Park Street
Rochester, Vermont 05767
www.ParkStPress.com

Park Street Press is a division of Inner Traditions International

**Library of Congress Cataloging-in-Publication Data**

Names: Papaspyrou, Maria, editor. | Baldini, Chiara, editor. | Luke, David, editor.
Title: Psychedelic mysteries of the feminine : creativity, ecstasy, and healing / edited by Maria Papaspyrou, Chiara Baldini, and David Luke.
Description: Rochester, Vermont : Park Street Press, [2019] | Includes bibliographical references and index.
Identifiers: LCCN 2018035491 (print) | LCCN 2018037534 (ebook) | ISBN 9781620558027 (pbk.) | ISBN 9781620558034 (ebook)
Subjects: LCSH: Goddess religion. | Hallucinogenic drugs. | Feminism—Religious aspects.
Classification: LCC BL473.5 .P79 2019 (print) | LCC BL473.5 (ebook) | DDC 282.092—dc23
LC record available at https://lccn.loc.gov/2018035491

Printed and bound in the United States by McNaughton & Gunn, Inc.

10  9  8  7  6  5  4  3

Text design and layout by Virginia Scott Bowman
This book was typeset in Garamond Premier Pro with Jensen, Gill Sans, and Avenir used as display typefaces
Artwork used with permission.

To send correspondence to the author of this book, mail a first-class letter to the author c/o Inner Traditions • Bear & Company, One Park Street, Rochester, VT 05767, and we will forward the communication, or contact the authors directly: Maria Papaspyrou at **www.towardswholeness.co.uk**, Chiara Baldini at **https://chiarabaldini.academia.edu**, and David Luke at **https://www.gre.ac.uk/eduhea/study/pswc/staff/dr-david-luke**.

※

*This book is dedicated to those young girls and boys (and all genders inbetween) growing up in these difficult times. May you find inspiration in these words and bring their seeds into the future, so that a better world— more just, more balanced, more psychedelic, and more feminist—can emerge from the ashes of this one.*

# Contents

❧

## PART 1
### Archetypal Dimensions of the Feminine Principle

PART 2

# Ancient Roots of Female Shamanism

PART 3

# Embodied Paths to Ecstasy

# Acknowledgments

We the editors wish to express our enormous gratitude to all the writers and artists that have generously contributed their work and energy for this volume with great enthusiasm, knowledge, and passion. They are all listed in the pages that follow and have been a great team to collaborate with over the course of three years.

We would like to thank Inner Traditions for expertly supporting and housing this project throughout its journey, especially Jon Graham for opening the doors to this book by trusting its message and integrity, Kelly Bowen and Manzanita Carpenter Sanz for guiding us through the intricate publishing process, and Patricia Rydle and Kayla Toher for carefully and meticulously metabolizing this anthology to its final form and structure with incredible editing expertise. There were many others behind the scenes who fine-tuned the production of this book, and we are thankful for their efforts toward the end result.

We thank William Montgomery for his skillful, precious editing help "in service of the goddess" while staying in Portugal, and to all those who have crossed our paths and have inspired our work, either directly or indirectly. We are lucky to be part of a vibrant web of soulful and inquisitive hearts and minds.

We would like to express our respect and gratefulness for collective spaces like Boom Festival and Breaking Convention that have offered us transformative initiations and have supported the emergence and expansion of consciousness and collaborations.

We pay homage to Maria Sabina, the first woman shaman to be recognized as such in modern culture, to Kai Wingo, who was planning to participate but crossed over to the other side while this book was in the making, and to all our allies and guides from the otherworlds.

Most importantly, we would like to thank our families and our partners, Stuart, Diogo, Anna, as well as Bridget, the starry little future seed, and friends who have nourished and sustained us along this winding path.

We are truly grateful and moved to witness how much human energy and potency can gather around ideas that really matter! Without all of you, this book would not exist.

# Psysterhood

### Allyson Grey

The voices and cries of our psychedelic sisters, from Sappho to Maria Sabina, are connected through a secret language that transcends time. We carry the mysterious womb of creation within us. We birth new realities. We are Maya, the divine veil of materiality. We are spider women, spinning stories of connection. We are the Earth Mother now desecrated. This impressive volume demonstrates the generous genius of the Goddess. Our spiritual sisterhood unites us with an often-silenced majority. Now it is our turn to tell our story.

At age seventeen in 1969, I moved to college and began tripping fairly often: journeying with psychedelic friends, camping around a fire in the Rocky Mountains, a daylong bicycle ride, dancing to Led Zeppelin at an art school party, and even alone, observing in the quad. This ritual of socially interactive self-medicating healed me, opened me, deepened me. Every experience, both enlightening and terrifying, enriched my consciousness and offered great learning.

In 1971, influenced by Ram Dass's essential book *Be Here Now,* two friends joined me in my tiny college bedroom intending to witness the "white light." With only that aim and a dark, quiet space, after three years of psychedelic journeys, I saw the infinite, interconnected glowing light. It was the glue of the universe, like white neon, defining edges and permeating every being and thing. Secret writing, an untranslatable symbol system, appeared to me as the language of the Almighty force of the universe. The sacred language washed over all surfaces in the room and floated through the air like moving ribbons. This inexplicable vision lifted the veil on material reality and revealed a divine intelligence, speaking in a visionary language of the spiritual nature of all things.

Looking around my room, beholding the genderless, disembodied energy of the Almighty, it all made sense to me. *God* was the word invented to describe this. In my heart, cultivated in the Jewish tradition, this realization was aligned with all that I intuited about Adonai (the secret Hebrew name of God, literally meaning "Almighty"). In my experience of the white light, the facade of material existence became transparent, revealing a luminous holy realm. I was introduced to the possibility of realizing the holy in every moment.

God contact turned my life upside down. From that point onward my mind changed. I began meditating with the Yogi Bhajan community in Provincetown, Massachusetts. Friends changed.

It was psychedelics that introduced me to my beloved, lifelong partner, collaborator, and best friend. In 1975, after he experienced his first LSD dose at a party in my apartment, he shared with me his overnight transformation from suicidal nihilistic atheist to full-on mystic. This was the first man who had ever declared to me that he had seen God, and I knew I had found my soul mate.

Witnessing the mystic realm of visionary reality connected us with a clandestine family, an underground international love tribe united by higher visions. Psychedelics have catalyzed an evolution of gender consciousness and balance across ethnic and racial divides. The expansion of consciousness and conscience resulting from altered states calls for cognitive liberty and decriminalizing sacred substances to restore their sacramental status. I am more than happy to do my part. Invited to speak in praise and gratitude of my psysters is an honor I cherish. The remorseless oppression of women, over half the world's population, is a blight on our species and can likely be blamed for moral and ecological degradation. In a rare television appearance from 1975, Simone de Beauvoir displayed her grasp of this injustice when she stated:

> In the Middle Ages, and in the Renaissance, the female physician had much power. They knew about remedies and herbs, the "old wives" remedies which were sometimes of great value. Then medicine was taken away from them by men. All of the witch-hunts were basically a way for men to keep women away from medicine and the power it conferred. In the 18th and 19th centuries statutes were drafted by men that prevented women—who were imprisoned, fined, and otherwise persecuted—from practicing medicine unless they had attended certain schools, which did not admit them anyway. Women were relegated to the role of nurses, of Florence Nightingale, as aides and assistants.

Psychedelics call in fair-mindedness and a world that works for everyone. Yet at many psychedelic conferences, women have been underrepresented as featured speakers. Accomplished, innovative women are called to step up and become recognized as bright minds and vocal leaders. The study of the voice of women is only a few decades old and growing rapidly. Women are changing *herstory* with their emerging voices in this evolving discussion. This would be a good time to thank the Women's Visionary Congress for their important work in the United States.

As this book celebrates the feminine, we should note the goddess Seshet of ancient Egypt, who is credited as the inventor of writing. The name Seshet means "she who is the scribe." Seshet is often portrayed writing with a stylus on a palm stem, bearing notches as she records the passage of time. Egyptian art also frequently depicts Seshet with a seven-leafed plant, likely cannabis, that appears to sprout from the crown of her head. Over the plant is always a protective umbrella, shaped like a breast, with a round nipple pointing up to heaven. Spell 10 of the Egyptian Coffin Texts states, "Seshet opens the gates of heaven for you" (Buck, 1935).

Mystic language is a sign of the Divine. Maria Sabina was the Mexican *curandera* medicine woman who introduced psilocybin mushrooms to the world in 1955. Speaking of her altered-state encounter with secret writing, the holy woman said, "I also see the words fall, they come from up above, as if they were little luminous objects falling from the sky. The language falls on the sacred table, falls on my body. Then with my hands I catch word after word" (Rothenberg, 2003, 73). For Maria, the sacred language was a tool she used to heal members of her community.

May the words of this volume bring healing to our culture.

Hail, *Psychedelic Mysteries of the Feminine,* for bringing together dozens of empowered women and our male allies to create this anthology. The altered state has made us present, even indignant, activated, and vocal about the injustices that intolerably persist. United, our voices are strong and are shifting cultural presumptions. Grateful thanks to all my psysters for sharing their deepest wounds and highest healings, modeling a path toward eco-consciousness, love, health, creativity, and gender balance, with the potential to transform our species and our world.

ALLYSON GREY is a painter and social sculptor. With a graduate degree from Tufts University in Boston, Grey has long been an art educator, arts organizer, and muse to artists worldwide. Since art school in 1975, Allyson has collaborated and shared a studio with her husband, artist Alex Grey. The Greys cofounded the Chapel of Sacred Mirrors, a spiritual retreat center for artists in

Wappingers Falls, New York. Together, Allyson and Alex have painted onstage in dozens of cities in front of thousands of dancing young people at festivals and arenas across five continents, including Broadway theaters in New York City. As longtime advocates of "cognitive liberty," a growing international "sacramental culture" has embraced the Greys as mapmakers and spokespersons of the visionary realm. Turn to plate 1 of the color insert to see art by Allyson Grey.

# INTRODUCTION

# The Genesis of Feminine Consciousness

In 2015, during Breaking Convention—a biennial multidisciplinary conference on psychedelic consciousness held in London—a panel was curated by Maria Papaspyrou under the name *Femtheogenesis*. The intention was to bring together a collective of female voices from psychedelic culture that would explore the links between the feminine principle and altered states of consciousness. What emerged were five compelling, soulful, and inspiring presentations that ignited the hearts and minds of those who spoke and those who listened. When the panel discussion was over, the editors of this book—Maria, Chiara, and David—felt compelled to collect more voices and to spread all of the stories far and wide, for it is our belief that the world is ready for their message.

This book is the product of the times it emerges in, times of immense sociopolitical, economic, ecological, and spiritual upheavals and transformations. These are times that put our individual and collective value systems to the test, and we are called to reflect deeply on how we exist on this planet and in relation to one another. There is a recognition that for humanity to survive, we are called to restore the balance between the opposites, to support wholeness and unity.

This book wishes to be a small yet important step in that direction.

It moves in service toward an emerging paradigm of a co-creative relationship between the masculine and feminine principles. In so doing, it allows the female and the feminine to emerge, be heard, and be known, may it be about women's perspectives or the feminine expression inside any human being. In particular we feel that the psychedelic scene, where this book emerges from, has the potential to be deeply involved in this process of rebalancing, for it holds the seeds of awareness of the "bigger picture" of wholeness and oneness—the unity beyond duality.

This work therefore is the fruit of the merging of two different yet resonant cultural currents, the one propelling what has been called the *psychedelic renaissance,* the other bringing forth the regeneration of *feminine consciousness* as part of *fourth-wave feminism.* In this it gives voice to those researchers and activists taking over two of the most relevant struggles of the sixties and pushing them to the next level.

In the pages that follow a great weaving has taken place. You will hear the passionate voices of those involved in psychedelic scientific studies and research, the flourishing expansion of festival culture, or the reconnection to indigenous wisdom and its message of oneness with nature. You will witness the rediscovery of the sacred "technology" of plant medicines cross-pollinating with activist campaigns addressing structural and systemic problems derived from gender discrimination. You will journey through the growing interest in reframing the dynamics between the masculine and the feminine polarity, the psycho-spiritual effects of the reemergence of the goddess archetype on an individual and a collective level, and a growing awareness of the political and social consequences of gender inequality on a global scale. You will view the wonderful and inspiring artwork that some of the visionary contributors to this anthology have produced.

Feminine consciousness, when intermingled with psychedelic knowledge, carries and reveals the essence of inclusivity, interconnectedness, and balance. These perspectives strive to emerge into our collective consciousness from a distant past, with the purpose of importing much-needed values into the systems and paradigms they aim to upgrade. In many ways one needs the other to avoid the risk of remaining closed off to the very essence that permeates its own philosophy.

In psychedelic conferences, journals, books, and research projects the lack of diversity in terms of class, ethnicity, gender, and religion is still evident, and this absence generates a need of being reflected upon and collectively addressed. These matters have energy that, if gathered and harnessed, can propel the psychedelic paradigm where it should be leading from: the forefront of inclusivity, celebrating diversity and oneness, bridging the splits and threading the paradoxes.

This is the gap that this book wants to bridge. This is a labor of love and dedicated research of more than two years, combing the work of established researchers, Ph.D. students, modern medicine women, artists, therapists, anthropologists, historians, and many more. In these pages you will find structure and abstraction, research, dreams, whispers, and screams walking side by side, complementing, augmenting, and holding each other.

We start in the depths of time and soul, in the collective archetypal lands of equally bright light and darkness, the depository of humanity's psychic inheritance. The journey begins with Maria Papaspyrou, who explores the links between the archetypal feminine, altered states of consciousness, and nature, discovering that their shared qualities have also been the very reason for their suppression. She argues that the archetypal feminine is a psychic construct that belongs to both men and women, and restoring it is a collective responsibility. The work of Patricia 'Iolana is next. She explores two paths to Goddess consciousness in support of our connection to the archetypal feminine, the archetypal analytic, and the embodied ritual, illustrating how they can deliver us to deep psychic work with the anima. The next chapter is Tim Read's essay on inner encounters with the transformative powers of the dark and devouring aspect of the archetypal feminine through altered states and holotropic breathwork. He equates such a journey to an ego death-and-rebirth experience, leading to a closer relationship with the archetypal self.

From the archetypal realms we move toward the nearest human expressions of these spaces, the shamanic rituals and lore of different lands and times. In this section of the book Max Dashu gives a well-researched account demonstrating that women have been shamans and oracles since time immemorial, defying in their rituals what is considered humanly possible. Her essay takes us through the African, Asian, American, and European continents, providing a much needed view into diverse cultural expressions of shamanic customs and practices across the world. The rest of the chapter focuses on female shamans harnessing techniques of ecstasy and altered consciousness in healing and purification rituals, both in southern and northern Europe. Moving on, the *maenadic* rites of Dionysus described by Chiara Baldini are seen as the missing link between primitive goddess shamanic traditions and the practices of the witches of modern Europe, enticing the spirits of both women and men in rites and rituals that transcended binary sexual identity. Carl Ruck's essay explains how symbols connected to both masculine and feminine sexual organs, together with the use of psychotropic substances, were used in Mystery religions of ancient Greece as a way to underline the importance of the balance and union of opposites as the core of mystical knowledge. In the case of northern Europe, Maria Christine Kvilhaug introduces us to the *vǫlvas* of Norse mythology. These were highly respected women, carriers of ancient knowledge pertaining to powerful rituals of witchcraft and shamanism, which were able to affect people, animals, and the environment.

The conclusion of the chapter on shamanistic practices leads to the next stage of this book, into the realms of the embodied experience as a source of wisdom and, ultimately, of life itself. Christa Mackinnon begins by highlighting the links between the archetypal feminine and Earth, underlining the patriarchal domination process of both. She explores the importance of embodied work and shamanic trance dancing as a process of reclaiming the vitality of the feminine principle. Alana Bliss reveals how giving birth can be seen as a highly psychedelic, ecstatic, and even orgasmic experience, considering how the body, through the release of specific hormones, supports this journey into an altered state. The following chapter by Shonagh Home introduces us to some very special women using techniques of altered states in therapeutic contexts, thus reclaiming women's heritage as shamanic healers within the current cultural paradigm.

From the realm of the body, we move toward the definition of principles inspired by a feminine perspective. Kathleen Harrison gifts us with her psychedelic wisdom on those feminine qualities of awareness that can support the recognition of aliveness and consciousness across creation—from plants, to animals, to the Earth itself. This enables the triggering of a cultural process wherein communication channels can be established to support and promote the thriving of life. Next, Anna Luke defines radical uncertainty as a fundamental aspect of existence that has been deeply undervalued by the prevailing patriarchal culture. She argues that plant medicines might offer a much-needed bridge back to a certain reverence for darkness and a capacity to tolerate uncertainty, as an increasingly urgent social and environmental need. Eleonora Molnar concludes this section of the book with an essay on bioethics within the context of psychoactive substance use. She discusses the detrimental effects of their transgression and how as a community we need to maintain a collective voice, able to safeguard ritual spaces for the exploration of altered states of consciousness. She particularly references shamanic circles, but her notes and words of caution are relevant to any setting where people's vulnerability should only be matched with an adequate level of integrity on the part of the space holders.

From feminine perspectives we follow the trail to a place of current thoughts and ideas, tracing the edges of a new cultural paradigm through contemporary gender discourse. Lorna Olivia O'Dowd challenges the notion of "femininity" against generalizing notions of the normalized "masculinity," claiming how psychedelic research and particularly indigenous shamanic practices involving psychoactive plants can offer a way of disrupting binaries in favor of a more fluid and complex vision. This is echoed in the next essay by Cameron Adams and Timothy Davis, which challenges those associations of psychedelic substances with feminine entities commonly claimed within the psychedelic community as inconsistent with ethnographic research. They claim that any gendered associations are derived through our cognitive and cultural filters and bias. They go on to posit that the psychedelic experience can actually allow us to transcend societal norms, beyond a binary perspective on gender, as exemplified by shamanic practices supported by transvestism and gender fluidity.

The perfect container for decomposition and deconstruction is the vessel of the creative process, wherein inspiration functions as a channel for the mysterious forces inhabiting our deeper psychic layers. Martina Hoffmann shares with us that her creative process moves her beyond any preplanning of what she will depict on the canvas, allowing herself to be in service of the ineffable creative energy springing from within. She thus unfolds her creative expression, drawing from visionary experiences of altered states, often channeling the manifestation of feminine presence and energy. This connection to inner and outer realms that moves the creative process is also echoed by Amanda Sage, who herself has found the faces of many feminine archetypes flowing through her paintbrush. Her work is her offering to the world, to awaken a call to action, a remembering of who we truly are and where our collective potential lies. Alana Bliss reminds of the sacred nature of giving birth. Omolewa closes this section by stirring the soul in the direction of the wondrous creative force held in women's bodies.

The final section of the book is dedicated to feminist psychedelic activism; it is a space to seed ideas toward collective action. Annie Oak talks about the creation of the Women's Visionary Congress as a way to gather a council of wisewomen experienced in psychedelic knowledge. She discusses the core values they have been building on to develop a sustainable community of inquiry. Adam Aronovich offers a significant critique about the current medical ethos that pervades Western psychiatry. He offers thoughts on an alternative, postpatriarchal, postcolonial, inclusive medical model that returns the spirit, the intuitive body, and the heart back into the treatment, much in line with the healing process supported by plant medicines. In the next essay, Nadia Erlam uses a feminist filter to explore the current drug classification system and reveal its discriminatory bias against neurodiversity. Nadia illustrates the power struggles and the colonial trajectory that hide behind the criminalization of psychedelic substances. As the book nears its end, Charlotte Walsh offers us a meticulous critique of the current state of drug laws while illuminating a way to move forward. She asserts that the current propaganda-based drug classification system is violating the fundamental human right of altering one's consciousness, constituting an infringement on the principle of cognitive liberty. She argues that unless this fundamental right is respected and upheld, conditions for a more just society that is able to support the flourishing of humanity's full potential will never take hold. A final coda punctuates the end of the book, summarizing what we hope to have achieved in these pages.

Because this book aims to fill the underrepresentation of female speakers in the psychedelic community, we agreed that we would prioritize female voices, but we also felt that male voices belong in the space too. However, we are aware that the contributions only offer a portion of the whole picture. In fact, the feminine that has begun to find voice and space is predominantly cisgender white middle-class, and we need to acknowledge that a gap still remains. This anthology wishes to contribute to opening the way to the new postpatriarchal paradigm. We hope that an increased number of diverse voices will soon find the inspiration to "come out of the closet" and bring forth their unique and precious perspectives.

~

**PART 1**

Archetypal Dimensions of
the Feminine Principle

# 1

# Femtheogenic Consciousness

## Archetypal Energies of Regeneration

### Maria Papaspyrou

*Femtheogens* is a compound word made up of *feminine* and *entheogens*. *Entheogens* is yet another compound word derived from *entheo* and *genesis*. It refers to the mystical and sacred properties of the psychedelic experience. *Femtheogens,* through its roots in *entheogens,* refers to the feminized sacredness of the experiences such substances can induce. *Femtheogens* is as much a word as it is a concept. It refers to the capacity of the entheogenic experience to revive the broken Sacred Feminine and filter its essence through to us. This capacity is enhanced by the strong connections between the archetypal feminine and the entheogenic experience. The two share qualities that can heal, transform, and support the expansion of our consciousness. These qualities are also major points of suppression for both, as they run counter to our Western mind-set and emergent social paradigms.

## Archetypal Feminine Realms

In trying to reveal some of the feminine nature and quality, I will be focusing on the archetypal feminine. Archetypes are inherited psychic systems that are deeply buried within the collective strata of our unconscious, serving as primal inner maps of our human nature. These collective psychic entities are primarily expressed through symbols and metaphors. Their fundamental task is to mediate between unconscious depths and consciousness, facilitating integration of the two and enabling our potential for wholeness. The feminine archetype is not a singular entity. It manifests in a multitude of aspects, and, like all archetypes, she occupies a spectrum that ranges from light to darkness. As an archetype, the feminine is always and ever present, inhabiting the depths of our collective unconscious where the archetypes reside. From here she addresses us both individually and collectively. In our collective disconnection from the archetypal feminine voice and essence we have lost our ability to integrate her energies and offerings. But her essence is relevant to every one of us, because the feminine is an elemental pattern we all carry within ourselves, whether we are a man or a woman. And she is also relevant to everything around us, because the feminine is the one half of the Divine Androgyne, which is the deepest archetype that permeates all of creation.

Gareth Hill is a Jungian analyst who has explored the intrapsychic aspects of gender. He has divided the feminine in her static and her dynamic aspect, mapping out the deepest and most essential qualities of the feminine force. The *static feminine* (Hill 1992) is connected to motherhood and nourishment, gestating deep primal secrets of creation within her body. She can conceive the potential of life and give birth to it, participating in the great mystery of manifesting a soul into material life (Vaughan-Lee 2013). In that mystery, the feminine participates in the forces of creation and regeneration. It is this feminine link to regeneration that makes her central to our collective healing process. Woman magic and earth magic are linked; they both create and nourish life

(Campbell, Moyers, and Flowers 1991). The static feminine is impersonal like nature, and serves the collective goals of life on Earth, which are the preservation of all species and survival. For our early ancestors, the feminine link with nature was at first a point of worship, until man tried to control, manipulate, and suppress the force of the feminine and nature, creating a deep imbalance in his relationship with both.

The *dynamic feminine* (Hill 1992) is represented by a surrendering watery flow "towards the new, the non-rational, and the playful" (17). She is spontaneous, responsive, intuitive, and forms according to what fate brings her way. She receives her wisdom by engaging with direct experience and is receptive to knowledge that belongs to the deep inner worlds. She opens us to sublime encounters and owns the spaces of spontaneous realization. She is connected to the creative and regenerative aspects of chaos and supports the expansive creative synthesis of new possibilities and subsequent evolution. The dynamic feminine represents spaces that can be fascinating and ecstatic as well as terrifying and disorienting, and these are watery transient spaces that as a society we have learned to resist.

In today's society, the Goddess has lost her lineage and her priestesses. In the absence of her guides, she meets us in the land of the unconscious (Woodman and Dickson 1997) and the realms of altered consciousness, where her feminine work can go on undisturbed. She communicates with us through the archaic symbolic language of dreams and imagination. In our Western world we focus on language, which is the ordered and rational container of experience—a masculine principle. The realms beyond that space belong to the feminine, and there we meet that which is beyond words.

The words we hold the feminine in control her essence and energies. By holding the feminine in words like *irrational, emotional, hysterical, subjective,* and *chaotic* we have linked her with energies that our societies have always feared and tried to control. However, the word *feminine* refers to the soul (Baring 2013). It is a reference to the cosmic thread that connects us to each other and to the rest of creation. It acknowledges our interconnectedness and place within a cosmic sacred order, linking us to life and the Divine.

The myths we have held the feminine in have also denied her true essence. In the Garden of Eden, Eve took a bite from the apple of the sacred tree of knowledge. This was a mythos that repressed both the feminine and expanded awareness into sin within our consciousness, merging them with the shadow side. Mythologically and symbolically, this was the onset point of ego development for our species. To leave the garden was to gain self-awareness; up until that point we lived in the unconscious Eden. Today, in our predominantly ego-driven reality, we still keep femtheogenic consciousness in exile; we systematically maintain its inferiority, and we remain suspicious of its depth and potential. The feminine and entheogens have been suppressed because their force and energy could not be assimilated by our species. We have distorted both to a diabolical form and seen them as dangerous and seductive forces that threaten the status quo. The primordial temptress and the *evil* snake were separated in our consciousness from what they and the apple really stood for: the potential for transformation.

## Femtheogenic Consciousness

How we relate to the points below can have a profound effect on how we experience and relate to the world around us, and in effect recalibrate our moral compass. But for that to happen, we must resurrect the true and deeper essence of both the feminine and entheogens from the tenebrous depths of our unconscious, where both have been repressed by patriarchy. Patriarchy, both outer and internalized, serves the status quo, casting a heavy shadow toward anything that threatens its structures. It is in that collective shadow that the feminine and her potential reside.

The links between the archetypal feminine and entheogenic spaces offer us a glimpse into their great force and power, but also into what has been the basis of their suppression. Once their links unfold, a triptych emerges. It contains the feminine, entheogens, and nature, revealing their interconnectedness and how each contains and reveals deep aspects of the other.

## The Links Between the Archetypal Feminine and Altered States of Consciousness

One of the major insights femtheogenic consciousness opens us up to is the awareness of connectedness and oneness. Our developing ego consciousness created the illusion of separateness, which has eroded our connection and relationship with Earth, each other, and the deepest nature of our own selves. Operating from a fragmented, disconnected, and desacralized state, we lost our knowing of the primary symbiotic links that held together humanity, nature, and spirit. From that new consciousness of separateness and humanity's attempts to deny its vulnerability against nature and the great chaotic forces of the universe, our relational structures became increasingly hierarchical, with our species in the dominator's position. And from that narcissistic bubble, all we can recognize in the mirrors of the world around us is ourselves (Woodman and Dickson 1997) and our own needs. We have assumed that our needs allow us to control and manipulate all natural resources, and we have been attacking the forces of creation that have sustained us for centuries and our links with anything that truly nourishes. We have created a crisis that is environmental, social, and spiritual.

Femtheogenic consciousness operates in the spheres of oneness. This oneness is a spiritual connection that reveals the reflections we emit to each other. We are all mirrors of our shared humanity, and we all hold each other within ourselves. This oneness is not only a metaphysical idea (Vaughan-Lee 2013). It is the oneness that chaos theorists have called "the butterfly effect," wherein a butterfly flaps its wings on one continent and causes a hurricane, weeks later, on another. This is the oneness that reveals itself in the intricate dance of cause and effect. It is the oneness of quantum physics and the oneness in Rupert Sheldrake's (2011) theory of morphic resonance.

The feminine consciousness is by nature aware that everything is connected. This is a knowledge the feminine has always carried in her body's centers of creation, where all life emerges and regenerates from. Similarly, in the infinite realms of entheogenic channels, we can witness the threads of our interconnectedness and interdependence. Here we encounter the pulsating presence of Indra's net and meet the potential of reawakening our links with each other, nature, the divine, and ultimately—ourselves. The invisible space of singularity that femtheogenic consciousness reveals us to contains Eros at its core. To recognize its presence is to awaken to the most powerful force in the universe.

The next femtheogenic consciousness link is boundary-dissolving experiences. Our societies are based on divisive boundaries that maintain the illusion of our separateness, and the ultimate and most dreaded boundary to cross is the dissolution of the ego. The ego has been a big part of our evolution, and as a concept in itself it can have many useful functions. What is dysfunctional is our need to hold on to it. The ego needs to undergo many deaths if we are to transform into a more authentic version of ourselves. We need to peel through the layers to reach through to the core of who we really are.

The essence of feminine consciousness is based on the elementary feminine experience of boundary dissolution, motherhood, where the "other" is contained within oneself. That symbiotic bond between mother and offspring is not merely a physical one, for it extends way beyond the physical birthing process. Entheogenic experiences are also, by their very nature, based on the dissolution of boundaries on various levels. In these realms, the divisive lines between past, present, and future, us and "other," conscious and unconscious, masculine and feminine, dissolve. This dissolution is the most threatening aspect of entheogenic consciousness for individuals and the general status quo (McKenna and Hagerty 2007). Both the Great Goddess and entheogenic journeys deliver us to a point where in order to evolve we need to transcend our boundaries and release ourselves from the ego-driven mirage of our delicate reality.

The next femtheogenic consciousness link relates to chaos. We have battled for generations to tame chaos because we have perceived it to be one of our greatest survival threats. It hasn't always been like that. The early Gnostics and alchemists recognized chaos as a vital element of the creative process of transformation. Today we relate to chaos as a state of disintegration rather than a stage of transformation. We have failed to acknowledge the inherent order it contains because its nature is creative rather than linear—it is not to be imposed, it is to emerge (Woodman and Dickson 1997). In its field reside the rhythms of matter and the deeper wisdom of the creative process.

To our ancestors, the Goddess was linked with nature. Nature held the archetypes of the Great Mother on one end, seeming to give continually in a limitless way, and the Devouring Mother on the other end, turning ruthless and unreserved. Our early ancestors gradually viewed nature as a chaotic force that needed to be controlled, and they reflected that onto the feminine, installing our unconscious collective link between the feminine and chaos. But the archetypal feminine, in its *dynamic aspect,* has a creative link with chaos, and that is a link with the transformative and regenerative aspects of chaos.

Entheogenic journeys embrace chaos and its transformative potential and teach us it is a valued stage in our unfolding process of individuation. During a deep entheogenic journey we are taken apart and then put back together. Chaos gives birth to a new order that is of greater complexity than before, a step further on our evolutionary journey (Papaspyrou 2015). A big part of what drove our connection with nature, the Goddess, and entheogens underground is our collective difficulty to be with chaos. Femtheogenic consciousness holds the potential of reviving that relationship in a meaningful way.

The next femtheogenic link relates to the vital cycles of life, death, and rebirth. To our early ancestors, the feminine powers of fertility and birth were a reflection of the cosmic regeneration they witnessed in nature. Nature's wisdom taught them that death is a stage of regeneration rather than an end in itself. Today we relate to death with dread, unable to face its vital essence and relate to it on a deeper level, and we are immersed in a collective and all-encompassing denial of it. The goddess Kali is a powerful archetypal feminine symbol of the regenerative wisdom. In Kali's terms, the goddess who gives life is the goddess who takes life. Creation gives place to destruction, and destruction that is in service to life gives place to creation, a ceaseless movement that is indifferent to our ego's demands for survival (Woodman and Dickson 1997).

According to C. G. Jung, "the descent into the depths always seems to precede the ascent" (Jung 1968, 19). We can only recover our inner gifts and treasures by meeting the dark side of the archetypal feminine: the devourer and the transformer. Similarly, the most potent entheogenic experiences that people report the greatest and most profound changes from are journeys within a supportive set and setting, unfolding into the ultimate spiritual experience of ego death. Femtheogenic consciousness allows us to flee our ego, if only for a second, and receive the wisdom that necessitates and even welcomes death. That is not to negate the painful experience of crossing the transition portals of change, death, and loss. But it does allow us to access the femtheogenic wisdom that teaches us that on a soul level, things are very different, because our souls know that every end is a drop in a vast ocean (Woodman and Dickson 1997).

The next femtheogenic link relates to time. Time is a major symbol in our society and one that we have learned to treat as a fixed and static construct. But the feminine rhythms of regeneration reveal *timelessness*. The archetypal goddess of birth contains a soul that moves through various birth canals. She participates in a mystery that intersects time. She moves us out of *chronos* into the territory of *kairos* that holds the eternal moment—the past, present, and future—in unity. Entheogenic spaces also hold timelessness, revealing to us, within a journey, mysteries that defy our ordinary experiential parameters and boundaries, allowing us to move through past, present, and future in extraordinary ways. Through femtheogenic consciousness we come to witness and experience a very different sense of time.

The next femtheogenic link is creativity. Patriarchy has suppressed our creative forces by focusing on logic and the mind. But femtheogenic consciousness supports the creative dimension of our evolution. The feminine is the creative matrix of life for our species. She resonates with the patterns that belong to creation. The archetypal feminine is also linked to experience, immersion, and surrender; yielding and responsive, she channels the energies of imagination. Entheogenic journeys are highly creative spaces. They *speak* to us through symbols, images, and feeling states that are carried forward by visions. These openings create metaphors that connect us to that which is beyond words or beyond immediate perception. These are the same spaces that the artists, the visionaries, the mystics, and the shamans navigate and draw their inspiration and wisdom from. But our societies have not acknowledged the creative and ultimately healing potential of these spaces, and we only relate to them as chaotic, destructive, and dangerous.

Femtheogenic consciousness carries a particular kind of *knowing* that our culture has long neglected and avoided, estranging us from the watery initiations of femtheogenic awareness. Our cultural estrangement from feminine and entheogenic sources of intelligence has deprived us from knowledge that penetrates deep within the reaches of the invisible. Femtheogenic knowing is intuitive, nonlinear, and informed by the creative source. It has the potency to reveal us to the invisible, and that includes the invisible corners of our psyche. This is where our shadow lives. Claiming our shadow and its darkness helps us cultivate compassion for ourselves, and in reflection, for others. This is where we encounter the limitations of our human nature and where the heart works on forgiveness. The mind carries the logic while the heart carries the wisdom (Woodman and Dickson 1997). In this deeply reflective space, dualities fall through; here we can heal the psychic divides we have succumbed to and invoke the restorative inner forces of integration.

Femtheogenic consciousness opens us up to spontaneous, instinctual, and authentic ways of living. In trying to shield ourselves from our impermanence and lack of control, we have learned to perceive the world and reality as concrete. This concreteness offers us a "safety," but it can also lead to staleness and deadness, which is ironically the very thing our egos are trying to avoid. We operate from a state of doing unable to tolerate a state of being (Woodman and Dickson 1997). Femtheogenic consciousness embraces change and impermanence, aware that this is the foundational basis of evolutionary drives.

The true essence of the feminine is not bound by rules or order. She exists in a freedom that is full of potential. She is not identified with the social personas that we are predestined to hold on to in our patriarchal society; she is receptive to experience with a sense of self that is expansive. Entheogens too, by dissolving our egos, allow us to die and rebirth infinite times within the space of a few hours, shaking away our social masks and helping us question the unquestionable. In these spaces we can encounter wholeness and a natural intelligence that is buried deeply within us. The dissolution of our personas facilitates the ultimate goal of development and individuation—the growth into one's true Self and potential. Who we become under the guidance of femtheogenic consciousness can be far wider and broader than what the stagnant social matrix allows us to ever imagine.

The final femtheogenic link I will explore is the unconscious. The unconscious is an entity that is not containable in a rational system of causality. In the symbolic world of Jungian analytical psychology, consciousness is carried by the masculine while the unconscious is the terrain of the feminine. And indeed, the feminine and entheogenic experiences have been relegated by society to the collective unconscious depths. It is the dynamic feminine that is linked to the invisible symbolic spaces of our psyche, and she communicates these spaces into our consciousness through imagination and altered states of consciousness. Entheogenic journeys raise unconscious material into consciousness, allowing us to access our undercurrent realms. Femtheogenic openings to these deep spaces can create the potential for our conscious and unconscious selves to meet and integrate, paving the way for our psychological journey toward wholeness. It is through psychopomps and mediators between states of consciousness that Self can truly emerge.

## The War on Femtheogenic Consciousness

Patriarchy is a paranoid state of consciousness that tries to suppress any potential for power or anything that threatens its structures. It has actively waged a war against both the feminine and entheogens. Patriarchy is a power system that breeds unjust hierarchical power relations, teaching us that our value as a person is linked to our position in its structures. We adopt its worldview, wear our personas, and come to believe that we actually are what we appear to be.

Today, patriarchy's attack on the feminine is a collective responsibility. We are part of a culture that attacks nature and the feminine in all of us (Woodman and Dickson 1997). We all have to delve deep within ourselves and recognize where we have played our own part in her oppression and betrayed her essence. In our masculine culture we have lost our knowledge and connection to her ancient mystery traditions and have denied her wisdom in the rational and scientific world we have created and surrounded ourselves with. By dissecting the essence of the feminine and throwing its essential elemental patterns away, we have deprived ourselves of the potential of connecting with the feminine wholeness, the unifying principle of creation.

Men have also been wounded and alienated from patriarchy's attacks on the feminine. The devaluing of the feminine has damaged the feminine within men, because we all hold a part of that archetype in our psychic depths. Patriarchy has also alienated men from the feminine outside themselves, by splitting them between their need to idealize the feminine and their fearful need to dominate and control her (Woodman and Dickson 1997).

Patriarchy has also been in conflict with entheogens. Patriarchy has traditionally favored substances that maintain boundaries, create a mindless state, and support the status quo (McKenna and Hagerty 2007). Entheogenic experiences deliver us to the land of ambiguity, helping us question what it all means and why things are as they are. These experiences allow us to consider alternative possibilities that are usually more planet- and people-friendly. They cut through our cultural conditioning and offer us a wider lens to examine what we call *reality*—that which is beyond our dominant cultural paradigms. They catalyze imagination and the expansion of our consciousness. And very importantly, they reawaken and unify the fractured feminine and filter her essence through to us, reviving and transmitting her essential regencrative and restorative energies. It is no coincidence that during the psychedelic wave of the fifties and sixties and under the influence of psychedelic expansions, all forms of oppression were questioned. It was during this time that the ecological, antiwar, and feminist movements emerged, amongst others—seeds that are still growing today.

Entheogenic experiences make the maintenance of rigid hierarchies unsustainable, and that poses a major threat to patriarchy (McKenna and Hagerty 2007). Patriarchy, in response to that threat, has done a very good job at making us believe that the use of psychedelics is an immoral and antisocial threat. Patriarchy has also validated the criminal persecution of cognitive liberty, which is the freedom to alter or enhance one's consciousness.

## As Within, So Without; As Above, So Below

The recovery of the femtheogenic energy is integral for reviving the political, social, economic, and spiritual desolation we are currently facing. On an individual level, we have neglected our hearts and deprived ourselves of the sanctuary of community and relationships. We have become increasingly self-conscious, but that is not built on self-knowledge and self-awareness. In our internal and external state of alienation we increasingly give in to diseases of the mind and the body.

But nothing exists in isolation, as femtheogenic consciousness knows and teaches us all too well. The individual psyche is a reflection and a microcosm of the cultural macrocosm, and our individual crisis translates to a horrifying social crisis.

In our target-driven societies, we have forgotten how to care for each other and ourselves. We have forgotten how to support and honor our elders and have abandoned our youth to the mercy of a ruthless media that shrinks their souls and neglects the development of their highest potential. In the meantime, we are busy waging wars of ideology, religion, and race (Vulliamy 2011). We are facing overpopulation and tragic issues such as hunger, water shortages, sanitation, and the spread of infectious diseases in various parts of our world. These concerns are not being effectively addressed.

Our individual and social crisis also extends to the ecology around us. We have ravaged our rain forests, we have overfished and depleted our seas, we have contaminated our rivers, we have excavated our mountains, and our ever-increasing demands for food and technology are depleting Earth's vital resources. Our exploitation of Earth and its resources is amounting to ecocide, as we irreversibly disrupt ecosystems that species depend on. Our ecocidal tendencies are also linked to our genocidal tendencies as we wage wars on the basis of diminishing resources (Baring 2013).

The moment of crisis activates the potential for deep transformation. All birthing initiates in the darkness. We have to face our shadows before the "old solidified ego boundaries can be shattered" (Woodman and Dickson 1997, 36), and through the cracks the possibility of something new can emerge.

## Invoking Archaic Vestiges: Anima Mundi

At the dawn of human consciousness, our early ancestors lived in a symbiotic relationship with nature. In their concrete and magical thinking, they created mythologies in which nature was personified through the Great Mother, powerful and vital in the threading of life and death. This image was one of our earliest collective blueprints on the nature of God. When the Sun God replaced the Earth Goddess, we lost that connection to nature and became alienated from the most profound source of life and wisdom.

That divine source of creation, the soul of the world, was once known as anima mundi. Anima mundi was the spirit that resides within the center of every living thing (Woodman and Dickson 1997, 36) and held the knowledge that there is consciousness within matter. Our ancestors used sacred ritual to activate this light of the world soul, invoking a communion with creation where light spoke to light (Vaughan-Lee 2013).

In our current Western cosmological framework we relate to anima mundi only as a concept, as we no longer live a life that is aligned to its principles. We have desacralized nature and forgotten that the world is alive. We no longer relate to this light within nature or within ourselves. We have disconnected from our imaginative and intuitive potential, and we have lost touch with the magic stuff.

Meditations, mantras, breathing exercises, and entheogens can all activate aspects of the inner technology of our species; they belong to the magical side of our human experience (Vaughan-Lee 2013). They return us to an embodied wisdom and transform our ego consciousness to a soul consciousness. A connection with anima mundi, the world soul, can bring us back into connection with our own soul.

## Mythopoetic Metamorphosis

The ultimate developmental goal in Jungian psychology is individuation; the growth into one's full potential. We cannot individuate unless we integrate our shadow material. Patriarchy has repressed the feminine and its values in our collective shadow, and until we retrieve and integrate her essence in our psychic development we will continue to act out our neurotic fantasies and endanger our survival on this planet.

There has been a lot of talk about the return of the Divine Feminine. The return of the Divine Feminine is essentially a new mythology for challenging the existing patriarchal structures and for the expansion of our consciousness. It speaks of a change in our attitude toward nature, our planet, and our own bodies. To release the Goddess is to cultivate a relationship to the deep cosmic source of our psychic lives and come to care for all creation (Baring 2013). The Divine Feminine asks us to transcend our divisive ideologies, to hold a responsible presence on this planet, and to foster emotional intelligence for the generations that are to come.

The masculine and the feminine are the fundamental archetypal energies of life that make up the entire universe. They are complementary and compensating forces. We are being called to create new mythologies that integrate the alchemical union of the lunar feminine wisdom with the solar masculine consciousness (Baring 2013). The archetypal union of the masculine and the feminine principles holds the promise of wholeness. A healthy future needs to be balanced by the Divine Androgyne.

Evolution for our species at this point is no longer a matter of physicality; it is now a matter of interiority (Woodman and Dickson 1997). We need to go within and discover who we really are away from the social personas we have adapted to. To enter the core is to awaken the light that resides within the core of every living thing; to enter the core is to invoke the anima mundi.

The feminine, entheogens, and nature can only be liberated after we challenge the patriarchal systems and the systemic nature of oppression. On an individual and a collective level we are seeking greater truth and freedom. We are one step away from assuming responsibility and participation, which is where our true freedom lies. For all of these energies to transform we need the strong container of the Goddess, and entheogens are a powerful channel of the feminine voice and essence.

They bring us into alignment with the sacred core and remind us of the divine purpose of being alive.

The revival of femtheogenic consciousness can support the emergence of a planetary consciousness. Our crisis is a crisis of consciousness. The world's wounds and imbalances are a reflection of our own wounds and imbalances (Vaughan-Lee 2013); first we have to rescue our own souls. That is how we participate in the mystery of oneness. When sentient matter becomes a vessel for the enormity of the soul we can transcend the alienated and fragmented levels of consciousness our one-sided materiality binds us to. "A world that is not connected to the soul cannot heal" (Vaughan-Lee 2013, 5). Femtheogenic consciousness can guide us in a creative relationship toward our deepest Self, and its myriad outward reflections.

# 2

# In Search of Goddess Consciousness

## Archetypal and Embodied Paths to Interconnectivity

### Patricia 'Iolana

There are various paths one can take to attain what author and Jungian analyst Jean Shinoda Bolen (1994) deems *Goddess consciousness*. This essay offers two routes to this consciousness—from many that are gaining momentum in both the United States and the United Kingdom. While both paths focus on an underlying theme of interconnectivity, one is derived from the analytical and archetypal psyche while the other is accessed through embodied, physical experience.

Bolen (1994) offers an *analytical* pathway to Goddess. The path of the psyche emphasizes a series of elevating shifts in consciousness that lead to Goddess consciousness and the central tenets of interconnectivity and interrelatedness. This route seeks to expand the psyche beyond the confines of the body. The *embodied* pathway, exemplified by the methods offered through the Beltane Fire Society, requires the body to be the portal for the psyche. Through drumming, dance, guided meditation, and ritual one can raise one's level of consciousness and help to raise Goddess consciousness in others.

At the heart of both pathways is Jung's archetypal anima.

## Jung and the Archetypal Anima

In Jungian analytical psychology, the conscious psyche holds a door to self-introspection through the *unconscious* psyche; this doorway offers a way to raise one's *consciousness,* to shift away from an *ego-centered state* toward an understanding of physical and psychic interconnectivity—toward the central core of Jung's psychology: *wholeness* and *individuation* (Jung 1995). Often, this new conscious information radically shifts one's perception of the world and one's integral place within it.

At the center of Jung's path of self-introspection and his model of the *collective unconscious* is the anima (Goddess), who, for Jung, is "the feminine and chthonic part of the soul" (1968, 59). Believing Goddess to be wholly immanent, an internal psychic force as opposed to an external or *transcendent* deity, Jung's analytical psychology focuses on a long-term path of individuation that culminates in the union of Self and the anima. Jung wrote at great length about the archetypes of the collective unconscious but gave "special reference to the anima concept" (1968, 54). Jung deified and anthropomorphized the anima: "With the archetype of the anima we enter the realm of the gods, or rather, the realm that metaphysics has reserved for itself. Everything the anima touches becomes numinous—unconditional, dangerous, taboo, magical" (1968, 28).

Jung aligns the anima with the *realm of the gods* and envisions the anima as the purveyor of self-knowledge. Jung writes, "for the anima can appear also as an angel of light, a psychopomp who points the way to the highest meaning . . ." (1968, 29). To reach the anima, Jung's path requires a series of psychological advancements in one's consciousness. The resulting Goddess consciousness that stems from a union with the anima (Goddess) is a prerequisite in Jungian and post-Jungian models toward individuation and Selfhood. This is not a process of faith or belief, but a practice devoted to the psyche and the power of the collective unconscious.

Three unique, contemporary Western women have built upon Jung's archetypal Goddess consciousness through their individuation memoirs: Jean Shinoda Bolen, Ph.D., Sue Monk Kidd, and Phyllis Curott. I will cite examples that will allow us to understand the differing ways they approach and build upon Jung's anima as Goddess and discuss how each navigated a path to obtaining Goddess consciousness.

## Goddess Consciousness

Jean Shinoda Bolen advocates for *Goddess consciousness*. She writes, "Many books have been published about the Earth as Gaia, feminist theology, goddess archaeology, women's spirituality, planetary consciousness, deep ecology, paradigm shifts, and other areas of thought that support the thesis of an emerging 'goddess consciousness'" (1994, 270). In Bolen's construct, Goddess consciousness is awakening to the interconnectivity, compassion, and Eros-based knowledge that she believes has been neglected, disparaged, and repressed in Western culture.

Goddess consciousness includes both feminist and ecological political agendas centering on empowering women and highlighting our communal responsibility toward Mother Earth. Bolen combines Jungian analytics with contemporary spirituality: Goddess is an archetype. However, Goddess consciousness is inherently sacred: "it is only through a Goddess consciousness that matter can be perceived as having a sacred dimension" (39). Bolen draws from multiple sources when it comes to invoking Goddess, including Merlin Stone: "Somewhere in our souls, women remember a time when divinity was called Goddess and Mother" (81). Through her work, Bolen intends to help craft substantial and life-affirming feminine-based archetypal mysteries for the West. Her task is to open other women and men up to her understanding of a post-Jungian Goddess consciousness that is eloquently summarized in her memoir, *Crossing to Avalon*:

> We must remember how and when each of us has had an experience of the Goddess and felt healed and made whole by her. These are holy, sacred, timeless moments, and as numinous as they may have been, without words they are difficult to retrieve. But when someone else speaks of a similar experience, it can evoke the memory and bring back the feelings, which restore the experience. Only if we speak from personal experience does this happen. This is why we need words for women's mysteries, which, like everything else that is of women, seems to require that one woman at a time birth what she knows. *We serve as midwives to each other's consciousness.* (1994, 79–80, emphasis added)

## Interconnectivity

At the heart of Bolen's Goddess consciousness is the model of *interconnectivity*. Referring to a state of being connected by an unseen thread, interconnectivity also refers to the parts of a system that interact with and impact one another. In *Crossing to Avalon*, Bolen describes her vision of this web of interconnectivity: "I have often felt myself to be a point of light connected to everyone I have ever loved or mattered to, each also being a point of light, in turn connected to those they love, so that somehow, we are all part of a vast web of twinkling lights. I think that each individual light can grow brighter or dimmer over the course of a lifetime, and that whenever a light goes out on this web, if affects me" (203).

However, this perception of interconnectivity is not the sole realm of post-Jungian psychology; it is also found in systems theory and in a variety of faith traditions including Charismatic Catholicism. Margaret Starbird, a reformed Catholic, echoes Bolen in her memoir *Goddess in the Gospels*: "I am now persuaded that all of reality is interwoven, a fabulous tapestry of silken threads linked with tiny knots behind the fabric . . . interconnected by the unseen hand of the Weaver" (Starbird 1998, xi, 114). Interconnectivity is also found in contemporary Goddess-centered faith traditions. Post-Christian Sue Monk Kidd writes: "Goddess is that which unites, connects, and affirms the interrelatedness of all life, all people. Being related is at the core of Divine Feminine Being. She is the dance of relation. . . . The Divine co-inheres all that is" (2007, 155, 159). These authors exemplify how many adherents in contemporary Goddess-centered faith traditions refer to interconnectivity as a "web" whose image echoes both Indra's net and the Buddhist wheel—where all things are connected from a single source. In this post-Jungian belief system, the center of the web is Goddess. Through this web, we are connected to each other and to the Divine. Realizing one is interconnected to every particle in our known universe can shift one's paradigm from a life of isolation and disconnection to a model of union, wholeness, and the greater responsibility toward others and the natural world.

Bolen took Jung from the confines of the clinician's office and offered the world a post-Jungian route to Goddess and Goddess consciousness. A source of inspiration to those who follow, Sue Monk Kidd and Phyllis Curott build on Bolen's Goddess consciousness in disparate but personally unique thealogical ways.

## We-Consciousness

Sue Monk Kidd's journey to Goddess began in the Southern Baptist Church. Her memoir, *Dance of the Dissident Daughter*, describes her shift from the (old) Christian concept of separation between God, humanity, and nature to the (new) consciousness of connectivity that is emerging in the West. Unlike Bolen's analytical approach, Kidd is a post-Christian who writes specifically for other Christian and post-Christian women. Whether it is called *Goddess consciousness* or *We-consciousness,* as Kidd refers to it, these two proposed forms of consciousness are one and the same—a call for elevated consciousness and interconnectivity. Kidd's memoir exemplifies the shift in consciousness that Jung marked as instrumental in individuation—union with the anima as Goddess—in the contemporary post-Jungian world.

She writes about being lost in the Self (blind to the injustices that surrounded her), having several *awakenings* to the reality of her situation as a woman in the West, and finally coming to embrace a shift from I (the self) to we (the interconnectivity that union with the anima brings). Kidd writes, "We-consciousness is knowing and feeling oneself intimately connected with and part of everything that is, and coming to act and relate out of that awareness" (2007, 154). Seeing the world as a web where we are all connected through its strands remains a vital philosophy today underpinning spiritual, environmental, and political movements across the globe. Kidd writes, "This new feminine spiritual consciousness will help us recognize that humans, having special abilities, are responsible to the rest of the earth, not superior to it" (2007, 162).

## Interconnectivity on the Quantum Level

Wiccan high priestess Phyllis Curott also espouses a Goddess consciousness of interconnectivity in her 1998 memoir, *Book of Shadows*. However, Curott returns to the source of Jung's theory on the interconnectivity of consciousness—quantum mechanics.

Quantum mechanics may prove the model of interconnectivity inherent in Goddess consciousness. What fascinated Jung and many adherents of Goddess, is that if *consciousness is quantum*, and everything is interconnected and can affect each other then, by conclusion, conscious intent can affect the world around us. This key idea of the human capacity to consciously affect and change, for better or worse, the physical world around us is the foundation for a vast array of magical work (witchcraft, Wicca, druids, shamans, healers and the like included).

According to Suzanne Gieser (2005), one of Jung's patients was

Nobel Prize–winning quantum physicist Wolfgang Pauli. Discovering their shared interest in quantum reality and its effect on consciousness, Pauli and Jung's relationship continued post-therapy; they collaborated on the 1955 joint publication *The Interpretation of Nature and the Psyche*. Like Jung, Pauli held unique views, as Lisa Zyga articulates: "Pauli favored a hypothesis of 'lucid mysticism,' a synthesis between rationality and religion. He speculated that quantum theory could unify the psychological/scientific and philosophical/mystical approaches to consciousness. Pauli's perspective was influenced by the philosopher Arthur Schopenhauer, whose views on reality were in turn influenced by Eastern religions" (2009, 2).

Pauli and Jung both inhabited that liminal space between science and religion, attempting to make sense of how the quantum world around us functions on the psyche. Jung's relationship with Pauli was, in large part, responsible for the quantum theories of interconnectivity being an integral component to his psychological models and paths of consciousness-raising.

Curott's use of theoretical physics also adds another important element to the theory of interconnectivity as quantum level mechanics point to an alternate dimension; in her 1998 memoir, *Book of Shadows,* she writes: "Quantum reality is another level of existence, another dimension. Here the energy field is the underlying order, a hidden or shadow reality of our daily lives. We see solid material objects as separated from one another—a rock, a table, a human being—but on the quantum level, they are all actually bundles of vibrating, interacting energy. And though we perceive them to exist separately, these energies—the rocks and tables and ourselves—are interconnected" (8).

Recent research in the field of astrophysics is validating these theories. UCLA professor Tommaso Treu is researching dark matter, dark energy, and something often referred to as the *cosmic web*. In a talk sponsored by the W. M. Keck Observatory in July 2016, Treu spoke of how his research into gravitational lensing appears to indicate a cosmic web of filaments of dark matter that give rise to galaxies. What Treu is proposing in his theory exponentially expands the theory of interconnectivity from the natural world surrounding us on Earth to the cosmic world and *the creation of universes within the cosmos.* In other words, Bolen's original model of human and natural interconnectivity has now been expanded to include the known and unknown universes and the *power of creation.*

Despite modern scientific breakthroughs in the understanding of our quantum world, these theories remain contrary to the deeply ingrained and patriarchal paradigm of man separate from and in dominion over the natural world. Modern science appears to prove long-held beliefs about the interconnectivity of the cosmos and the cosmic web's ability to create alternate universes. However, there is still a long road before these various theories of interconnectivity become more mainstream—and thus available to more people.

## Embodied Ritual Work as a Path to Goddess Consciousness

If analytical psychology, quantum mechanics, or astrophysics are not the route one wishes to take to an interconnected Goddess consciousness, there are other physical paths available. The power of the psyche plays an important part in embodied ritual—offering the believer a portal to an elevated form of consciousness. When focused on Goddess, the attainment of Goddess consciousness can either be the intent or a by-product of embodied ritual work.

What do I mean by *embodied ritual work?* There are many rituals that can be performed that require little or no embodied participation of the adherent—an excellent example of this would be candle magic, where once lit, the body's work is done. So, an embodied ritual is one where the adherent's physical body is *used as a tool or vehicle in ritual* such as the tasks of ritual cleansings or blessings, ritual dance, or drawing down the moon. This last is a sacred ritual where the Goddess is "drawn down" into a human body willing to be the vehicle for communication with the Divine. The body is an active participant and tool in the ritual. This is an important distinction from the analytical and archetypal technique because it is the body that will open the pathway for the psyche to elevate in consciousness. This powerful method is often referred to as *ecstatic* or as *a technique of ecstasy.*

Attaining a higher level of consciousness, and in this case Goddess consciousness, is possible not only through ritual but also through activities such as drumming, dance, and guided (and unguided) meditation. The key element is that the body must open the pathway for the psyche. While these kinds of embodied rituals can be performed by a solitary practitioner, the powerful energy that can be raised by a group with the shared intention of attaining a higher level of consciousness can be psychologically and spiritually transformative and offers an excellent way of validating and/or corroborating one's experiences. Nowhere have I observed this power—amplified by hundreds of people extended to thousands serving as witnesses in the contemporary festival culture— than with the Beltane Fire Society (BFS) in Edinburgh, Scotland.

For nearly three decades, in Edinburgh, the Beltane Fire Society has been publicly celebrating the holy days of Beltane and Samhain. Over the years, the organization has grown from a handful of people to hundreds of volunteer members. I joined them in 2009, and this section is grounded in my experiences over six years and my participation in over a dozen different celebrations with BFS. Because of the variety of roles offered to the performers, BFS provides a powerful example of how drumming, dance, guided meditation, and ritual can be used to actively raise an individual's or a group's consciousness and interconnectivity. Each fire festival is uniquely designed by the volunteer members, and the groups and stories are ever changing. And yet the larger narrative remains as the union of Goddess as Maiden to the Green Man at Beltane and the union of the Cailleach (or Crone) to the Winter King at Samhain. As a troupe, our goal is to celebrate and recreate this journey and ultimate union; but the magic of raising Goddess consciousness is left to the smaller groups that make up the whole society. The key elements of drumming, dance, meditation, and embodied ritual work are central to the groups who are dedicated to the ritual aspect, rather than the performance aspect, of this festival journey.

## Drumming

The psychological therapeutic effects of drumming are gaining interest in contemporary psychology (Muller 2015), and science is proving that group drumming offers physical, emotional, and psychological benefits including raising one's sensitivity and awareness to group interconnectivity. Drumming also holds a wealth of therapeutic benefits, from stress reduction to an improved immune system (Schwarcz 2014). However, when drumming is used to raise one's level of consciousness as a ritual act, it can be an embodied path to Goddess consciousness. The rhythmic nature of drumming can allow the body to move in repetition, freeing the psyche to open and wander as it will. This is a crucial component of drumming; allowing the body to be *lost in the moment* grants the psyche the opportunity to begin to unconsciously explore. When the body is absorbed in the primal and repetitive rhythm, the psyche can move from the constraints of the individual, and project both outward toward personal expression and inward toward interconnectivity, compassion, and the primal urge to connect with the Divine.

## Dance

As with drumming, dance also requires the body to surrender to the psyche. In the late 1970s an American dancer named Gabrielle Roth created a movement meditation she called "5Rhythms" wherein participants dance in a free-form fashion, allowing the psyche to wander to higher forms of consciousness. The whirling dervishes also exemplify this method of meditative dance. Groups within BFS have used dance in the same way Roth had intended: as a form of meditation to free the conscious psyche. Particularly when paired with one of the society's many drumming groups, the dancer moves without intent or thought, swaying to the primal rhythms by instinct rather than a choreographed movement.

Dancers can use this skill to either raise energy—that can later be focused elsewhere—or to allow the psyche to cross the portal to a higher form of consciousness. Not only does this give the individual the opportunity to explore consciousness outside of the physical body, it also allows all the dancers to share a common experience, offering a sense of bond and unity among them. These two key elements are often utilized by the performing groups within the society as pathways to Goddess consciousness and to developing a group bond. Dance may be an element the smaller group brings to the larger ritual and celebration, or it may be used strictly in the rehearsal process as a technique to achieve the group's goals.

### Guided Meditation

Although individual meditation is an indispensable tool to many faith traditions for unlocking the conscious and unconscious minds, some groups within BFS utilize guided group meditations in the rehearsal process specifically to raise the group's consciousness toward Goddess. Given that Goddess is the central character in the story we are telling, it is important that, as a group, we each find an individual connection to Goddess as well as creating a collective archetypal mythic narrative. Hours of open and honest discussions about our personal beliefs and experiences precede a group-guided meditation, in order for the guide to ascertain how the meditation can actively include the various beliefs held within the group into one integrated group understanding.

Guided meditations require advance preparation and start with an intention. What does the meditation want to achieve? Is the goal to connect with one (or all five) of the elements? Is the goal to invoke or create a useful archetype? Or is the goal to find a way to create or strengthen the individual's union with Goddess? Once the intention is set, the task of the guide is to safely take the individuals on a conscious journey that, often, can be transformative. The key to guided meditation is to introduce new knowledge or offer the opportunity for the individual to gain fresh information or experience through the mediation journey. As with most groups within the society, a large part of the rehearsal process centers upon the Goddess at the heart of the festival (be it the May Queen or the Cailleach). In this rich mythological environment, opening one to Goddess consciousness is perhaps easier with the support of the group members and organizers.

Oliver Wendell Holmes Sr. (1858) wrote: "Every now and then a man's mind is stretched by a new idea or sensation, and never shrinks back to its former dimensions" (502). And nowhere is this more evident than in opening the psyche to Goddess and Goddess consciousness. Once people are aware of Goddess, they cannot unknow Her. Once people learn that consciousness can exist outside of the ego-driven self to a point of connectivity with all that surrounds them, they cannot forget their interconnectivity. They can no longer walk alone, oblivious to the world around them.

### Ritual

Ritual is perhaps the most complex of the modalities as a path to elevated Goddess consciousness because it often requires that the adherent already possess a level of union with Goddess that they bring to the ritual. This prior knowledge and experience, however, is not always the case, and many rituals have been performed, especially within BFS, where participating individuals bring no prior knowledge. This offers the other members of the group the opportunity to share their own stories and experiences and introduces these individuals to the various understandings of Goddess as they pertain to the celebration.

Over the years, I have participated in many rituals as a member of BFS—both rituals for private group work and public rituals during the festival itself. In my experience, rituals in private group work are far more effective than they are in the public sphere of the festival night where the thousands of spectators and photographers challenge concentration and focus. As members of the society we often tread a fine line between performance and ritual, and it takes a strong psyche to stay in the moment of the ritual during a public festival that might be witnessed by over ten thousand people. This is why most group rituals are performed during months of rehearsal leading up to the festival night. Some rituals are performed to strengthen the bond between the members of the group, such as a naming ceremony. Other rituals are created to dedicate a group, or groups, to a specific deity, such as the Morrigan—a Celtic goddess and warrior queen who reigns over birth, battle, and death. Some groups that place more emphasis on the ritual aspect of the society rather than the performance will hold rituals with their members on a weekly basis. Not only does this create union with Goddess, it also creates firm links in the individual's psyche to the levels of consciousness that permeate the natural world outside the individual ego. This bond is strengthened through each succeeding ritual, whether that be with the group or in the privacy of individual space.

Whether groups within BFS use drumming, dance, guided meditation, embodied ritual, or any other method of consciousness-raising is strictly the choice of the group leaders, supported by input from the members of their group. However, the grand intent is often the same: to develop the bonds of interconnectivity within the group, and their connection to Goddess, in service of the festival.

From my own experiences and observations from within BFS, we *can* serve as midwives to each other's higher consciousness as Bolen (1994) suggested. This interconnected shift *from I to we* is palpable not only in the various post-Jungian paths to Goddess consciousness but also in the consciousness-raising interactions within the festival groups and the wider society itself.

# 3

# The Dark Feminine

## Mediators of Transformation

### Tim Read

## The Nurturing Feminine and Numinous States

Fusion therapy was controversial even among the psychedelic psycho-therapists of the 1960s. Two women, Joyce Martin and Pauline McCririck, both trained as psychoanalysts, developed a method of LSD psychotherapy that involved close physical contact between client and therapist during the session. It was felt to be particularly suitable as a corrective experience for people with a history of early emotional neglect, for the treatment sought to instill—at a deep level—a repara-tive and embedded experience of a good mother. During the LSD ses-sion the client would lie on a couch covered in a blanket while being held in a close embrace, as a mother might hold her child.

Czech psychiatrist Stanislav Grof, who had extensive clinical and research experience with LSD psychotherapy, underwent a session of fusion therapy with Pauline McCririck. He describes a profound regres-sion where he became a nursing infant on the breast of a good mother, then a fetus in a good womb. He felt nourished by both the milk and the blood of his mother, and this held a strong sense of the sacred for him. The session culminated with an expansion into the transpersonal domain and a sacred union with the Great Mother Goddess. He described his session as profoundly healing; one of the most powerful experiences that he had with entheogens (Grof 2006).

Psychedelics bring the gift of numinous experience; there is simply no other method that provides such open access to a heightened archetypal consciousness. The numinous is the principle that underlies all religion; it is a mystery that can hold and induce both terror and awe. Its essence is mediated by an amplification of meaning so that the power and resonance of meaning challenge our ego structures and our prevailing way of being in the world. There is enormous potential for growth, but the more powerful the instrument, the greater the risk of damage if the experience is insufficiently supported or integrated. Of course, dosage and set and setting are of the utmost importance.

The crucial point about the idea of the numinous is its bivalence, with both dark and light manifestations. Thus incomplete or partial forms of numinous experience can have a nightmarish primitive quality with an abrupt and capricious character. However, this crude stage, with its ominous tone, has the potential to be transcended as the numen reveals itself and the process unfolds, eventually becoming integrated by the more rational elements of consciousness (Otto 1958).

Thus our encounters with the Divine Feminine in high archetypal penetrance states may not always have the highly positive emotional quality that Grof encountered in fusion therapy. The emotional tone may also be ominous or dread-filled. But these experiences can be worked with, supported, and transmuted; indeed, the learning from such difficult experiences can be of immense value.

## The Devouring Feminine

One afternoon Ramakrishna—a nineteenth-century Bengali saint and devotee of Kali (among others)—watched as a beautiful woman ascended from the Ganges and approached the grove where he was meditating. He could see that she was about to give birth; in a moment the baby was born, and she gently nursed it. Then suddenly her appearance changed so that she became monstrous and horrible, and she took the infant in her jaws and crushed it. Swallowing the corpse, she returned to the Ganges and disappeared (Nikhilananda 1942).

How can eating babies bring forth growth? The literal mind struggles to plumb the depths required. And yet if the baby is seen as metaphorical, if it represents our ego structures, our wants, our desires, and our attachments to superficial structures, then perhaps the answer starts to take some shape.

The dark aspect of the feminine is challenging. It seems much easier to maintain the deodorized archetypal image of the feminine offered by our cultural conditioning as characterized by the Virgin Birth, the saintly smiling Madonna, Isis, and Lakshmi. But we are poorer if we cannot hold a more nuanced version of the feminine. By averting our gaze from the shadow of the feminine we also disown our own shadow, both on an individual and collective level.

So when we first encounter the dark feminine she tends to appear in primitive forms. If the archetypal feminine has been alienated and rejected, the first meeting with it is likely to be difficult, gnarled, jagged, and dreadful. She approaches from the shadow, which can be frightening, even paralyzing. She is Medusa rather than Athena and the assistance she offers may be subtle and mysterious. But the prize, if we persist, is that we process our shadow, accommodate our demons, expand our consciousness, and move to a closer relationship with the archetypal Self. This is the journey of ego death and rebirth.

The Hindu goddess Kali is associated with death and destruction. Although she can be worshipped as the benevolent mother goddess, she is perhaps better known for her dreadful aspect. She epitomizes the dark goddess and is usually depicted as black. Kali is also the penetrator of Maya, the world of illusion, of ego structures. Thus does Kali represent a mutative process; she will bring you to your demons but she can also be the demon slayer. Indeed, she feeds on demons and is usually depicted with a garland of severed demon heads. But she is also god-dess of salvation, a symbol of triumph over death. She is the principle of consciousness, the infinite darkness. She holds the threat of madness as ego dissolves. But with her grace, ego can be reborn in a transformed relationship with the primary energy of archetypal Self.

## Salome and the Anima

Swiss psychiatrist Carl Jung pioneered the development of archetypal psychology until his death in 1961. He was a masculine man grow-ing up in a patriarchal world, and his journey inevitably involved an integration of the feminine—which he termed *the anima.*

The anima is a transpersonal concept. She is that part of our psyche that has a feminine flavor, but she is also something other, acting as a mediator between ego and that which lies beyond our individual psyche. We need help from the anima to engage usefully with our shadow. Indeed, dealing with our anima involves facing our darkness and engaging in the complex web of Maya before we can begin to disen-tangle from it and disentangle from it in service of our psycho-spiritual development. The engagement with the anima/feminine is a process of supreme importance for our psycho-spiritual development.

Jung went through a transformational crisis lasting four years, a high archetypal penetrance state that has parallels to the psychedelic expe-rience. He developed various techniques to engage with and integrate the material that was flooding out of his unconscious. His first active imagination journey took him to another world—a place that felt like the land of the dead where he met two figures: an old man and a beau-tiful young woman. He was Elijah and she was Salome, the blind girl of whom he was "distinctly suspicious" (Jung 1983, 205). Salome is the symbol of the femme fatale, the voluptuous dancing girl who seduced old men and demanded the head of John the Baptist. No wonder Jung was wary. And yet Jung was also intrigued. Whom did Salome represent and why had she appeared to him? In pondering these questions, the encounter with Salome paved the way for Jung's progressive integration of the feminine and was a crucial step in his healing and growth.

Jung also describes how the anima principle can be seductive in a way that can promote a disengagement with reality. Like the Sirens of the *Odyssey* or the whispering Lorelei of the Rhine, they can steer us onto the rocks. But the anima also provides a window into our deep unconscious if we can but ground it; our intellect—our rational mind—is needed for this task. Hence Jung's dyad of the old man representing the saturnine principles of Logos and sight in the eternal world as opposed to Salome's entirely different form of perception. An excess of the Elijah archetype leads to rigidity, but he is necessary to add some form and shape to the more fluid but archetypally nourishing feminine. I suggest that holding the dynamic tension between Elijah and Salome is a useful model for managing any psychedelic or high archetypal penetrance state.

## The Destructive Feminine and Holotropic Breathwork

After the use of psychedelic drugs had been made illegal for research and clinical use in the United States in the mid-1960s, Stanislav and Christina Grof developed a nondrug method of accessing an expanded state of consciousness. This method—holotropic breathwork—induces the entheogenic state by hyperventilation and by loud and archetypally evocative music.

The potency of holotropic breathwork has been compared to a low to moderate dose of psilocybin. This means that the ego structures are not overwhelmed as may occur in a high-dose LSD or ayahuasca session. This is helpful to integration as it makes material from the nonordinary state more accessible to the conscious process. Holotropic breathwork has been developed to make a setting as supportive as possible and optimize integration using a variety of methods. The fundamental premise of this work is that there is an inner healing intelligence, a power within that is inherently supportive, so that any challenging material that emerges is to be welcomed as an opportunity to process material that is helpful to our progress.

I trained in holotropic breathwork with Grof and his team for five years beginning in 2003. I found that the training afforded a safer, gentler journey through some of the territory that Jung encountered during his transformational crisis. The training provided access to numinous experience and support for the failure of some ego structures that inevitably follows, together with an opportunity to address the shadow and deeper layers of trauma. Part of the ego (perhaps more influenced by Self archetype) volunteers for the process. However, other parts of the ego structures tend to resist strongly, and new and powerful, sometimes subtle, ego defenses arise. Self beckons while ego quakes.

The session that I will describe here was my third. My first session some six months previously had given me, to my surprise, a taste of divine light and love and cosmic oneness. It was a life-changing, paradigm-busting, and thoroughly disorienting experience. Numinous experience is enormously stimulating; a whole new cosmos had opened up to me and shown me how little I knew and how much I wanted to learn. But one side effect was that I desperately wanted to touch that place again; I had a yearning that preoccupied me. And yet the doors of perception had slammed shut again. It was tantalizing.

So this was the mood that I brought with me as I lay down on the mat and started my session. I had traveled far and waited some months for this opportunity. At the retreat setting in the desert; Grof had been teaching and Jack Kornfeld had been taking us progressively deeper into Vipassana meditation. My mind-set was primed, the setting was as good as it gets, and I wanted very much to touch the Divine.

But in nonordinary states you do not always get what you want—you get what you need! As my session progressed, I was having a frustrating time. Indeed, I seemed to be stuck in my thoughts and my desires and I felt like a very limited human being who just could not leave the chattering mind behind. Grof had been teaching us about the states of mind associated with the second perinatal matrix, the no-exit state before birth when the uterus is contracting with extraordinary power, crushing the baby. At such times we are apt to feel a profoundly bleak futility and hopelessness, and this was indeed where I was heading. In holotropic breathwork we are encouraged to amplify, to make it bigger, to surrender to whatever comes up. So I surrendered; then I seemed to go through a threshold, and I found myself in another landscape.

A massive female figure reclined at ease beneath the crust of the earth. She seemed a few miles long, judging by the tiny figures of the humans above her. She was propped on one elbow and surveyed the scene above her: the devastation, the mud, the craters, and the ghastly landscape of the trenches of the First World War. She seemed calm and at ease while above her men lived out their little lives. I saw them die like ants. I watched as other horror stories from our collective history played out before my eyes.

I was in awe; she seemed more real to me than everyday reality. I was frightened, although I knew I was being shown something important. It was as though I were frozen. Hoping she wouldn't notice me, I stayed as still and unobtrusive as I could. I was holding two conflicting emotions: the desperate sorrow for the grief that we cause each other with our stupid conflicts, but also gratitude and reverence for this supernatural being who was watching us, holding us, even with tenderness, while we went through our collective developmental agonies.

An experience of this nature requires careful integration. The integration process has layer upon layer. There is low-hanging fruit that is easy to pick, but some of the fruit lies in the higher branches and one has to reach for it. This takes time and patience. It is probably inevitable that some of the integration process is challenging to our existing way of seeing the world and ourselves. But if done properly, I think it will generally reveal something of our shadow and birth a little more of ourselves into consciousness.

To state it briefly, my first insight was, of course, to reaffirm that history has a developmental trajectory; that humanity is still at an immature stage of development. The dark lady (for that is how she seemed to me) was like a mother watching toddlers. It seemed to me that the metaphorical trenches in which we find ourselves—the breathtaking suffering, man's inhumanity to man—these are but necessary developmental steps in the evolution of our collective psyche. How else do we learn about the futility of war and collective trauma if we do not experience it fully, deeply, and viscerally? This is how we grow from our tribal ethnocentricity to become true citizens of a global humanity, perhaps even a cosmic collective psyche. Maybe I knew this before, but I felt as though this understanding was seared into me now. The Divine Goddess was certainly giving us some tough love but at least she was *with* us, her lap was just beneath—although we do not see it.

This type of insight can lead to the perspective that everything that happens in the world, however bad it seems, is actually pitch-perfect; that there is a bigger, teleological picture that is oriented toward growth. The trap here is that while focusing on the bigger picture, it can become possible to lose focus on the smaller, more human picture. Indeed, I became aware in the aftermath of this experience that perhaps I was losing something, perhaps even becoming emotionally disengaged from the immediacy of my everyday experience. It became clearer to me that if there is a bigger picture, it is that much more important to bring care, compassion, and love to all we see in the trenches of everyday life. As Ram Dass suggests—life could be a statement of love and compassion—and where it isn't, that's where the real work lies.

As my integration progressed and my understanding deepened, the main gift seemed to be an opening of the heart and some loosening of the armor that had accumulated over the years. It seemed to me that this armor had a masculine quality, perhaps something to do with the patriarchal structures that had dominated my formative experiences. Now the barriers to compassion seemed to be dissolving, leading, I believe, to an increased capacity to care, to parent, and to nurture. My yearning for cosmic oneness had left me. That initial experience had done its job—and thus I had let it go. My job now was to try to be here with both feet firmly planted on planet Earth—and to try to be of some use. This was the gift of the Goddess.

## Dismemberment

A client of mine, Hannah, had been to an ayahuasca retreat hoping to get some relief from long-term difficulties with social anxiety. But during the first sessions she became frightened and paranoid. She thought that she was in a dangerous place with people who might do her harm; their faces seemed twisted and malevolent. She decided to leave while still under the influence, and the facilitators simply watched her depart. She had a terrifying journey home using public transport. The next day everything seemed so much worse. She felt paralyzed with anxiety that now had a paranoid tinge; she had a crushing sensation in her chest, and she felt utterly alone and helpless.

For me ayahuasca carries something of the same dark transformational feminine energy as Kali, the Mother Ayahuasca archetype having a quality different from other entheogens. Where holotropic breathwork asks respectful questions of the ego defenses, ayahuasca is more confrontational, especially at higher dosage. Ideally the ayahuasca ceremony will allow the process to fully unfold, but one of the dangers is an unresolved process where people leave with the work unfinished and the psyche deeply troubled and fragmented.

Stanislav Grof suggests that people who have had an unintegrated psychedelic experience or high archetypal penetrance state need to return to a similar layer of psyche in order to work through and process that experience (personal communication, August 7, 2016). People who fall into this category often attend holotropic breathwork retreats. Indeed, I met and worked with Hannah during such a retreat. Given her first experience with ayahuasca, it had taken her a great deal of courage to try holotropic breathwork.

The schedule that day of our retreat called for two breathwork sessions. She felt her way cautiously during the first breathwork session and seemed to satisfy herself that it was safe enough to immerse more fully during her second session. It would be an understatement to say that Hannah's next breathwork session was a powerful one. She was in a state of acute mental and physical distress for much of the time. She had a crushing feeling in her chest and we worked with her intensely, using focused release techniques. After a couple of hours, she settled and indicated that she wanted to be held. One of the female facilitators lay on the mat with her for the last hour, holding her, perhaps as a mother would hold a child. This version of fusion therapy occurs from time to time in breathwork.

After the session Hannah talked the experience through with her sitter and spent some time drawing a mandala and writing as part of the integrative process. In the evening group she told us that she had felt an Inca sorceress crushing her chest in a torture device; she was malign and wanted to hurt Hannah. The face of this being started to change into the faces of the people who had hurt Hannah in the past, and included even the twisted faces of the facilitators in the ayahuasca session. Part of her wanted to run out of the room and escape, but we had discussed this scenario beforehand, and, with our encouragement, she was able to stay with her feelings and remain. Then she transitioned into another place that had an entirely different tone, the malign faces fell away, and she felt a state of great peace and love. She was in the arms of her mother at last, then all mothers in the world, then a more abstract sense of union with the Great Mother, the Divine Goddess herself.

## The Crushing Feminine

The existential despair, futility, and hopelessness of a bad trip is one of the most challenging experiences we can encounter in a psychedelic session. It is not immediately obvious that this has anything to do with the feminine, but Stanislav Grof brilliantly linked these dark-night-of-the-soul experiences to an aspect of the birth process. This aspect occurs when the uterus starts to contract, the paradise of the supportive womb is lost, we are rhythmically crushed, the cervix is still closed, and there is no escape.

Grof found that many of his LSD psychotherapy patients were hindered in some important ways in their adult lives because of unresolved emotional trauma around the process of their birth. Thus, in accessing this profoundly dark material we allow the possibility of trauma resolution, of healing. Grof developed his insight during the course of a personal high-dose LSD session wherein he found himself in a claustrophobic nightmare, a hellish no-exit situation representing the ultimate existential crisis. He felt his entire existence was absurd and pointless and he could think of no positive or redeeming features. As well as feeling existentially trapped, he experienced a sense of pressure on his head and jaws. He felt crushed and had difficulties breathing. It suddenly came to him that he was reliving his biological birth.

He subsequently found that many patients and clients in LSD psychotherapy and holotropic breathwork had a range of similar experiences, which seemed to validate his theory (Grof 2005). This is an extraordinary insight that I believe will be Grof's lasting legacy to developmental psychology. Psychoanalysis has long held the newborn infant to be oblivious to the birth process, a blank slate that is exquisitely sensitive to the nuance of feeding and the relationship with mother, which acts as a powerful template for personality development. But Grof argues that this completely misunderstands the developmental template provided by this extraordinary journey toward our birth, the death/rebirth involved in that journey, the trauma, the fight for life, and the eventual deliverance.

This entire process is driven by the feminine in different aspects and holds profoundly archetypal qualities. The womb is the source of biological support but also the place of cosmic union. Sometimes the womb can become toxic, especially just before birth is triggered. The onset of labor with its pulverizing force is a primal threat to the organism, the ultimate existential challenge. At this stage the cervix is closed so there is no escape, no hope; we are ranged against insuperable forces, we are being crushed by the feminine. Then, as the cervix opens, it becomes possible to make progress, and the life-or-death struggle begins through the birth canal toward the external world. As the baby emerges, its previous life comes to a decisive end.

The mother, the feminine principle, first conceives then nourishes in the uterus before paradise is lost as the devastating crushing begins. This is followed by the epic journey of expulsion before being held with love again, in a different form in the outside world. Reexperiencing this cycle and surrendering to it in a nonordinary state of consciousness enables some resolution of deeply held traumatic residue, which can echo loudly in the ways that we lead our lives. Without working through it in an expanded state of consciousness, this material is very difficult to process. It is not necessary to go through a birth process in the session, although some people do; often it is more of an archetypal, symbolic journey that is therapeutically effective nonetheless.

We find this is borne out in the holotropic breathwork retreats we participate in. This is one of the gifts of serious work in expanded states of consciousness: deep, sometimes subtle wounds can be healed. In resolving the trauma of our first encounter with the destructive aspect of the feminine we can become more fully born, more completely alive, and ultimately more conscious of who we really are.

∿

**PART 2**

# Ancient Roots of Female Shamanism

# 4

# Woman Shaman

## Uncovering the Female Ecstatics

### Max Dashu

At the lip of the water, the Norse *vǫlva* sits on a weathered boulder in a mountain forest. She is engaged in *útiseta*, "sitting out" on the land for inspiration. She may remain in silence, gazing, for hours out of time. She may chant, reaching out and opening her arms, calling to spirits. She dances to them, moving in rhythmic pulses, releasing and imbibing vital essence. She touches her head to the stone, entering into deep communion with the Earth. She may immerse her body in the pure chill waters; they open her awareness into their depths. Or she may watch a great bird circling over her, listening. As the vǫlva reaches a profound state of consciousness, foreknowledge comes to her: "The fates I fathom, yet farther I see | See far and wide the worlds about . . . " ("Vǫluspá," 3–4, 29, in Hollander 1962, 6)

Her spiritual wisdom and experience of "the nine worlds" causes people to seek out the vǫlva for counsel, for healing, and for solutions. They invite her to their homesteads to hold *seiðr*. She mounts the high seat and is surrounded by a chorus of women or of young people. They sing enchanting melodies that enable her to enter trance and to prophesy. She wields a *vǫlur* (ceremonial staff), from which her spiritual office of vǫlva is named: "staff-woman." It is shaped like a distaff, the spinner's wand that folk culture associates with goddesses, the Fates, ancestors—and the power of ordinary women. It is part of the long history of the witch's wand, so vividly remembered in fairy tales (Dashu 2016).

## Oracular Women in Africa

In southeastern Africa, the *makewana* dances beside the Pool of Malawi, invoking the python spirit that dwells within the ancient rain shrine. She is the highest religious authority in Chewa country, consulted on all matters of importance. Her title means "Mother of Children"—all children—mother of all the people. She belongs to a long line of women who have each been designated by spirit selection, according to known, recognizable signs and manifestations. The *makewana*s wear a spiral shell and carry an ebony staff. They have the power to call rain and prophesy (Apawo Phiri 2000, 23–33). So did the rain shrine prophetesses of the Diola in Senegal and the Mujaji line in the Lovedu country of South Africa.

Female oracles were prominent in the borderlands of Uganda, Rwanda, and Congo at the turn of the last century. These *bagirwa* were named after an ancestral queen Nyabinghi whose oracles they were, and whose spirit they channeled when they put on the bark cloth veil. They had political as well as spiritual authority, as shown by their guidance of numerous revolts in the early twentieth century (Dashu 2007).

In Zimbabwe, a series of lion oracles guided the Shona people from a cave sanctuary at Mazoe. They were titled Nehanda after a princess of the Mwanamutapa Empire who founded the shrine around 1450. Even older was the hill sanctuary founded by the great seeress Kasamba in the time of Bantu migrations into southern Africa, as recounted by oral histories of the Goba people. She was revered as an ancestor at the shrine, where successor priestesses became her oracles and wielded the authority to select kings.

Old Chinese sources describe the *wu* as performing invocation and divination, healing, driving off evil spirits, and performing ecstatic rain dances. Many powers were attributed to the *wu* in their ecstatic ceremonies: "They could become invisible, they slashed themselves with knives and swords, cut their tongues, swallowed swords, and spat fire, were carried off on a cloud that shone as if with lightning. The female *wu* danced whirling dances, spoke the language of spirits, and around them objects rose in the air and knocked together" (Eliade 1972, 454). The archaic character for *wu* depicts shamans dancing around a pillar, waving their long sleeves. In the third century BCE, the *Guoyu* says that the *wu* worked with spirits in their ceremonies. It identifies *wu* as a female title, stating that male shamans were called *xi* and the females *wu* (the *wu* character is incorporated into the *xi* glyph as the meaning-bearing radical). Several centuries later, the oldest Chinese dictionary, *Shuowen Jiezi*, underlines the word's female signification, describing the *wu* as an invocator (*zhu*), "a woman who is able to render [herself] invisible, and with dance to invoke gods to come down" (Erickson 1994, 52).

For centuries the Mapuche people of Chile have been guided by medicine women called *machi*. They invoke the Powers (in both female and male forms), prophesy, heal, and act on the weather. A *machi* enters sacred consciousness by chanting, drumming on the *kultrún*, and mounting the *rewe*. This spirit pillar is a ladder into other worlds, a tree hewn and carved with ancestral images. Branches of the *foye* tree are tied to it with other offerings. The *machi* also leads the *nguillatun*, a great ceremony in which the entire community asks for blessings as they dance rounds (Bacigalupo 2007).

Aztec codices produced shortly after the Spanish conquest show women presiding over the *temezcalli* (sweathouse). An invocation to the Grandmother sung by one of these healing priestesses was written down: "Mother of the gods and us all, whose creative and life-giving power shone in the Temezcalli, also named Xochicalli, the place where she sees sacred things, sets to right what has been deranged in human bodies, makes young and tender things growing and strong, and where she aids and cures" (Nuttall 1901, 128). These were the ancestors of present-day *curanderas*.

Some indigenous cultures of Mexico preserved these invocatory chants. One of the great masters of incantation was the Mazatec *curandera* María Sabina, "a woman who knows how to swim in the sacred" (Estrada 1977, 139). Laying on of hands was part of her healing practice. In her *veladas* (all-night candle ceremonies) she blessed and shared the entheogenic psilocybin mushrooms that she called *los Niños Santos* (the holy children). These, along with her incantations and prayers, enabled her to enter into deep states of consciousness: "I let myself be carried off. I don't resist, and I fall into a deep well, endlessly, and I feel a vertigo. When the Niños Santos work inside my body, I talk to them, I ask them the favor of blessing us and teaching us the way, the truth, the healing. That they will give us the power to dredge out the evil, in order to end it" (Echevarría 1979).

Among the Kashaya in northern California, the great *yomta* Essie Parrish was one of the *Bole Maru* dreamers of the Pomo. Her honorific title *yomta* means "song," and she carried chants for healing and ceremonies in the traditional roundhouse (Dashu 2010a). She danced with two doctoring staffs as recorded in photographs and in the 1953 film *Pomo Shaman*, where she heals disease by the power of water:

I believe in creation. From the beginning, in my dream and in my vision, it was shown to me how the world was created. My way of doctoring is about creation. This water is creation. Without the water, we could not live. Without the water, the things of the world would fail. Everything fails without the water. . . . We couldn't walk without the water. Our blood couldn't circulate without the water. . . . When I take out disease, after I put it in the water, it disappears there in so many minutes. It doesn't stay, it doesn't lay in the ground, it doesn't stay in the basket—it disappears. . . . Wherever I go, in stranger-places, I have to call on the Spirit. [Pause] Do not doubt this work, because it is spiritual. (Heick and Mueller 1953)

Women are thought to have a special capacity for these spiritual gifts in many parts of the world. In the far northeast of Asia, the Chukchi have a proverb: "Woman is by nature a shaman" (Czaplicka 1914, 243). Maria Czaplicka detailed many Russian sources that referred to a pre-ponderance of female shamans in Siberia, especially among the most north Asian ancient peoples (Heick and Mueller 1953).

## Constructing Shamanism as a Male Domain

Despite this emphasis on the feminine, scholars have often slighted the female dimension of this realm of spiritual experience. Mircea Eliade notoriously believed that women shamans represented a degeneration of a profession that was originally all male. Yet he was hard put to explain why so many male shamans customarily dressed in women's clothing, or wore symbolic breasts on their shamans' coats, or assumed feminine-gendered behaviors. He insisted that the strong feminine charge around shamans' regalia and behavior "does not appear to indicate any priority of women in the earliest shamanism" (Eliade 1972, 258). He did not bother to supply any evidence for this claim.

The projection of "shamanism" as a masculine sphere ignores the predominance of female shamans in many cultures. This was true for the ancient *wu* of China and *mikogami* of Japan, as it still is for the *mudang* in modern Korea and the *yuta* in Okinawa, for the *izangoma* and *amagqirha* in South Africa, the Karok *eem* in northern California, and the *machi* in Chile. In the Philippines also, the *babaylan* (Visayan) and *catalonan* (Tagalog) have been overwhelmingly women. The female pattern holds true for the *völur* in medieval Scandinavia and the much-maligned European witches in all their varied names who were described as engaging in shamanic flight, shape-shifting, prophecy, and healing.

Many cultures recognize both women and men as shamans (but it can take quite a bit of digging through the literature to locate the women). Women are well represented among the *belian, wadian,* or *dukun* in Indonesia, for example, and in many cultures of Africa and the Americas. There certainly exist cultures where male shamans predominate (though even there, many are gay or transfeminine). And some cultures throw up direct barriers to women, as many institutionalized priesthoods do. In Yunnan, the Jinuo and the Nakhi say that the shamans were once women, but that men took over that sphere, now emptied of females. So the global picture is complex and variegated.

## Oral Histories of Women as Original Shamans

The masculine-default theory also fails to account for widespread traditions that the first shaman was a woman. The Puyuma of Taiwan credit a woman named Udekaw. The Magyars spoke of a woman named Rasdi. For the Jinuo of Yunnan, it was two women, Mili Jide and Mupu Shaode, who not only originated the ceremonies but also taught people to forage, farm, and herd, and invented weaving and irrigation. In the Baikal region of southern Siberia, the Buryat say that a shepherd girl was the first *udgan;* she received her gift from an eagle sent from on high. Evenks say that the old women who guarded the road to the dead were progenitors of all later shamans (Jacobson 1993, 174).

The oldest Japanese book, the *Kojiki,* describes the ecstatic dancer Ame-no-Uzume as the foundational *mikogami.* Koreans recount how the "thrown-away" princess Bari Gongju became the first *mudang.* In the Bwiti religion of Gabon, an aboriginal Babongo woman called Disumba discovered the entheogenic plant *iboga;* she is called "the beginning of Bwiti" (Fernandez 1982, 321–22). Other accounts say that Benzogho, a Fang woman, started the Bwiti ceremonies after learning about this ecstatic medicine from the Babongo forest people. In eastern Indonesia, the Toradja of Sulawesi recount that the first *bajasa* was a woman who fell ill and was taken to the sky world to learn the healing arts—a theme of initiatory illness or "spirit sickness" common all over the world.

Looking deep into the past, archaeology and rock art are rich in images invoking women. In ancient sculpture and painted ceramics, ancient women dance into ecstasy, shape-shift into birds, deer, or polar bears, and fly in the spirit (for examples, see Dashu 2013). The women pour libation, lay on hands, drum, and shake the gourd rattle or the sistrum. They chew *huachuma* cactus buttons in Perú, *Amanita muscaria* in Siberia, and psilocybin mushrooms in Mexico. They direct power with their staff: the *vǫlur* (Scandinavia) or the *khatvanga* (south Asia) or *thyrsos* (Greece).

These sacred wands are still around: there is the Huichol *muwieri*, the Tuvan *tava* with its many strands, and the *ileeshin* of Nana Burukú, a curved bundle of raffia or palm that must never be held by a man. The divinatory mirror of ancient Afghanistan has a Tibetan counterpart in the *mélong*, the initiatory mirror of the dakinis, by which they impart *rigpa*, or true vision. Shamans in north and central Asia wear the mirror on their robes, and use it to divine, heal, and chase away negative spirits.

Around the world, historical sources and orature (oral literature) show women acting as healers, herbalists, oracles, diviners, ecstatic dancers, and dreamers. They are priestesses of the ancestors, like the *nganga* who consecrate and keep the *minkisi* in the Congo. Medicine women in North America act as guardians of sacred bundles, teach reverence for the waters, and lead the way to protect them. Ancient Kemetic women are depicted with ceremonial fans, which are still used in Korea and in the Yoruba religion. In Vietnam and Korea, women are still dancing the old divinities, carrying over and preserving their ancient melodies and litanies. Women keep these ways alive in spite of tremendous cultural pressures that work against female leadership and against indigenous spiritual heritages.

## Reinterpretations of "Shamanism"

There is not enough space to do justice to all these traditions, only to sketch out the vast terrain that is missing from most accounts of *shamanism.* I have *italicized* that word because it has come to mean so many things to different people, often drifting far from its origins. The word *saman/shaman* comes from the Tungusic languages of the Evenk, Even', Nanay, Manchu, and related peoples in northeast Asia (Dashu 2010b). Anthropologists adopted the word *shaman* from Russian ethnographic literature about Siberia because they were trying to fill a linguistic gap for a concept that had been stripped from most European languages (see Dashu 2011b for a discussion of the word *shaman,* its borrowings and transformations, and the politics of cultural appropriation).

In the colonial era, European outsiders projected their own ideas on indigenous ecstatics, portraying them as prestidigitating magicians, fraudulent tricksters, even as frenzied mad people. In the Americas they frequently called them "jugglers"; in Africa, "witch doctors." To understand where these negative depictions came from, we have to back up further, to the suppression of parallel spiritual ways in Europe itself. The persecution of pagans and the witch hunts that followed targeted ecstatic practices that were part of folk religion. The priesthood interpreted them through its lens of diabolism, decreeing that all non-Christian deities were "devils." They demonized the folk goddesses beloved by the common people—and any chants, dances, and ceremonies connected with them, with land spirits, or ancestors. Over many centuries, European culture became deeply stained by the ideology of "devil worship" forged in these persecutions.

The "Enlightenment" reaction to the witch hunts put an end to the torture trials and burnings but failed to reconsider negative attitudes toward the animist, magical culture of the common people. Instead, there was a rush to a rationalistic, mechanistic, and linear worldview, intensified by the capitalist obsession with wealth extraction. Church dogma was replaced with the new "modern" doctrine of scientism (which, however, retained its patriarchal dogmatism). The precious cultural knowledge of millennia of human experience was rejected as ignorance, even "savagery," in a process that has been described as "the disenchantment of the world" (originating with the poet Friedrich Schiller, the phrase was popularized by Max Weber in *The Sociology of Religion*).

All this resulted in an impoverishment of European culture. Lost were the words describing spiritual practices and experiences once held in common with other peoples around the world. Animist names for *life force,* like Anglo-Saxon *lyb,* or words for concepts of soul and vitality, like Old Norse *hugr* and *hamr,* dropped out of use. Ways of talking about these realities were wiped out or driven so deeply underground that they could only be shared in marginalized rural enclaves. And then the ideology of "devil worship" and "superstition" was turned against new targets during the era of European conquest and empire.

The practice and ways of medicine have political ramifications because they represent direct spiritual power, energy that cannot be controlled by man-made hierarchies or systems of domination. They place us in direct contact with *khaos* in its original sense of the primordial vastness (and even in its more recent scientific meanings, from quantum physics to meteorology, to the flight patterns of bird flocks). Shamans connect with the core of being, the resonant whole, and oppressive social orders perceive this as a threat to their authoritarian control. They cannot tolerate cosmologies that emphasize relatedness, that delve into the ineffable, timeless cycles of creation and destruction.

Women's spiritual power is seen as a threat to male supremacist systems. They recognize its potential to overturn the social controls that sustain domination, exploitation, and injustice. So they respond to female spiritual power with violence and persecution. They call it evil and unnatural and attempt to repress it, as in the European witch hunts, in Confucian attacks on the *wu* in China and the *yuta* in Okinawa, or witch hunts still going on in India and Nepal, Papua New Guinea, or South Africa.

We can't understand these sacred ways without putting women back in the picture. In academia, *shamanism* quickly came to be framed as a masculine preserve. Tungusic cultures did not restrict the title *sama/shaman* to males, as shown by the Manchu tale "Nishan Shaman," which paints its female protagonist as the greatest shaman. But "Western" academicians reshaped *shaman* according to their own prevailing masculine default. They applied *he, his, him* so consistently that it was often impossible to determine if any female shamans existed in the cultures being discussed. It was as though women did not exist; nor were they worth considering in shamanic studies.

More insidiously, the assumption of masculine gender for *shaman* became so pervasive that when writers did mention female shamans, they added a feminizing suffix (Russian *shamanka,* English *shamaness*). The effect was to make women appear secondary, derivative. As these masculinizing preconceptions spread into popular culture, they gave rise to the neologism *shamen.* The second syllable of Tungusic *shaman* was equated to the English word *man,* so that the plural *men* was assumed for an (unrelated) Asian word.

This masculine default is still influential in current sources. At this writing, Wikipedia states: "The Buryat word for shaman is *бөө (böö),*" but this is only the term for *male* shamans. Then, the female title is listed in the second paragraph, under 'shamaness'" ("Shamanism in Siberia," Wikipedia). The masculine term is presumed to be *the* word, even when this notion collides with reality. Many north Asian languages have a shared word for the female shaman: Buryat *udagan,* Mongolian *idughan,* Yakut *udaghan,* Evenki and Lamut *udugan,* Nedigal *odogan,* among many others. These titles may originate with a name for Earth, *etügen,* which is also used for the hearth goddess (Czaplicka 1914, 243), or they may be related to the ancient Turkic word for fire (*ut, öt*). Yet another derivation is from the word *udkha,* "root, essence, supernatural ability" (Humphrey 1998, 53).

## Reclaiming the Real Power of Women

We desperately need another angle for what is often called "the Divine Feminine"—and for the very concept of "femininity." These are cultural definitions, and in the dominant cultures they are patriarchal: hyper-sexualizing, subordinating, and constraining. For this reason, many of us prefer to say "female," reclaiming our bodies and investing them with our own meanings, distinct from patriarchal commodification and the male gaze. The word *feminine* is loaded with cultural demands and restrictions on how we women inhabit our bodies, how we move and speak. We are tyrannized by cultural messages that imprint in us a sense that our bodies are not acceptable, that we must perform certain scripts, without being even entirely conscious of those demands. But still we feel their weight in our body-soul.

Women have been engaged in a prolonged process of throwing off these old cultural trances of the patriarchy. A big obstacle is the power of representation in media, which poisons the depiction of spiritual women. In the past decade, I've watched an explosion of pornified images labeled as "shamaness," "priestess," "witch," "medicine woman," "goddess"—even "Amazon"—spread across the internet (Dashu 2011a). They rehearse familiar female stereotypes: tightly posed with their breasts thrust out and their backs arched, their knees coyly drawn together, their toes pointed. This hypersexualized "pretty lady" stereo-type is all about external appearance and has nothing to do with the deep pulse of power within the body of a healer—the spirit-filled pres-ence of a woman in a deep state of unified consciousness.

The market-packaged harm of toxic prescriptive femininity is not what real female power looks like. That can be seen in the potency of the Karok or Pomo medicine woman, the Visayan *babaylan*, the dynamic presence of the *izangoma* in South Africa. It is also found in the insurgent culture that reclaims the witches, in their original sense of "wisewomen," and the old stories of women who go by night with the Goddess, with the faery hosts, the ancestors.

We are bringing transformative power to bear on the ways that toxic culture has imprinted itself on our bodies and damaged our psyches. We find pathways for that release: through walking out on the land, chanting, lamenting, deep crying, and laughter yoga, and by practicing other kinds of breathwork, meditation, qigong, and the circle dance. We learn how to get out from the cultural spells cast by the patriarchy, and the unconscious self-doubt and fears they have sown in us. Many women have a hard time relaxing into sacred dance because the external gaze weighs on them so heavily.

This is why ecstatic sacred dance is one of the pathways for releasing old wounds. It is now being rediscovered and practiced in many places. This form of dance is a way of praying with the body; transforming ourselves on material as well as psychic levels. We can do this alone and in community. It is a powerful way to uncover our authentic essence and to live it fully. We do this by going through the layers of emotion, the memory of trauma held in the body, and letting out the sounds. In this we break free of social conditioning to reclaim our wildness and oldness of spirit.

This reclamation has historical antecedents in women's ecstatic dances that were depicted in ancient ceramics of Anatolia, Iraq, Iran, and Pakistan; the rock art of the Sahara, South Africa, and Spain; the temple art of India; and Cretan and Mycenaean seals. Women's ceremonial dance survives in some parts of the world: the *ahouash* of the Amazighen/Berbers; the embracing circle dances of Adivasi women in India; and the *ganggangsullae* (moon dance) of Korea, done at night, sometimes until dawn. Bulgarian women kept the round dance alive, with many intricate and repetitive steps that induce an altered state of consciousness. That psychic shift is also prominent in the North African ceremonies of the *zar* or *bori*, an overwhelmingly female occasion of dancing in the spirits, and the entranced *sanghyang* of Bali. Rhythm also figures strongly in the shift to altered states of consciousness, whether it is with the frame drum, the clapping sticks of the Pomo, the *takuará* stamping tubes of the Guaraní, or the reclamation of the *djembe* in the African diaspora.

Many of us are seeking to recover our own ancestral heritages— whatever those are—and to find an authentic place to stand in our own truth. Those heritages may be lost, or survive only in torn fragments. As cultural exiles cut off from initiatory transmission, dealing with stress, trauma, or illness, our greatest remedy is to go back to the root: to seek inspiration directly from nature, from land and sea, from incantation and movement, from drumming and dreaming. This to me is the core of the women's spirituality movement.

There is a tremendous trove of knowledge to be recovered about women who dive into the ecstatic realm, beyond our personal selves and beyond the bounds of space and time. This rejuvenation of deep cultural memory is crucial to understanding who we are as women, and that our being is not defined by the dominant culture—or by any culture of domination. We need to understand that our access to these realms is not secondary or derivative from what men do. It is primeval, and it is our own. We enter the spirit worlds not in spite of our female bodies, but by fully inhabiting them, being grounded in their awesome capacities, and by expanding our awareness within them. We are rediscovering our original reality in the spirit of distant ancestors who are still present in our blood and bone.

# 5

# Her Share of Divine Madness

## The Role of Women in the Ancient Rites of Dionysus

### Chiara Baldini

*You may not remember,*
*But let me tell you this,*
*Someone in some future time*
*Will think of us.*

SAPPHO

## The Women of Amphissa

On a very cold winter day almost twenty-five hundred years ago, a group of women from Delphi arrived in the town of Amphissa after much aimless wandering on nearby Mount Parnassus. Tired, cold, and "not yet in their right minds," they flung themselves down in the market square and fell asleep where they lay. The local women saw them fast asleep in the middle of the town and, worried about the presence of many soldiers that were occupying Amphissa, decided to gather around them in silence to protect them. The following morning, when the strangers woke up, the local women gave them food and water and, after receiving the consent of their husbands, accompanied the strangers to the frontier, where they would be safe.

This story is narrated by Plutarch in *On the Bravery of Women,* inspired by a conversation he had with Klea, a high priestess of Dionysus at Delphi (Harrison 1991, 392). Apparently, the facts narrated by Plutarch took place around 354–353 BCE (Bremmer 2006, 39), when a group of *maenads*—women dedicated to the practice of an archaic ritual in honor of Dionysus—got lost while on their way to Delphi.

In this essay we will take a closer look at them. Who were the maenads? Why were they "not yet in their right minds"? What did they do on the mountain without the supervision of their husbands? How did the social and political context in which they lived react to their unusual spiritual practice? To start to give answers to these questions we will first inquire into the nature of Dionysus.

## God of Nature and Ecstasy

Dionysus is generally known today as the god of wine, sex, and intoxication, typically portrayed drunk, holding or wearing grapes, and trailed by his "riotous crew of nymphs and satyrs," an interpretation typical of the Hellenistic and Roman times (Dodds 1960, xi). In the classical age, the god still retained much of his primordial nature as a vegetation and fertility god (Otto 1965, 49)—an irresistibly beautiful androgynous young man representing the vital, irrational, untamed, lusty essence of wild nature.

In early literary sources he is referred to as "power of the tree," "blossom bringer," "fruit bringer," and "the sap in the plants" (Dodds 1960, xi). He is the "archetypal image of indestructible life" (Kerényi 1996), representing life's irresistible impulse to reproduce itself endlessly, manifesting as both the force that pushes a plant out of its seed and the urge of sexual attraction. In animal form he was commonly associated with the bull, the archetype of the masculine principle of fecundity and potency (Harrison 1991, 436).

His worship was very widespread all over classical Greece in the form of public festivals and processions marking the seasonal changes and the phases of wine making. In the Hellenistic age private initiations also became very popular, given their tantalizing mixture of loud, fast-paced music, frenetic dances, the drinking of wine mixed with herbs,. sexual licentiousness, and the enthusiastic release of emotions.

Initiations were open to everyone, including slaves, women, and homosexuals (Evans 1988), and this tolerance often stood in direct contrast with the moral values and civilized behavior promoted by the emerging Greek patriarchal society. Dionysian religion, in other words, was "expression of a religious attitude, and the memorial of a religious experience, different from anything implied in the cult of the traditional Olympian gods" (Dodds 1960, xi). Thus Dionysian worship, though very popular, was often vehemently opposed, and the inclusion of Dionysus in the official Greek pantheon was often questioned. But how did it all start?

## To the Mountain!

From ancient sources, it seems that as early as the eighth century BCE (Bremmer 2006, 39) there existed an archaic form of Dionysian rite practiced by women only. They would gather in local congregations called *thiasoi*, to then climb to mountaintops every two years to perform a mysterious ritual. *Thiasoi* were composed of women of different ages and "unmarried girls were allowed to . . . share the transports of the elders" (Dodds 2004, 270), evoking a touching image of young women carrying older ones up the mountain despite the discomfort and risks that such an extreme practice could involve.

The mountain ritual was known as *Oreibasia*, from *Eis oros!*— "to the mountain!"— and was mentioned in the *Homeric Hymn to Demeter* (seventh century BCE) and also by Alcman, Anacreon, and

Aristophanes before being extensively described in *The Bacchae* by Euripides in the fourth century BCE.

According to ancient iconography, maenads wore fawn skins and ivy wreaths and carried the *thyrsus*, a fennel stalk crowned with a pine cone. Their name comes from *meinesthai,* meaning "to go crazy," and has been translated as "mad one, rushing one, inspired one, raging one" (Harrison 1991, 389). Another name commonly used was *bacchantes,* from *bacchein:* "to revel," underlining the peculiar character of their practice. Bacchic rites, in fact, challenged the norms of socially accepted behavior for women, as evidenced by another attribute of Dionysus, *gynaimanes,* "he who drives women insane" (Kraemer 1979, 64). However, no matter how "insane" they were (or maybe *because* they were "insane"), maenads and their mysterious mountain gatherings have traveled across time and space in the work of countless artists, writers, poets, and researchers, who have been offering myriad interpretations of their myth. What did these women actually *do* on the mountain? What was the connection between the ritual practice and the participants' state of mind? How "insane" did they actually get—and why?

## Madness Divine

In many ancient sources maenads are depicted playing the *tympanon,* or frame drum, together with the *aulos,* a double flute also known as pan flute, considered "the orgiastic instruments par excellence" (Dodds 2004, 275). *Maenadic* music had therefore a repetitive, maddening quality, which was intensified by the repetition of words like *Eis oros!* and *Evohè!* an "ecstasy-producing self-hypnotic technique, probably used to increase the synchronization effect" (Bremmer 1984, 277). Their dance most likely included specific body movements, like throwing their heads backward and "hip-swaying" (Bremmer 2006, 39; Dodds 2004, 273), to intensify the entrancement effect and alter their perception.

Besides these ritual practices, the ingestion of mind-altering substances was part of Oreibasia. The consumption of wine, however, seems to be very unlikely as it was only available in spring (Dodds 1960, xii; Ruck 1982, 163). Therefore the use of other plant stimulants like mushrooms, roots, and seeds—considered "the wild botanic version of Dionysus" (Ruck 1982, 163)—was a better fit for the mountain ritual than the cultivated and "civilized" wine. Ruck also infers that the *thyrsus* functioned as a receptacle of wild plants, indicating the maenads' role as herbal gatherers. Another name for the fennel wand was *narthex,* etymologically derived as the "narcotic receptacle" (Ruck 1982, 162) and "a clear indication that the mountain orgy of the bacchantes entails a ritualized picking of the magical psychoactive wild plants which commemorated the intoxicants predating the cultivated art of viticulture" (Ruck 2015a, 9).

The nature and existence of ritual sexuality in *maenadism* remains a topic for debate. This is partly due to the relative scarcity of direct reports of such practices in ancient sources, with the exception of a few clues like this in *The Bacchae*, where the women are described as "hunting Aphrodite by themselves throughout the woods" (v. 688). As explained by Kraemer: "On the one hand the maenads are repeatedly accused of sexual immorality while in the possession of Dionysus, but often elsewhere in the same myth, and in *The Bacchae* themselves, they are defended from such accusations" (1979, 68).

What we can attest with a degree of certainty is that in the Hellenistic and imperial periods, once men also joined the cult, sexuality seems to have been an integral part of Dionysian worship. As Henrichs notes, "sexually unrestricted Dionysian groups . . . mushroomed during the Hellenistic period and provided the model for the ubiquitous Dionysian mystery cults of the imperial era" (1982, 147).

However, even if in a later period ritual sexuality might have provided a liberating experience of "reversal of the normal conventions of decency" (Henrichs 1982, 148), originally it was a "spiritual technology" inherited by primitive agrarian rituals, whose aim, besides reaching ecstatic peaks of rapture and divine inspiration, was to propitiate the fertility of both the people and the land (Frazer 1996, 156). On this point the late Layne Redmond, composer, author, and a renowned drummer herself, makes an interesting comparison between the use of drumming and sex in fertility rituals in connection with primitive goddess culture: "The association of the drum with fertility encompassed human sexuality. In many ancient cultures drums were particularly associated with feminine sexual energy. As instigator of creation, the Goddess manifested in sexual desire and union. The drum she held identified her with the primal rhythms of life apparent in the sexual act" (1997, 21).

These (and maybe more) ritual practices combined with a millennia-old expertise on how to use them were the "techniques of ecstasy" described by Eliade (1964) or the "driving behaviors" (Lewis 1971, 606–14) used by the maenads in their rituals to enter into a state of blissful rapture. This state was generally described as being possessed by Dionysus himself, but it can now be explained as the result of the skillful deployment of specific ritual behaviors: "The combination of physical exertion, thinner air, low temperature, lack of sleep, lack of oxygen and consequent exhilaration, all contributed to enter into an altered state and increasing susceptibility to visions. . . . Continuous subjection to the rhythms of the drums . . . has a synchronizing effect on the activity of neuronal cells in some centers of the brain. The external rhythm becomes the synchronizer of the activity of the brain; as a result the sound and the action 'possess' and control the participant" (Bremmer 1984, 278).

The experience provided "a sense of identity with a supernatural power" (Lewis 1971, 26), but also "a gift of illumination, in return for a surrendering of the self or part of the self, described in the classical language of mysticism as gnosis—a fusing of human and divinity—which is part of controlled spirit possession everywhere" (Lewis 1971, 57). For "controlled possession" Lewis refers to a cult that is based on the "deliberate cultivation of ecstatic states" (57), thus ascribing maenadism to a Greek version of a shamanic lineage sharing similar techniques and aims across time and space.

## They Work Strange Deeds

When discussing Dionysian madness, the words of Plato from the *Phaedrus* (370 BCE, trans. 1952) generally provide an explanation of how techniques to induce an altered state of consciousness were sanctioned in Greek culture as an accepted form of spiritual practice. The philosopher, in fact, has Socrates stating that one of the world's greatest blessings comes from mania, or divinely inspired madness. Dionysus, in particular, is said to reside over the telestic mania, the kind of madness triggered during initiation rituals or *teletai* (58), of which Oreibasia was an example (Burkert 1987, 19).

Greek society was already "male oriented and patriarchal" (Henrichs 1982, 38) and founded itself on principles of rationality, moderation, self-control and, in the case of women, chastity and fidelity. Thus, women alone on mountains practicing madness-inducing rituals raised many doubts, sparked rumors, triggered severe judgments, and generally contributed to a reputation of threatening invulnerability and scandalous sexual freedom. As Kraemer notes, what maenads did was not even "appropriate behavior of Greek male citizens" (1992, 40), and as Bremmer specifies: "the name *maenad* was essentially a poetic word which had decidedly pejorative connotations and which evidently reflected male disapproval of the female worshippers of Dionysus" (1984, 281).

*The Bacchae* by Euripides, and specifically the character of Pentheus, is a great example of how some men (and possibly some women) could react to maenads. Pentheus was the king whose kingdom was invaded by Dionysus, who convinced all women to follow him to the tops of mountains to perform his rites. The king, infuriated, sent a messenger to spy on them and report to him. In Murray's translation, the messenger reports:

> I have seen the wild white women there, o king, . . . and come to tell
> thee how they work strange deeds. . . . Like invaders . . . everything
> in sight they pillaged and destroyed. They snatched the children
> from their homes . . . flames flickered in their curls and did not burn

them. Then the villagers furious at what the women did took their arms. And there was something terrible to see. For the men's spears were pointed and sharp and yet drew no blood whereas the wands the women drew inflicted wounds. And then the men ran, routed by women! (vv. 664–711)

In this passage we see how maenads are depicted not only as raging invincible creatures, but also as hunters and dominators in an ironic reversal of roles, which must have sounded very frightening. Another myth circulating about maenads as hunters was that they practiced *sparagmos* and *homophagia*, the ritual killing of a wild animal with bare hands to then eat it raw. From a mythological perspective, the wild essence of the spirit of Dionysus was thought to reside in the flesh of the animal, making these practices into a sort of "primitive Eucharist" (Bremmer 1984, 267; Henrichs 1982, 159). However, even if the most famous scene of *sparagmos* is contained in *The Bacchae*, the actual performance of such a savage act is still contentious and generally considered belonging to mythical rather than historical maenadism (Bremmer 1984, 275; Henrichs 1982, 144).

This mixture between truth and rumor, madness and divinity, sublime beauty and frightening savagery accompanied maenadism throughout its history. Today still, in the comments of modern researchers we can often perceive similarly severe judgments over the behavior of the ancient madwomen.

## The "Feminine Thing"

*Le mènadisme est chose feminine.*
MARCEL DETIENNE

Ever since Nietzsche, a comparison has been made between Dionysian rituals and the dancing epidemics of the Middle Ages (see page 22 of the 2000 edition of his 1872 publication). And although the German philosopher is known to have supported the cultural and social need for the vitality expressed through Dionysian madness, he seems to only have done so for men and did not spend much time discussing female participation.

Later, the general approach has been to interpret the "epidemic" of *maenadic* rites as a manifestation of the need for spaces where women could "hysterically" release their suppressed emotions, thus fulfilling an all-too-female biological need. "What happened on Mount Cithaeron was hysteria in the raw," exclaims Dodds, referring to the *sparagmos* in *The Bacchae* yet sounding as scandalized as if it had happened for real. He goes on to explain: "By canalizing such hysteria in an organized rite once in two years, the Dionysiac cult kept it within bounds and gave it a relatively harmless outlet" (2004, 272), as if to say: men are keeping female hysteria under control by allowing women to run on mountains every now and then. After all, as he justified: "That the god should make his first converts among the women is natural in view of the narrow and repressed lives which Greek women commonly led" (xxvi).

Lewis, on the contrary, bravely states that: "It would no doubt be satisfying to male vanity to interpret the marked prominence of women . . . as the reflection of an inherent and biologically grounded female disposition to hysteria" (1971, 100). Instead, he proposes that the rites were a sort of tolerated infringement of patriarchal rules, or a "thinly disguised protest movement directed against the dominant sex" (31), still implying, however, that maenadism developed as women's reaction to the limitations imposed by men.

Kraemer, a feminist scholar, seems to agree with Lewis, dismissing any "appeals to the 'emotional' needs of women" as "unsubstantiated" (1979, 56) and proposing that Dionysiac possession enabled women "at least temporarily to defy their normal roles and participate in activities that were normally not permitted to them, within a framework which prohibited the exercise of any serious sanctions against them, since the possession was in most instances, understood to be amoral and irresistible" (80). However, considering that the rites originated in prepatriarchal times, Kraemer eventually concludes that: "the cult did not arise as a response to the devaluation of women, but rather became a means to cope with it" (80).

Henrichs then seems to postulate the need for releasing stress through physical exercise as a main motive behind the rites when he states that: "By all indications, the peculiar religious identity of the maenads had more to do with sweat and physical exhaustion than with an abnormal state of mind" (1982, 147). And Bremmer brings this theory even further when he makes a daring comparison with modern disco: "where we find the same phenomena of auditory and photic driving, headshaking and strenuous activity, which help modern youths to get through the boredom of everyday life: maenadism as a Saturday Night Fever avant la lettre—a sobering thought" (1984, 286). I personally agree that a comparison with the repetitive beats of electronic music is legitimate, but modern rave parties happening on top of mountains offer a much better parallel than "discos," and their spiritual dimension cannot be overlooked in favor of the possibility that they also afford an escape from boredom (Baldini 2010).

More recent research is now bringing back the spiritual aspect of maenadism, as articulated by Redmond, who states that "Mastery of the precise musical rhythms required to align the devotees' consciousness with the divine suggests a control and sophistication of technique that contradicts the historical image of wanton frenzied women" (1997, 131). With this statement Redmond reconnects maenads to the millennia old spiritual lineage of shamanic drummers they belong to, one that used dancing, among other techniques, to facilitate mystical experiences and not just to release stress, scream out the pain of patriarchal wounds, and act "as men."

## The Liminal Space

As a matter of fact, maenads left civilization behind and entered "into the wild" to enter a space of deep communion with untamed nature, mingling with wild animals, ingesting wild plants, and dancing to the point of forgetting who they are, thus becoming "wild with divinity" (Euripides v. 679). We find an example of such a deep communion with nature in this idyllic picture painted by Euripides:

> The entire mountain and its wild animals were, like them,
> in one Bacchic ecstasy.
> As these women moved, they made all things dance
> (vv. 896–98)

Furthermore, the objective of Oreibasia could be seen as a sort of "training in liminality," where participants navigated the "space in between" wild nature and civilization, human and animal, male and female, rational and irrational, using techniques that brought sanity by means of madness. In Dionysian rituals, Kraemer explains, "It is insane to be sane, sane to be insane" (1979, 67). Undergoing such a "training" thus allowed these women to have a firsthand experience of the paradoxical nature of reality, which only superficially seems to be "one or the other," but at a deeper level reveals itself to be "both at the same time." After all, ambiguity, paradox, reversal, duality, and contrast are all elements typical of Dionysian worship. This is evidenced by the god's epithet *dimorphos,* or dual form (Otto 1965, 9; Henrichs 1982, 158)—revealing a spiritual practice where the attainment of wisdom comes from the experience of the coexistence of opposites as a genuine manifestation of the Divine, forever ambiguous and paradoxical.

According to Bøgh, "the seeking of wisdom was one of the main drives behind Bacchic conversions, and it was seen as the 'understanding or knowing the truth of life and death and of good and evil'" (2014, 45). The attainment of this special knowledge (which renders the maenads in *The Bacchae* "blessed," "fortunate," "prudent") ended up influencing the initiate's entire life, going well beyond the frenzy of the moment (30). Moreover, the sharing of the ecstatic experience and of the knowledge thus derived allowed women to establish exceptionally close bonds with each other "not as a by-effect, but as the main result of the rites" (30). Initiation thus conveyed a permanent change, involving joining a group for life, developing a new religious identity and a lifelong commitment: "Being a [Dionysian] initiate is the whole story of one's whole life," explained an epitaph found at the entrance of a temple of Dionysus (Bøgh, 34).

This seems to contradict another common concept according to which Dionysian women were like "quiet housewives" (Bremmer 1984, 277) who turned into raging maenads through ritual practice and who then "came down from the mountain, resumed their normal lives and waited for the return of the ritual two years later" (Henrichs 1982, 147).

## In Search of the Goddess of Ecstasy

If maenadism was the continuation of an ancient shamanic tradition where wise and wild women were dedicated to ecstatic practices, what *was* this tradition and what do we know about it?

Jane Ellen Harrison, writing in the beginning of the twentieth century and probably the first ever female classical scholar, rightly pointed out in her *Prolegomena to the Study of Greek Religion*: "A god can only exist so long as he is the mirror of the people who worship him" (1991, 545).* In another work, she goes further: "How can a *thiasos* of women project a young male god? They cannot, and they do not, who then do they worship?" (*Themis,* 2010, 38).† The question that seems to arise here is: Was there an original female divinity that was then replaced by Dionysus?

As a matter of fact, Dionysus's name is first attested in a Linear B inscription found on the island of Crete and dating back to the thirteenth century BCE (Kerényi 1996, 68). There the celebration of the fertility of the land and of the cycles of nature were among the main

---

*Jane Ellen Harrison originally published this work in 1903.
†These words were originally published in 1912.

motives for religious rites. Techniques of ecstasy were central to spiritual practice, and women played a major role in the celebrations of rituals (Eisler 2011; Kerényi 1996). According to Kerényi, in Minoan Crete the main deity was a great goddess, dwelling on mountain peaks and bearing an "evident relationship with wild nature" (8), while the bull, later associated with Dionysus, was another main motif and "an exemplary manifestation of the deity in Crete" (13). This seems to indicate that Greek maenadism could have carried a reminiscence of those times, when ecstatic rites were officiated by women in honor of a great goddess of fertility and wild nature, and the bull was the ever-present metaphor of the male fecundating principle.

When her work was published in 1903, Harrison was seemingly the first to evidence the importance of the origins of the cult as a clue to the presence of women, when she remarked that the "Dionysian cult is linked to primitive Earth worship" (1991, 390) and it "bears to the end, as no other god does, the stamp of his matriarchal origins" (561). In 1912, she further stated that "*Maenadism* is only to be understood by reference to an earlier social structure, that known as matrilineal" (2010, xviii).

*The Bacchae* also offers a few clues that reinforce this perspective, since Dionysus comes to Thebes to protest that his mother Semele—which translates as "Mother Earth" (Harrison 1991, 404; Otto 1965, 69)—is not recognized anymore as a divinity. Dionysus could therefore be identified with the son of the primitive mother goddess and his cult a Greek adaptation and continuation of the fertility rituals of Neolithic times. Maenadism thus provides the missing link between primitive shamanic rituals in honor of Mother Nature present in many cultures worldwide and the surviving pagan tradition of Europe exemplified by the witches of the Middle Ages. As Vicky Noble explains it: "This ancient female lineage began in the Neolithic Age (or even earlier) and included priestesses of the Aegean Bronze and Iron Ages [the *maenads*]; the shaman women of Central Asia . . . and millions of shaman women murdered as witches during the European 'Burning Times'" (2003, 92).

As a matter of fact, the witches were thought to be copulating with a horned god (like a bull god) and were followers of Diana: "a goddess of woodland, of wild things, of nature in general and fertility in particular" (Frazer 1996, 156), denoting an uninterrupted tradition spanning millennia.

In summary, ecstatic dancing in mountain forests to the compelling sound of drums, ingestion of plants with psychotropic properties, indulgence in ritual sexuality, worship of a bull god—these are elements of an ancient female shamanic tradition that shared similar characteristics in most ancient cultures. Maenads were the Greek representatives of this lineage during the transition from primitive matrilineal earth goddess culture toward patriarchal society. This places them in both the role of the great-granddaughters of Neolithic herbal gatherers and worshippers of a goddess of nature and in the role of the great-grandmothers of the witches of early modern Europe.

The Dionysian cult did not originate as a release valve for repressed women. Rather it was the Greek expression of a prepatriarchal cultural paradigm wherein the main deity was once an earth goddess. Ecstatic rites were not peripheral or marginalized, but a prominent feature of religious life. Women played a fundamental role in the administration of those rites and altered states of consciousness were a "spiritual technology" used to attain mystical knowledge about the paradoxical nature of reality and humans' place within the natural world.

Maenadic rituals during classical Greek times functioned as spaces where women could escape the repressive rules of the patriarchy, but also as occasions to commemorate a distant past when women were wild and free, and nature was the dwelling place of the Divine.

# 6

# The Lady Who Served the Mystery Potion

### The Botanical Symbolism behind the Mysteries of Eleusis

### Carl A. P. Ruck

According to myth, the woman who first served the *kykeon*, did something obscene that made the goddess Demeter laugh (*Homeric Hymn to Demeter* 2.203). Kykeon was the mixed drink that was imbibed by the initiates of the Mystery celebrated annually for two millennia at the sanctuary of the "Two Deities" (*tó theó*) at Eleusis, near Athens. The Two Deities were Demeter and Persephone, mother and the daughter, but since the role of one (the daughter) would eventually devolve into that of the other (the mother), they were referred to as the Holy Duo. In the *Homeric Hymn,* the goddess Demeter had been grieving her daughter Persephone, who had been abducted by the lord of the netherworld, Hades, while gathering magical plants with a group of maidens attending her.

The jest that made Demeter laugh consisted of the woman exposing herself in front of the goddess. It was an obscenity, but a sacred one, which contributed to constellating the meaning of the initiation and was an essential element in the indoctrination into the secret of the Mysteries of Demeter and Persephone. How could such a base gesture trigger the insights deemed responsible for the betterment of the thousands of people who came to Eleusis to be initiated? What did the gesture symbolize, who was the woman performing it, and what can we learn from it about the history of one of the best kept secret rituals in ancient Europe?

## The Dwarfish Grotesquerie

The Lady who served the potion was herself the personification of the obscenity, a dwarfish grotesquerie who went by the name of Iambe, named for the iambic rhythm used in poetry to write scurrilous verse. However, the name was also a calque upon the whole series of names punning upon the *ia/o-* root that designated the homonymous word in Greek (*iós*) for the "arrow" and the "drug" or entheogen that anointed it with its "toxicity," so named for the *tóxon,* or poisoned bow. Shamans in classical antiquity commonly traveled in the spirit world upon the vehicle of the arrow with its toxicity.

The verbal root of the name Iambe occurs in the word for the "druggist," doctor as *iatrós,* and in the numerous mythical figures associated with entheogenic empowerment. These figures include Ion of Athens, the eponymous ancestor of the Ionian tribal group of Greek peoples, conceived from a magical crocus plucked in a cave beneath the city's acropolis. Other names derived from the same root are Iamos of Olympia, the etiological founder of its hereditary brotherhood of divinatory shamans, and the cow maiden Io, who was constantly in estrus from the bite of the cow fly (*Tabanus bovinus*), and even Iacchos, who was Bacchos (the chthonic Bacchus, the wine god Dionysus) personified as the joyous shout who led the procession of Eleusinian initiates.

Since the essence of the Mystery initiation at the Eleusinian sanctuary was something seen, a vision of "the holy"—although the hall of initiation was in no way suitable for a theatrical performance—we should expect that the kykeon served by Iambe was psychoactive. This could also be a possible explanation as to why her name belongs to the series of punning personifications upon the motif of the toxic arrow and other psychoactive symbols.

The abduction of Persephone by Hades is a frequent mythical motif of shamanic rapture accessed in rituals of herbalism. In the case of Persephone's experience, it was occasioned by the plucking of the *nárkissos* (*Homeric Hymn to Demeter* 2.8) (*Pancratium maritimum* or the sea-daffodil), depicted in preclassical Minoan frescoes, and specifically as a rite of visionary herbalism on a golden ring from Cretan Isopata. The flower's name belongs to the pre-Greek language, but it was assimilated into Greek as the verbal root for *narcosis* and *narcotic*.

## Dirty Dancing

Numerous figurines of Iambe survive that depict the nature of her obscenity. In some she clutches the lyre that would provide the musical accompaniment for her unseemly song and dance. Most characteristic of her obscenity is that her face is displaced to her belly, sometimes with a topknot of hair above, legs joined, and the vulva located at the bottom of her belly face. The exposed vulva is essential to her identity to the extent that she might even be considered merely an anthropomorphism of the sexual organ. Thus Iambe may also be depicted as she spreads her legs, riding upon a pig. The *piglet* was, in fact, slang for the *pudendum muliebre* (vulva), probably determined by the response of the *Suidae* (species of mammals that includes the pigs, hogs, boars, etc.) to the human pheromone.

Iambe's name is generally interchangeable with Baubo, who was the anthropomorphism of the *baubón,* or dildo, more commonly called *ólisthos,* or slipper, turning her into a sort of symbol of the union of the opposites, with both male and female principles represented in the same image. For this reason, Iambe's legs often appear as joined in order to better present a more credible likeness of a penis. In this, the topknot is the split meatus that emerges from the foreskin, rather than the fanciful *chevelure* of the female's pubic hair. Even thus, however, Iambe's basic identity remains the vulva, and the *baubó* normally referred to the "belly."

Going back to the myth of Demeter and Persephone, I believe the obscene jest that cheered Demeter's grief was that Iambe offered the goddess a view through the spread labia of the vulva into her belly-womb, displaying that she was pregnant with a male child (Orphic *Hymns*, frag. 52), and thus offering another image of the union of male and female.

The dwarfish Iambe-Baubo could also be seen as a Greek version of the worldwide figure of the squatting goddess caught at the moment of giving birth. Examples occur from regions as diverse as the Aztecs of the New World and the sixth-millennia BCE birthing goddesses of Anatolian Çatal Hüyük.

## The Almond Gateway

The view through the gateway of the spread vulva is probably most famously represented by the Celtic *Sheila-na-gig*, an old woman with withered breasts and spindly ribcage, represented as she is pulling open the labia. The image of the almond-shaped (*mandorla*) vulva, also known in sacred geometry as *vesica piscis*, was then expropriated into Christianity as symbolic of the entrance into sacred space and incorporated into church architecture as an ornament above the gateways. In the initiation hall at the sanctuary of Eleusis, this vulva-like gate was represented by the doorway on the ancient shrine enclosed within the cavernous hall, surrounded by the stepped perimeter that accommodated the several hundreds of inductees. It was here, beside the doorway, that the hierophant proclaimed the child's birth as the culmination of the Mystery experience.

Going back to the role of Iambe in Demeter's myth, what perhaps cheered Demeter's grief could have been the realization that duality between two opposites can be transcended. In fact Iambe showed through her vulva that she was pregnant with a male child, almost like a hermaphroditic vision of a female with male attributes. Perhaps what Iambe wished to suggest to the goddess was that the kidnapping of Persephone by Hades and the transition into union between the male abductor and the abducted bride could also be seen as another such example of the merging of polarities.

Such merging of dichotomous antitheses is the essential experience of mystical vision. The primordial goddess, here symbolized by Iambe, was thus representing a sexual totality, an androgynous wholeness giving birth to the universe from the gaping cosmic vulva called Chaos, the "gaping aperture or mouth" (Hesiod *Theogony,* 124 et seq.*).* This primordial androgynous deity continued this manner of parthenogenesis until she externalized maleness as her procreative copartner in the form of Ouranos, whose name means "of the heavens." In Neolithic figurines her maternal female body is portrayed with an elongated neck, sometimes quite explicitly with the head in the likeness of the glans penis. She then evolved into the Cycladic figure of the bearded Aphrodite, eventually becoming the deified hermaphrodite of the classical period, sometimes depicted raising her garments, like Iambe, to display her paradoxically male genitals.

## Fungal Anthropomorphisms

This jesting dwarfish creature who served Demeter the kykeon could also be seen as a personification of the drink's entheogenic botanical content. Iambe-Baubo in the ancient folkloric tradition was an *englottogástor,* a "tongue-in-belly." The "tongue-in-bellies" are one in a group of dwarfish grotesqueries, more explicitly fungal anthropomorphisms belonging to the tribe of "shade-foots" or *skiápodes.* These are creatures with only a single broad foot, for which reason they were also called monopods.

In the *Birds* comedy (414 BCE) Aristophanes had Socrates engage in a profanation of the Eleusianian Mysteries by performing a rite of necromancy in the cemetery of the Kerameíkos, located in a swamp just outside the western gate of the city of Athens. The philosopher is described in the act of summoning the "tongue-in-bellies."

In this same swamp was also the very ancient Temple of Dionysus, which was opened just once a year for the Lesser Mystery, the prerequisite for the main initiation at Eleusis. The building was known as the "bull-stall" (*boukólion*). Here the Basilinna, a ceremonial position held in ancient Athenian religion by the wife of the king, or Archon Basileus, was prepared by a group of elder women for her sexual engagement with the god Dionysus. It was this enactment that constituted the Lesser Mystery, and resembled Persephone's abduction by Hades followed by her rebirth commemorated in the Greater Mystery at Eleusis.

The secret encounter between the wife of the king and Dionysus could be seen as a shamanic rite of sexual rapture accessed, as indicated by the temple's designation as a bullstall, by an appropriate psychoactive agent. This agent was a mushroom, a plant long associated with bellowing or mooing bovines. In Old English there was no name for mushroom, only metaphors, as characteristic of things too sacred to name. *Mushroom* is one of those metaphors, assimilated as early as the Elizabethan era from the French *mousseron,* itself derived from Late Latin *mussare,* to "moo/bellow," from Greek *muká-esthai,* to "bellow." *Mushroom* is onomatopoetic for this bellowing sound, which, as early as the classical period of Greece, mushrooms emitted as they sprouted from the ground (Aristias, frag. 6, probably from his *Perseus* tragedy).

In later tradition, these "shade-foots," or mushroom-shaped creatures, were perpetuated in medieval lore and depicted in Christian architecture. Their fungal anthropomorphism is well-known, as indicated by C. S. Lewis's *The Voyage of the Dawn Treader* (1952), part of a series of narratives for children titled *The Chronicles of Narnia.* The fact that shade-foots move around by jumping on their only foot could relate to the sudden bursting of the mushrooms from the ground. Shade-foots are sometimes anthropomorphized as parasols, and the parasol is a metaphor for the mushroom traceable back to Sanskrit and the Vedic soma sacrament.

More anthropomorphisms are identifiable around the world and over vast amounts of time. In Lucian's fantastical *True History* (second century CE), we find another mushroom anthropomorphism as the *Caulomycetes* (cover mushrooms), a tribe of mushroom warriors who wield the fungal cap above their heads as shields. They are obviously quite small if the cap is big enough to provide their cover. These warriors recall the berserkers, and more particularly the "*haoma* wolves," an elite band of Persian Achaemenid warriors, obviously involved in ritual lycanthropy, like the wolf cults of the ancient Spartans. The Persian Zoroastrian version of soma was the Avestan *haoma*, known to the Greeks as *[h]ómomi*, the moly (*mólu*) of Homeric tradition and associated with wolves and foxes, given that canines are fond of the intoxication it affords. The berserker tradition was widespread throughout ancient Europe and is documented in the time of the second-century Roman emperor Trajan as involving mushrooms in his encounter with the Dacians of Thrace, who were named the "wolf-people." The particular species of mushroom is probably the *Amanita muscaria* since it best fits a panoply of metaphoric attributes and is the only mushroom noted for the enhanced physical stamina that it accesses. All of this indicates that the sources of these creatures and their dissemination throughout Europe can be traced back to the soma-haoma potion.

## Food of the Thunderbird

Not only was the "tongue-in-belly" recognizable to Aristophanes's audience as the fungal identity of the Iambe of the Eleusinian Mysteries, but Aristophanes reveals another metaphor for the sacred mushroom. The parody of Socrates's necromancy was immediately preceded in the comedy by the entrance of the Titan Prometheus with his phallus, the obligatory appendage of his costuming, swaddled in drapery until its unfurling as a parasol. Prometheus, the creator of man, stole celestial fire from the gods. Aristophanes reveals him as a "shade-foot" as he hides from the gods above in the shade of his parasol. For the theft of fire, Prometheus was chained to a mountain, where daily an eagle feasted upon his liver.

The liver functions as the filter of the body's toxins, affording it the highest concentration of any poisons ingested. It was thought that the liver was a microcosmic model of the cosmos, making it thereby the seat of divination. From the divine fluid that dripped from the Titan's gnawed liver sprang a magical plant that grew with a double stem (Apollodorus Rhodius, *Argonautica*, 3.856). No plant sprouts from the ground with a "twin" stem except the Amanitas; its *stipe* (stem or trunk) thrusts both up and down as the mushroom fruits, producing the characteristic shape of a dumbbell. The Amanitas are commonly called raven's bread because these birds, and others, are fond of its intoxicating quality. It is also eagle's fare, as documented in the folklore of the New World and the tales of the thunderbird.

Another of the creatures summoned in Socrates's necromancy are the sycophants, the ones who tattled on people who had been just recently prosecuted for performing the Mystery ceremony in their private homes with guests at their symposia or drinking parties, apparently profaning the sacred potion by abusing it as a recreational drug. Among those accused was Alcibiades, the notorious disciple of Socrates. The sycophant is literally the person who "exposes the fig." It is a term of reproach for a despicable type of person who turns state's evidence for the prosecution. The fig, however, is an obscene gesture with the hand, the thumb protruding between the clenched forefinger and middle finger, imitating the penis/clitoris lurking between the labia of the vulva. The fig is both womblike, with its profusion of seeds enmeshed in its rosy menstrual flux, and also masculine, resembling the scrotum of the testes beneath its neck like the penis. The fig revealer or sycophant is a flasher exposing the genitals, the revelation of Iambe-Baubo that made Demeter laugh.

## Persephone's Abduction
## and the Bacchanalia

The child in Iambe's belly, revealed as she served the Mystery potion, was essential to the meaning of what the Eleusinian initiates experienced. Iambe had first offered Demeter a drink of red wine. This she had refused.

Persephone's abduction can be placed in the context of bacchanalian plant-gathering rituals. Hades, the abductor of Persephone, was interchangeable with the chthonic persona of Dionysus (Nonnus *Dionysiaca*, 31.144; *Orphic Hymn* 57; *Suda. s.v. "Zagreus"*), who was also believed to be the sexual counterpart of the queen Basilinna in the Temple in the Swamp, in the "bull stall" ritual that recalled ancient fertility ceremonies.

The rituals of Dionysus mediated his dual botanical manifestations as the wild mushroom and as its cultivated version as the fungal yeasts that grow the wine upon the juice of the harvested fruit. The bacchant revel celebrated the former and was a version of the same motif as Persephone's abduction. The emblem of the bacchants was the thyrsus, a fennel stalk carried by the women of Dionysus in their forest revelries. The thyrus was a symbolic container for the gathered wild plants, prototypic of which was the mushroom. In common culinary nomenclature the stipe of the mushroom was termed its thyrsus, underlining the connection between the Dionysian cult and the use of hallucinogenic mushrooms.

So why did Demeter refuse to drink the offered wine and instead prescribed to the Eleusinian initiates the mixed kykeon? The meaning of the Greater Mysteries also resides in Demeter's acceptance of her daughter's abduction (rape) as a transition to matrimony, in which the rapist becomes her son-in-law. The wine was intended as the antithesis to the wild plants collected by Persephone when she was abducted, because it was a plant that was "domesticated," and its cultivation was equivalent to the wild maiden turning into a married woman. The botanical equivalent of the cultivated vineyard was the plowed land planted with its crop of grain, particularly the barley, *Hordeum vulgare,* which was the main ingredient of the kykeon. The ingredients of the Mystery drink were kernels of barley and the mint fleabane in an aqueous medium. It was not a beer or any alcoholic product; grain will not ferment unless its kernels are mashed to convert its starch to sugars upon which the yeasts might grow.

## Fleabane

As the wife of Hades and mother of his child, Persephone could visit her mother, Demeter, for only two-thirds of the year, analogous to the seed that, after being underground, sprouts into a plant in spring, constituting a potent insight into the importance of plants to understand the symbology of myth, a principle further reaffirmed by nature of the kykeon.

The plants contained in the potion can be seen as representing Persephone's transition from maiden to bride and the broader transition from humanity's primordial state toward its civilized form. The wild fleabane (*Mentha pulegium*) was used as an insecticide and was personified as the maiden Minthe, the concubine of Hades, thus symbolizing prostitution, nonmarital sexuality, and primordial toxicity. The psychoactive agent in the kykeon, the fungal growth *Claviceps purpurea,* known as ergot, could be seen as the mediator between the wild fleabane and the cultivated barley. As a wild fungus growing on cultivated foodstuff (barley), ergot thus reconciles the wild with the civilized. From a symbolical perspective it mediates the transition from Persephone's "wild" maiden status to her domesticated version as the bride of Hades.

In a broader sense it also affords the vision of the reconciliation between the civilized world (in its infancy during the ancient Greek culture in which the Eleusinian Mysteries developed) with its primordial "wild" precedents, both in terms of agricultural knowledge and societal norms. However, this vision of reconciliation was only accessible to those who knew the secret of how to extract its psychoactive agent, namely, the two Eleusinian families in charge of preparing the kykeon over the centuries and the initiates.

This ergot potion was considered something superior to the normally available intoxicants and it is said to have been replicated by Alcibiades in the recreational profanation of the Mysteries initiation. The psychoactive agent is lysergic acid amide (LSA), a natural version of LSD, and the same entheogen known as *ololiuqui* extracted from morning glory seeds in Mayan shamanism. The extraction process produces an oscillating stasis of ergine. Its mirror isoergine is achieved by hydrolysis of the ergotamine toxin in an alkaline aqueous medium obtained by the addition of bone ash, in commemoration of the inaugural plowman offered as victim.

In the enactment of the Mystery initiation, the initiates journeyed in the spirit upon the vehicle of the kykeon to visit Persephone and Hades via the cave of the Ploutonion at the critical moment that she was about to give birth. They resurfaced in the hall of initiation through the vulva-door of the central shrine building, simultaneously reborn along with the Mystery child. Fleabane was an abortifacient, while ergot was employed in the pharmacopeia of midwifery to control postpartum bleeding (Pseudo-Dioscorides, 2.100), constituting another dichotomous antithesis where the wild and its cultivated counterpart were united and reconciled.

In the netherworld, the initiates had been welcomed as visiting guests of the infernal couple (Hades and Persephone), and thereby were from now on forever obligated by the sacred relationship of reciprocal hospitality (*Homeric Hymn* 2.485–89). The netherworld would visit their houses offering prosperity and fecundity and, when they died, they would travel to a realm with which they had already established a debt of hospitable accord.

## The Meaning of the Mystery

Plato explicitly described that what was experienced in the Mystery initiation was a face-to-face encounter with deity (Plato *Phaedrus*, 250e et seq.). As a Neoplatonist, the Christian Paul described his own mystical rapture in exactly the same terms (1 Cor. 13:12; 2 Cor. 12:2–5). As enacted in all the scenarios for such Mysteries, the initiate experienced a symbolic death as a preparation for enhanced living. At Eleusis, the initiate, in the words of Cicero, "learned the beginnings of life and gained the power not only to live happily, but to die with better hope" (Cicero, *Laws*, 2.14.36). The entire evolution of civilized modes of culture and the analogous hybridizing of primitive toxic plants into the foodstuffs upon which life depends became a personal experience in the vast expanse of limitless time. Life henceforth was lived with confidence in its antecedents and its cosmic projection. The vision of the Mystery afforded a reconciliation and union of the dichotomous worlds of the male and the female, as well as the wild and the civilized. This allowed initiates to grasp one of the essential paradoxes on which the universe is based: the coexistence of opposites and thus the inherent possibility of overcoming duality.

# 7

# The Vǫlva

## *Women in Norse Witchcraft*

## Maria Christine Kvilhaug

Scandinavia was one of the last parts of Europe where paganism was practiced. Christianity settled slowly during the twelfth century, but ancient practices were maintained or else remembered for centuries after. While monasteries provided a new class of scribes and literary scholars, ancient beliefs and rituals still survived. So did many myths, legends, and religious poetry—many of which found their ways into countless history books and sagas written down during the twelfth to fourteenth centuries. Even if these sources may have been altered and colored by the Christian beliefs of the scribes, many modern studies have shown that the written sources possess a great deal of genuine transmissions. The scribes were scholars and historians who faithfully sought to render the oral traditions as correctly as possible, even when they condemned them. These scribes were also close in time and culture to what they described—Old Norse paganism was still fresh in memory and partly practiced for centuries after the conversions. For these reasons we know more about Old Norse pagan beliefs and practices than we do about most other non-Greek and non-Roman pre-Christian traditions.

In the *Ynglinga Saga,* written by the renowned Icelandic scholar

Snorri Sturlusson in the thirteenth century, Old Norse witchcraft is described in detail. We hear that the god Óðinn knew several "sports" (power activities) constituting the art of magic. The most powerful of all these techniques was *seiðr*. With this art he could see the past and the future and cause changes in the fates of others—for better and for worse. It was an art of controlling destiny through divination, and no art brought with it more power. But we learn that despite the superior power of this art, it had so many "unmanly" aspects that men could not practice it without shame. Thus, even if it had been practiced by the head god of the pantheon, it was still an art best handed over to the *gyðjur*—the priestesses. Even though Óðinn was regarded as the original teacher of these "sports," we learn earlier in the story that this art was in fact originally practiced by women—Óðinn and the other Aesir gods had actually learned the art of seiðr from the goddess Freyia (Sturluson 1979).

Lots of scholars have discussed and wondered what this "unmanliness" indicated—why the art was "shameful" for men while acceptable to women. Nobody knows for sure, and this is not the subject of this article. Suffice it to say that the art of seiðr originated with a woman or goddess and, albeit practiced by men, was considered to be a feminine sort of art. What is more, the women who practiced this art were highly respected, and their profession had divine counterparts.

The *Edda* poems were orally transmitted poems about gods and myths written down in Iceland during the eleventh to thirteenth centuries. One of the most famous and important poems is the "Vǫluspá"—from *vǫlva,* meaning "witch, seeress," and *spá,* meaning "prophecy, divination"—which I like to translate as "the divination of the witch." This poem reveals the origin, destiny, and end of the present universe while indicating that there were other worlds before, and that another world will emerge after the apocalyptic end of the present one. The entire poem takes the shape of a séance of oracular seiðr performed by a vǫlva who appears to be divine.

## The Wands of the Vǫlvas

*Vǫlva* was the official title for a woman who practiced seiðr professionally. We do not know if there were other sorts of practitioners, but we do know that the title of a fully fledged female practitioner with a proper standing in society was called a *vǫlva*. The title is derived from the word *vǫl*, meaning "wand" or "staff." We are immediately reminded of Gandalf's staff or other magical staffs, such as those in the Harry Potter tales. And indeed, graves belonging to magical practitioners often do include staffs of all sorts and sizes—these women certainly held staffs of office. We do not know exactly how the Norse *vǫlur* used their staffs, but we do know that their art of divination was similar to shamanistic rituals of divination and that there had been ancient bonds between Siberia and Scandinavia. According to the ethnographer Vilmos Diószegi, female shamans in Siberia often carried staffs that they shook and rattled, instead of a drum, in order to enter a state of trance (Diószegi 1968, 229–41, 255, 309).

Interestingly, in the term for *staff* in this case, the *vǫl* is the same as the term for "horse penis." In one saga short story known as the *Vǫlsa þáttr,* the penis of a sacrificed stallion is preserved by the "house-Freyia" (the lady of the house) and passed around the table during a family ritual. Simultaneously, songs were sung about its power and ability to sexually please the giantesses, to whom the *vǫl* is dedicated, and with a plea that Óðinn himself will assume the power of the *vǫl* in order to please the giantesses. The title *vǫlva* appears to mean "wed to the wand."

Briefly summarized, the poem "Vǫluspá" explains that the god Óðinn seeks the prophecy of a vǫlva by giving her precious jewels:

> *Host Father (Óðinn) chose for her*
> *rings and jewels*
> *for her wise counsel*
> *and her spells of divination*

*she saw widely, so widely*
*into all the worlds.*
(KVILHAUG TRANSLATION OF "VǪLUSPÁ," STANZA 29)

The vǫlva begins her prophecy by demanding the attention of everybody in the entire universe. She declares that she remembers a time before time itself, and that she herself existed back then, remembering the nine worlds that came before the present (Kvilhaug translation of "Vǫluspá" stanza 2).

The vǫlva proceeds to tell of the creation of the present world, grown to spurt out of the Well of Origin; the oldest *norn* (fate goddess); how everything was arranged; how human beings were given thought, warmth, and desire; then how the first war started. All this leads up to the moment when Óðinn finally becomes so worried that he seeks the vǫlva for a séance of seiðr in order to understand what is happening and where it is leading—the present moment in that poem. Then begins a vision of the apocalyptic future paving the way for a new and better world in the end.

## The Vǫlva's Practice of Seiðr

The first war in the world is strongly connected to the first time a vǫlva appears among human beings on Earth. Most scholars agree that this is a tale of how Freyia and the Vanir came to be with the Aesir gods (and of how seiðr was introduced to them). The first stanza describes an attempt to burn and stab the witch called Gullveig (Gold Power-Drink), but she conquers death every time. The reference to a "power-drink" in her name is clearly an indication of her association with the "precious mead" of memory, poetry, and resurrection that is so crucial to many Old Norse myths, and which is always kept by a magical female of the underworld. This Norse sacred drink is mythically linked to the "nectar of immortality" of Greek myths, with the vision-inducing haoma of Iranian Zoroastrianism and with the soma of the Indian Vedas. It may have had its real-life counterparts in psycho-tropic drinks, but nobody has ever been able to prove exactly what kind (Kvilhaug 2004, 2013). After this trial (a trial of initiation, probably), she appears as a fully-fledged vǫlva doing what vǫlur did—traveling the land, helping people everywhere, and teaching her art to the women:

> *She was called Heiðr (Bright, Open Space)*
> *when she came to the settlements*
> *the Vǫlva of good prophecies*
> *she knew spells/magic*
> *she made seiðr wherever she could*
> *she made seiðr with a playful mind*
> *she was always loved*
> *by ill/wicked/bad women.*
> (KVILHAUG TRANSLATION OF "VǪLUSPÁ," STANZA 22)

The last line is a bit puzzling. The adjective *illr* is directly related to the English word for "ill" as in "sick," and it would make sense that "ill women" loved her, since she could heal them. But in Old Norse, the word primarily meant "wicked" or "bad." The word *brúðar* would refer to "women" but literally meant "brides," and I cannot help but wonder if we are speaking of "bad brides" here, as in women who were not exactly housewife material. For the vǫlva was not, by any account, a married woman but one who was independent, traveled as she pleased, and who, unlike most women in this largely patriarchal society, had a status completely independent of males and male relatives.

In many shamanic traditions, there are myths of the "first shaman"—a divine being who introduced the arts of shamanism or sim-ilar practices (Diószegi 1968, 110–14). I regard the myth of Gullveig/ Heiðr as a myth of the first vǫlva to introduce the art of seiðr.

The most famous and detailed descriptions of seiðr in Old Norse sources take the form of oracular or divinatory seiðr. Like many such descriptions, we see hints of breathing techniques designed to induce an altered state of consciousness. Other descriptions hint toward secret rituals and the application of songs, also as a part of inducing a trance-like state in which the practitioner may see what had before been hidden about fate, and reach communication with spirits.

In the *Saga of Hrolf Kráki* we hear of one such séance, where the purpose is to discover the whereabouts of two wanted boys:

> Then a vǫlva called Heiðr arrived. The king told her to use her art to divine what she could learn about the boys. The king held a magnificent feast prepared for her and had her placed on a high *seiðhjallr* [a platform or seat where the *seiðr* was practiced]. Then he asked her what she could see of the future, "Because I know," he said, "that much will be made clear to you. I see that there is great fortune in you, so answer me as quickly as possible." She wrenched open her jaws and yawned deeply, and this chant emerged from her mouth. . . . (Byock 1998, 6)

The vǫlva called Heiðr speaks forth her prophecies about the whereabouts of the boys that the king is chasing, and all her prophecies are spoken in poetical riddles. The vǫlva is corruptible, however, for when the queen—wanting to protect the wanted boys (her own brothers)—offers a gold ring to the vǫlva, she declares her own previous prophecies as false. The king is angry and commands her to tell him the truth, threatening her with torture if she doesn't. The vǫlva proceeds: "Her mouth gaped wide, but the spell became difficult. Finally she spoke this verse. . . ." (Byock 1998, 7).

The vǫlva solves the problem of loyalty by speaking forth true prophecies, but uses the metaphorical language of poetry to disguise what she really sees, in effect warning the boys who have hidden in the hall. Solving a poetical riddle takes time, and her maneuver gives the boys and herself enough time to flee the king's hall.

The most famous and most detailed description of a séance of oracular seiðr is found in the *Saga of Eirik the Red*, chapter 4, where we hear of Thorbjǫrg Litilvǫlva. The nickname Litilvǫlva—"Little Witch"—is explained: she was the youngest and last living member of a group of nine vǫlur who had accompanied the Icelandic families in their emigration to Greenland. At the time of the séance described, she is an older woman, but has retained her nickname. As with the other vǫlur, she was invited by the lord of the hall. This was during a great famine. She was treated respectfully and was somehow above or beyond normal ranking systems—she treated people the way she wanted to and not according to their rank: "Around her waist she wore a . . . belt with a large pouch. In that she hid the magical equipment she needed for her divinations. . . . When she entered, all felt that they owed to greet her with great reverence. She returned the greetings exactly as she felt like according to how she liked the person or not" (Hreinson 1997; Kvilhaug's translation of Eskeland 1907, 14–20).

We also get a quite detailed description of the ritual and of the importance of women's contribution: "The morning after, when dawn had come, they gave her the things she needed to perform the seiðr. She asked the women for help, if they knew the words of a spell called 'Invoking the Spirits' [vardlokur—vard = spirit, guardian, loka = to call, lure, invoke]. But there were no such women present. Then they searched the household for someone who could. . . . Then the women held hands and made a circle around the seiðhjallr [a special platform]. Þórbjörg [the vǫlva] sat on top of it" (Hreinson 1997; Kvilhaug's translation of Eskeland 1907, 17–18).

Finally, we learn that the ritual of divination depended upon calling the spirits for aid—a trait that makes this form of oracular divination very similar to classical shamanism.

Then Guðrið sang the spell-song so beautifully than none of them who were present thought they had ever heard a song performed with a lovelier voice. The vǫlva thanked her for the song and said that now many spirits had arrived, and that they had thought it was beautiful to listen to the song so well performed—"but before they have wanted to separate from us and not listen to us. And now I see well many things that before were hidden, for me and many others." After that, one after the other came before the prophet woman and each asked what he or she most wanted to know. She had many good things to say, and it usually happened as she said it. (Hreinson 1997; Kvilhaug's translation of Eskeland 1907, 14–20)

Summing up the story: the vǫlva travels the countryside during summer and is invited to feasts prepared in her honor and treated with great reverence. After eating a highly symbolic meal she listens to the questions and the concerns of the people. Then the household goes to sleep, and we are not told what the vǫlva does during night, if she performs any "night rituals" like in the Arrow-Odd example. The following morning, the séance itself takes place outside, with the vǫlva seated on a high *seiðhjallr*—a platform raised for the occasion. The women of the household stand around her in a circle. One of them sings a song to invoke the guardian spirits, after which the vǫlva declares that the guardians/spirits have arrived and that she can now "see what was before hidden."

She offers a prophecy to all the members of the household. Most importantly, she divines the end of a long-term famine and bad weather, a prophecy that soon comes true. It would seem that the divination belongs to the category of "operative divination" where the future is in fact affected by the divination itself. As such, seiðr is more than just divining the future, it is also a way of changing or influencing it; a way of taking control over fate. "Veleda was an unmarried woman who enjoyed wide influence over the tribe of the Bructeri. The Germans traditionally regard many of the female sex as prophetic, and indeed, by an excess of superstition, as divine. This was a case in point. Veleda's prestige stood high, for she had foretold the German successes and the extermination of the legions" (Rives 1999, 8.2).

## The Germanic Precedent
## of the Norse Witch

In the literary sources, Norse witches have their predecessors in the German tribes described by Roman authors such as Tacitus in his *Histories* and in his *Germania*. Most German tribes nurtured groups of women known to the Romans as *matronae*—"mothers." These "mothers" traveled with the war bands and the armies and gave strategic counsel to the war leaders based on oracular divination. They also performed sacrifice and other religious services. As well, descriptions exist of particular women who were used as oracles, much like in the ancient Greek and the Roman traditions (i.e., the Oracle of Delphi). One such woman was Veleda of the Bructeri, who two thousand years ago led her people in revolt against the Romans through her prophecies. It is now generally thought that Veleda is not actually a name, but a title, meaning "seeress." According to Tacitus, she had divine status among the Germans. How much power she had in her own right and how much she was the pawn of tribal leaders who needed a religious legitimizing of their actions is not known.

Veleda performed her divination while seated in a high tower much like the Norse witches were described as seated on a high platform during their séances.

The Viking Age Oseberg burial (Norway, 834 CE) is the last in a number of Germanic priestess-graves of a kind that date back to the early Iron Age in Europe. From about the fifth century BCE there is ample evidence for "widespread reverence for a prophetic, staff-bearing goddess" as well as countless female burials in which high-standing ladies were buried with magical amulets, the sacred wand, and ceremonial and practical equipment. All of this was useful for the practice of a mead-offering ritual that evidently was practiced among German as well as Celtic tribes during the Iron and Viking Ages. The Norse witch-goddess Freyia and her human vǫlur seem to be direct descendants of this ancient European "cult" (Enright 1996).

## Other Applications of Seiðr

When seiðr is mentioned and described in the written sources, it's almost always connected to rituals of divination. But as we learned before, there were other techniques by which a crafty "sport" could be practiced. Spell-songs could be used for many purposes—invoking spirits, waking the dead, surviving in other worlds—and for healing. Snorri tells us that the vǫlva Gróa came to help Thor after he was injured in battle: "She sang her *galðr* [spell-songs] over Thor until the piece of stone loosened [from his flesh]" (Eggen 1978, 104, author's translation).

In one *Edda* poem, we learn that the valkyria Oddrún arrives during a difficult birthing. Her estranged friend, young Borgný, is giving birth in secret. After some bickering, the valkyria sings until Borgný, painfully, manages to deliver:

> *richly sang Oddrún*
> *powerfully sang Oddrún*
> *bitter spell-songs*
> *for Borgný*
> (KVILHAUG TRANSLATION OF
> "ODDRÚNARGRÁTR," STANZA 7)

Not all magic was as helpful. Indeed, black magic was practiced by some. In the *Ynglinga Saga,* chapter 13 (Sturluson 1979), we hear of a scorned woman, Drífa, who buys the services of one Hulð Seiðkóna in order to avenge her broken heart on the man who never returned. The victim Vanlandi dies from the attack of a supernatural female spirit called "the Mare" (Mara), who rides him to death at night. The Mare has been sent by the witch. It is interesting to note that Hulð is not referred to by the title *vǫlva* but as a *seiðkóna*—perhaps a significant difference.

We are well accustomed to the concept of a male hero saving a damsel in distress in legends, myths, and folklore—and it happens often enough in the sagas that relate stories from the oldest saga lore. But in

Norse sagas there are also several stories in which a female hero actually saves a young man in distress. Women, often partly supernatural, acting as advisers, teachers, healers, and even as warrior protectors, keep showing up to save the day for young heroes-to-be. For the most part, women stand particularly strong as protectors when the enemies are supernatural demonic beings.

In the story of Swan-White, the maiden and her female companions travel all the way from Denmark to Sweden in order to save young Ragnar and Thorvald from monsters (Elton 1905, book II). As soon as the maidens, riding, observe the two young men, they are impressed with their masculine, youthful beauty and desire to dismount at once. However, Swan-White, being more perceptive, declares that she can see monsters taking swift leaps and flinging themselves over the beds, that these are demons at war, forbidding them entry, and that a horde of furious ghosts are drawing near. She calls out to the boys, complimenting their beauty (!) before she warns them of the monsters, telling them to get away "lest you yield your most gracious bodies to be the prey and pasture of the vilest hordes" (Elton 1905, 21).

It should be noted that her suggestion that the young men ought to avoid fighting the monsters is a challenge—she is testing their response to see if they are fearless and courageous before she is ready to offer her gift. Fortunately, Ragnar responds like a proper warrior hero, ready to fight, which means that she can protect him without causing shame on him for wanting to hide behind her skirt—he still has to hide behind her skirts, but at least he did not want to. She passes the night in combat against the throng of foul monsters: "At return of daybreak she perceived fallen all over the fields diverse shapes of phantoms and figures extraordinary to look on and among them was seen the semblance of the evil sorceress who had sent all these demons their way. Swan-White piles all the bodies in a heap and burns them, and this done, she won the throne of Sweden for Ragnar, and Ragnar for her bed" (Elton 1905, 21).

Another powerful female companion is Harthgrepa (hard clasping fist), a nursemaid, foster-mother, warrior woman, sorceress, and shape-shifting giantess. Her story is told in *Gesta Danorum Book I* (Elton, 1905). Saxo Grammaticus, the twelfth-century, deeply Christian author, took the opportunity to describe magical creatures:

> It is worth the knowing that there were in old times three kinds of magicians who by diverse sleights practiced extraordinary marvels. The first of these were men of monstrous stock, termed by antiquity giants; these by their exceeding great bodily stature surpassed the size natural to mankind. Those who came after these were the first who gained skill in divination from entrails, and attained the Pythonic art [a reference to the Oracle of Delphi and a reference to the divination rituals associated with *seiðr*] . . . they also held the repute of being divine. . . . Both of these kinds had extreme skill in deluding the eyesight, knowing how to obscure their own faces and those of others with diverse semblances, and to darken the true aspects of things with beguiling shapes. But the third kind of men, springing from the natural union of the first two, did not answer to the nature of their parents either in bodily size or in practice of magic arts; yet these gained credit for divinity with minds that were befooled by their jugglings. (Elton 1905, 5–6)

Harthgrepa dressed as a man and followed her beloved foster-son Hadding on a quest to avenge his father and claim the throne of Denmark. Upon their journey the couple entered a dwelling at night, only to discover that a funeral of the master of the house was being conducted. It seems that a funeral was an appropriate setting for certain magical rites: "Desiring to pry into the purposes of heaven by the help of a magical espial, Harthgrepa graved on wood some very dreadful spells, and caused Hadding to put them under the dead man's tongue; thus forcing him to utter, with the voice so given, a strain terrible to hear. . . ." (Elton 1905, 7).

The dead man speaks, first a curse on her who brought his spirit out of death, and declares that it is against his will and purpose to declare "tidings"—before he declares them anyway. The tidings are prophesies, warnings against the demons that are going to attack the couple very soon. The prophecy uttered by the corpse continues by declaring that whereas Hadding will survive the attack of the supernatural monsters, Harthgrepa is doomed, as a punishment for her necromancy. The prophecy turns out to be true—Harthgrepa fights the monsters and protects Hadding, but she herself is torn to pieces. Hadding goes on to become a great man, but always grieved the loss of his crafty foster-mother.

In one old text, Jordanes's *History of the Goths* (551 CE), chapter 24, we learn that just as the first settlers on Greenland brought with them a coven of witches, so did the earlier Goths bring with them a coven of women when they left Sweden for the continent during the first century CE. This was a type of women known as the *haliurunnae*. The term is a Latinized version of some Old Norse title that could likely, in my opinion, have been *heliurúnar*—"runes of Hel." Runes could refer to "secrets" or "symbols," while Hel equated with "death." These women knew the secrets of death, and likely held high esteem in the homelands, since they accompanied the migrating tribes. Yet after having emigrated, they somehow managed to get into conflict with the king, Filimer. They were accused of necromancy and dispelled from the tribe. Four hundred years later, people believed that the invasion of the Huns from the East was the long-term vengeance of these witches upon the Gothic tribes.

If nothing else, this legend shows, among many other sources testifying to their existence, that the memory of women practicing witchcraft and divination lived strongly in the minds of people several centuries after the conversions to Christianity, and that the loss and expulsion of these women may have been a traumatic event in its time.

PART 3

Embodied Paths
to Ecstasy

# 8

# She Dances and Trances Again

## Exploring, Healing, and Developing Feminine Aspects through Trance Dance

### Christa Mackinnon

The origin of the feminine principle stems from the primordial concept of the Great Mother, created by our early tribal ancestors in reverence to the earth and the cycles of nature. The Great Mother was seen as the wild, inclusive, and sacred force of life, death, and rebirth, carrying within her *being* the dimensions of earth, sky, and underworld, and the vital cycles of life reflected in the moon, sun, stars, plants, trees, animals, and humans. From her being emerged all of life, which she sustained through the nourishment she provided, and everything dying returned to her to be reborn again.

The feminine was consequently primarily identified with the amazing ability of the female body to gestate and birth life, defined as the life-giving, nurturing, and sustaining force, the creative vessel that contained, birthed, nurtured, and protected. In that capacity, the feminine was honored and respected. Over time, the feminine also became associated with heart-centeredness, with emotions—compassion and love—

with the sensual, the intuitive, the relational, and connecting, with the flowing, yielding, and responsive, and with the unconscious and the deep and dark psyche.

Over millennia, we developed from our tribal hunter-gatherer existence into what we now define as civilized societies. We became more powerful users of tools and resources. We established agriculture, individual possession, and territories, and later we industrialized. We started building cities and civilizations, fighting territorial wars, and we grew in number. While all of this was happening, our ways of seeing the world, our values, our thinking, and our power structures, as well as our spiritual systems, changed. The feminine, the sacred Earth womb-creatrix, was replaced by the masculine, the all-powerful sky godhead, and the elemental relationship with the Earth Mother gradually changed from reverence to exploitation. In the process we went from female goddesses and priestesses to male and female deities, and then to the dominance of the male gods and priests.

These gods were often fierce, war-oriented, powerful creatures, competing with each other, while progressively subordinating and disempowering the Sacred Feminine. This became increasingly evident in ancient Greece around 500–400 BCE and later in the Roman Empire when, for instance, Isis, the dominant revered goddess, had to make way for the Christian God. This subjugation of the Sacred Feminine reached its first culmination in the Judaism of the biblical era, from which Christianity and Islam evolved. In these three monotheistic religions of the book, the one masculine God in the sky is firmly established. The Sacred Feminine is replaced with the guilty, sexually alluring woman, dangerous and therefore in need of taming. The Holy Virgin Mother was subordinated to the father and her son. Both archetypes, the "virgin" and the "whore" with all their disturbing attributes, as well as the split of the female body, remain unintegrated in our present-day consciousness.

The long process away from the sacred, embodied Earth Mother to the disembodied sky god went hand in hand with the suppression and devaluation of "woman," who found herself increasingly—at the latest in Genesis—in the wrong garden. This was a garden in which the female was created from a rib of the male and subjugated to him. It was a garden in which humans were split from the whole and allowed to rule over other living creatures and the Earth (the feminine), and in which expanding consciousness through eating from the fruit of knowledge was forbidden. In this garden, woman was declared lustful, dark, disobedient, and wild, needing to be subdued, suppressed, and conquered. The symbol of the serpent, which was previously associated with the Great Mother's power to regenerate life and later with the feminine instinct, was vilified and became a symbol of evil (Baring 2013, 395). Woman as a physical and instinctual being was belittled, condemned, and forced into hiding. She was not considered to be a physical creation in her own right. Instead she was loaded with sin and shame for expressing her sexual physicality and declared responsible for the banishment from paradise, while her life-giving, instinctual abilities became associated with *a symbol of evil*.

The development that followed had devastating consequences for the feminine as one half of a balancing principle of the whole, and for women all over the world. Many factors played their part. And yet the suppression, raping, belittling, disempowering, and devaluing of women and the feminine could not have been accomplished without progressively valuing the disembodied, rational mind and without focusing on material development and possessions. Both formed the basis for the ever-increasing exploitation of resources, human as well as natural. The overarching aim was an increase in the production of goods and the creation and domination of territories and markets. In this, the strive for the advancement of production, profit, and power was held above life-giving and life-nurturing forces.

At the same time, women and the female body were gradually turned into commodities. Women and the female body could either be exploited for sexual pleasure, or needed guarding to ensure legitimate fatherhood of the (male) offspring who were destined to inherit possessions and territories. Parallel to this, driven by economic development as well as the advancement of science, value systems based on the masculine gradually dominated all levels of society. Educational systems increasingly placed their emphasis on the rational, logical, and analytical. When women were finally "allowed" to participate more fully in education and began to demand economic and social equality, they found themselves in worlds dominated by values and ways of thinking that required nurturing the masculine, the head-centered, analytical, rational, hierarchically directed, fight-oriented, and conquering forces within themselves.

The ongoing expansion of disembodiment in human development generally has increasingly split us from the part of ourselves that is rooted in nature—from the deep, dark, and intuitive psyche, which is the domain of the feminine. This has happened in alliance with masculine values and ways of thinking. Our agricultural, industrial, scientific, medical, and now technological development, our vast cities and urban lifestyles as well as our educational systems that are focused on the scientific and rational, have largely contributed to this split. This separation has also increased our fear of death. We now use technologies and scientific medical resources to prolong the human life span, divorcing ourselves further from the physical body and the natural cycles of life and death.

It is no surprise that the *masculine fear* of the deep, knowledgeable feminine side of our collective psyche—with its connection to the cycles of life, which include death of the body, as well as her link with the warm, rich, but also wild and dark Mother Earth—led all developing and imperial societies to suppress women's exercise of religious practice and authority. The ecstatically dancing temple women gradually disappeared from west Asia. Patrician imperial Rome tried to stamp out all women's Mysteries and later (mainly female) witches were burned in Europe. Countless indigenous, sacred Earth-based practices, from Polynesia to Alaska to sub-Saharan Africa and India, which were equally the domain of males and females, were suppressed and eradicated by

European conquerors and Christian missionaries (Mackinnon 2012). Many focused on the ecstatic ceremonies and dances, condemning the ceremonialists and trance dancers—especially the women—as uncivilized savages and devil worshipers. This suppression and eradication of the physically ecstatic spiritual life produced what Ehrenreich so pointedly calls *the eradication of ecstasy and joy* on a global scale (Ehrenreich 2007).

The move from the sensing body and connected heart to the thinking mind and disconnected head—together with the degrading, violating, and controlling of the female body for most of recorded history—not only kept the wild, sensing, instinctive, and heart-centered feminine suppressed, it forced it to adjust to masculine standards and behaviors in complex ways. This oppression of women included debilitating restrictions of clothing and behavioral codes and the suppression of sexuality over *body-beautiful ideals*. These ideals are currently taken to extremes via plastic surgery. They also include the "right to rape" in war. Until recently, this same "right to rape" was legal in marriage.

Adding to this, the expelling of the Sacred Feminine and the physically ecstatic from most of our religions, and the expelling of women from our church hierarchies, we can say that what has been done over many millennia to life on this planet, to the feminine aspect of the human psyche, and to women has produced separation as well as deep emotional and mental wounding. It has created shadow issues on a grand scale within the collective human psyche and, most importantly, has contributed to keeping us on a level of restricted consciousness.

## Searching for the Embodied Feminine and the Ecstatic through Shamanic Trance Dance

So, where are we now with the embodied feminine, the sacred, and the numinous? Despite all the positive changes over the last century and especially since the sixties, which have progressively brought more equality to women in various parts of the world, women's happiness has declined over the last few decades. A large and comprehensive study entitled "The Paradox of Declining Female Happiness," found that although women appreciate that they are more equal on monetary, social, political, and educational levels, in 2009 they described themselves as being less happy than in a similar study in 1970. Men's happiness rose in the same period (Stevenson and Wolfers 2009). Researchers state that this trend applies to all industrialized countries but find no obvious explanation. I strongly suspect that women now realize that being equal in the wrong garden, in societies that run according to patriarchal masculine systems, values, and principles, is not necessarily healing and nurturing their psyche.

The growing awareness that humanity's development has reached a point where a profound change is necessary has, over the last decade, resulted in a shift in women's movements away from "equality and wanting to succeed in a masculine world" to women searching for and rediscovering the feminine, while trying to heal, define, and express it. Hidden behind the veil, belittled, degraded, raped, persecuted, distorted, and devalued for many millennia, the feminine has become almost unrecognizable within the value systems of long-standing patriarchal societies. Although we sense that the desired change needs to redress the balance, we don't know how to access and implement the feminine and so bring it to the fore.

In this context it is important to distinguish between *equality* and *equal power of the feminine*. The fight for equality was a necessary intermediate step within the patriarchy to enable women's participation in society, to educate themselves, to develop their minds, and prove that they are as capable as their male counterparts. The next step has to be to explore and connect with the feminine, and to move us in the direction of implementing feminine principles in humanity's garden, which will contribute to necessary radical change.

To restore and revive the feminine we need to first understand that the feminine cannot flower in a disembodied form as intuition, sensing, feeling, relating, and being in tune with the natural cycles of life. Those depend directly on our connection with the body, on being embodied. Second, we need to understand that change cannot be accomplished without expanding consciousness, without accepting that the masculine focus on the analytical, unexpanded, rational, conscious mind, which has brought us much industrial, scientific and technological development and knowledge, has limited our view of ourselves and the world. It has, as well, limited our connection to the wider field. Thus we need to dive deeper to experience not only the feminine, but also who we are and what life is really all about.

This is where we can learn from the remaining traditionally oriented indigenous cultures. They are still connected to earth, nature, and spirit, and therefore quite naturally more to the feminine—especially from their ways of accessing the many layers of the inner and outer realities via expanding consciousness. I will focus on ecstatic dance in particular. These cultures, particularly their male and female shamans, have never stopped exploring the vast capacities of our minds and the underlying, wider fields through altering their states of perception. They also never stopped being *in the body* and utilizing embodiment in their spiritual work, mainly in the form of ecstatic dance. They understood that the body is a vehicle that is contained within the "spirit field," an expressed, manifested form of spirit, important for perception, information, and transformation. The poet, Jungian psychoanalyst, and author Clarissa Pinkola Estés expresses the importance of the body in her book *Women Who Run with the Wolves* when she writes: "The body records all that goes on. For those who can read it, the body is a living record of life given, life taken, life hoped for, life healed. It is valued for its articulate ability to register immediate reactions, to feel profoundly, to sense ahead. The body is a multilingual being. It speaks through its color, its temperature" (1992, 200).

Countless records of female shamans, ancient and contemporary, show that trance-inducing dance practices, with or without the ingestion of entheogens, are powerful tools. They expand consciousness and access the spirit worlds—or embody spirit power—useful in divination, healing, shape-shifting, inspiration, rites of passage, ceremonies, prophecy, achieving visions, and more. Max Dashu's (2013) accounts provide over forty images of artifacts and paintings depicting ancient traditional female trance-dancing shamans from all around the world. Current trance-dancing female shamans, initiated into traditional practices, can still be found worldwide in countries such as Mongolia, Siberia, Bali, Korea, Japan, Africa, Australia, the South Pacific, the Americas, and others.

Hi-ah Park, initiated into the classical shamanic Korean tradition in 1981, specializes in the art of ritual ecstatic dance. Her international work has sparked a renewed interest in and respect for this ancient Korean spiritual practice. She points out that movement is for many women the vehicle between the ordinary and the experience of ecstasy, the interface with spirituality. Her initiation consisted of many phases, with ecstatic dance being the main practice, leading her to the level of shape-shifting into a warrior, attacking herself viciously with sharp blades (*chaktu*) without sustaining a single injury. She then describes her final dance to freedom: "After I proved that nothing could harm me, I did the most vigorous dance of my life. At the peak of the dance, I seemed to fly up to the top of the tower, where I danced barefoot upon the chaktu. People later told me that my eyes didn't look human—that they had the luster of a tiger's eyes. As I stood barefoot on the sharp blades, I gained absolute freedom in time and space" (Park 1992). While traditional female shamans always danced themselves into trance states to create the energy flow through the body to lift themselves into numinous states, opening their bodies and minds for Spirit, contemporary practitioners have over the last few decades adapted shamanic trance dance in many variations. This form of movement has been pioneered in the West by people such as Gabrielle Roth (5Rhythms Dance) and Wibert Alix (shamanic trance dance). These and countless other adaptations have taught us that ecstatic dances are powerful tools for modern women to address and move through their wounding, to discharge it energetically from their bodies, and to let their bodies flow and express themselves. It also allows women to expand their consciousness, remove mental barriers, embody power, feel and express their wild and sexual nature, connect with Spirit, experience their blissful and ecstatic essence and joy, and often delve deeply into their instinctive knowing and wisdom. Or, as Caroline Carey, a British movement medicine teacher says, "I learned that the deeper I connected with my body, putting my roots into the deep depth of the Mother Earth, the higher I could expand my consciousness to receive knowledge, wisdom and insights" (Carey 2014, 17).

## Contemporary Trance Dance

I have facilitated shamanic trance-dance groups for women and worked therapeutically with women over the last twenty years. I found, as many others have, that contemporary shamanic trance-dance journey adaptations can play a major role in exploring, connecting, healing, and developing the feminine aspects. They work on three levels, which are distinct but also interwoven, influencing each other.

These levels include the physical, where a free flow of energy is necessary to reclaim and develop vital feminine aspects, such as connection to the rhythms of nature and women's own nature, wildness, sensory capacities, instincts, and intuition.

They also include the emotional/mental level, wherein ecstatic dance helps to access the deep personal and collective wounding of the feminine, which is held in women's bodies in the form of energy blockages and cellular memories. Here the aim is to release emotional energies arising from anxieties, deep sadness, and rage and thus gain fuller access to a wide range of feelings, but especially to the feminine aspects of heart-centered passion and compassion.

The third level is the spiritual/numinous/transpersonal, which can be experienced and worked with when "the dancer becomes the dance" and merges with the wider field. Here shamanic trance-dance journeys enable us to connect with the ecstatic dimension of the feminine as well as soul/sacred/archetypal aspects. Visions, teachings, and access to inner wisdom often accompany the experience.

Contemporary shamanic trance dance is often done in groups, in a sacred, ceremonial space, with Spirit invited. There is a preparation phase during which each individual dancer will formulate an intent of her dance. Usually the facilitator works together with a group of drummers led mainly by African djembes. It can be done with recorded music, but a group of good drummers can amplify the experience as they can take the dancers "up and down," adjusting to the energy in the room and also creating an energy field that supports the dancers.

When I facilitate women's trance-dance groups we always have a day of preparation. The dance begins in the evening and lasts until all participants have danced, in many cases, all night. A dancer usually dances between one to four hours until she falls down, or just stops, and stands still. Two to four people attend each dancer. They group around her to keep her safe, making sure she doesn't bump into anything, and they catch her when she falls, which enables the dancer to "let go completely." Done at night and around fires, this can become even more powerful, awakening the tribal roots of the wild woman within.

To illustrate how profound the experiences can be, and how they work for women on the mental, emotional, physical, and spiritual levels, here are three examples.

## Trance Dance Addressing the Wounding

The mental/emotional suffering of women is profound and deep reaching, stemming from many factors, as I have outlined above. But everybody who has ever worked with women in a therapeutic setting knows that much of the very deep female wounding is of a traumatic nature. It often stems from fear, anxiety, and even terror due to abuse, assault, molestation, rape, and other violations. Although the worldwide statistics paint a dark picture about the prevalence of these issues, I am not suggesting that every woman goes through such experiences.

Nevertheless, every woman seems to carry memories of such events, or some anxiety around such issues. They might be intergenerational or collective, but they still influence the individual female psyche. I have never experienced a women's group where you can't feel the energy changing, the tears flowing and rage surfacing, when one woman talks about a dream or an experience—or just theoretically—about violation, rape, abuse, or molestation. One of the most striking features of any trauma-reaction is dissociation—a splitting of the otherwise integrative way we process events. Survivors of rape, abuse, and assault usually try to split from the emotional realm as the feelings are too painful. Dissociating from feelings always demands a split from the physical, for feelings are experienced in the body. It is astonishing how dissociation reflects the *patriarchal split* between spirit and body.

Caroline Carey movingly and powerfully describes the beginning of her healing journey. Via the practice of shamanic dance, she accessed what was held and hidden in her body. This healing led to her transformation from a *dissociated out-of-body abuse survivor* to the highly respected shamanic medicine movement teacher she now is.

> I began to notice the effects dance had on me, how it lifted my spirits and put me in touch with a higher state of consciousness. . . . I would literally "see" images and shapes that gave me messages and taught me more about myself, as well as a deeper connection to the spirit world I had learned to love. Most importantly it made me feel. Not that this was comfortable to begin with, but somewhere inside I knew this was a very good idea. . . . I learned that by expressing my feelings and speaking out about things that were unhelpful to me, even unhealthy to my psyche; my body would begin to clear away what was old and no longer served me. (Carey 2014, 16)

A woman that I will call "Karen" demonstrates that trance dance is not necessarily pleasant for women at the beginning, but can heal great emotional wounds, clear away *the old,* and connect women with their hearts. Karen had attended quite a few of our trance-dance weekends and was at the time also in ongoing therapy. She was a "tough woman," who had spent ten years in the army and had only slowly begun to get in touch with her softer side. Haunted by incidences of violation against women that she witnessed in war zones and by her own childhood experiences of an uncle's inappropriate sexual behavior, she was extremely guarded. She easily accessed her anger, even raged about it all, but never accessed her vulnerability and therefore never felt compassion for herself and others. Quite unexpectedly in one of her dance journeys, she experienced a turning point:

A few minutes into the dance journey, my usual physical stamina seemed to leave me. I sank to the ground as I suddenly felt dizzy, my body began to shake and I started sobbing like a child. I shivered uncontrollably, but felt strangely safe, knowing that my group of women partners was around me. This went on for what seemed a long time. I vaguely heard people leaving the room, the drumming seemed to stop, but I just lay there, the shivering and sobbing coming and going in waves. At one point I heard the facilitator's voice, but I couldn't reply although I felt connected to her as she seemed to gently touch my back. In my mind I was all over the place. Images from my childhood—my uncle touching me, me hiding in the garden, me sitting on his lap—overlapped with images of crying, injured children and desperate women running away from attackers I couldn't see. I experienced a mixture of feelings such as shame, disgust, fear and, most unbearably, utter helplessness. When I became calmer, I felt a blanket being wrapped around me and then, suddenly, there she was, beautiful, innocent, almost pure and afraid: the child, the younger me, I had rejected for so long. This image, which was incredibly clear, moved me to a level of compassion and love I had never experienced for myself, let alone for others. After a while, without drums, and with the support of all the women around me, I stood up, held my child close, and I danced with her, gently and slowly my first dance of reconnecting, of compassion and caring, and of love for myself. Many followed, but this was the breakthrough.

## Opening to the Spiritual

While Karen's ecstatic dance provided some much-needed emotional healing and connected her with her heart, enabling her to feel compassion for herself and reconnecting her with a part of herself she had split off, Vicky's dance provided her with an experience that opened her to her spiritual self, connected her with the whole, and changed her concept of life.

At the beginning of my spiritual journey, I attended a weekend workshop for women, which involved a night of shamanic trance dance with drumming. During this each woman danced in the center of a group of other women, who provided a safety boundary for her to dance until she tranced out and either stood still or—in most cases—fell to the floor. During my dance I remember being conscious of the drum beat for a while until I seemed to become the drums, losing awareness of my surroundings and in a sense of myself. Then, suddenly I was standing on the edge of an incredible place, a place I can only describe as a "universe of love and connection," and all I had to do was to let it engulf me. I don't recall how long it took, but remember that I stopped moving, that my whole body pulsed, and it felt like it dissolved as it expanded becoming one with this indescribable space. I was for a long moment one with the cosmos and everything in it, and I understood in a flash, that everything—including myself—is connected, and I felt an almost unbearable love, joy, and gratitude. At this moment my concept of life changed. This was many years ago, but I haven't stopped dancing since.

## A Dance Journey to Explore the Feminine

The last ecstatic-dance journey I will describe is one of my own. I trance danced with the intent to connect with the feminine. This experience happened about an hour into the dance. I had overcome the urge to stop because I felt tired, and nothing much had happened a few times, but as I also enjoyed the experience I kept going and suddenly I felt weightless.

My body dances itself, effortlessly, whilst in my imagination I journey upward through the branches of my tree into the sky. I fly higher and higher at breathtaking speed, turning into a whirling sphere in the process until I suddenly have a vision, which overtakes me completely. I know that this is a vision, as it has all the hallmarks: it appears suddenly and takes over my whole being; I am unable to change it, and it has a hallucinatory quality. I find myself in the middle of a circle of women. I can see a flow of energy circling from one woman to another. My "seeing" is very strong, but nothing is said. After some time, I become aware that the energy is now also extending from the women toward the center, where I stand. One by one the women send out a stream of energy toward me until I turn into a rainbow-colored being of great radiance. I feel an overwhelming sense of bliss streaming through me, knowing that this is the "shining of my wholeness." This radiant rainbow-colored being is me, whilst I am also "all the women in the circle." This Being is indescribably bright. In fact, it is indescribable. Not a word is being spoken until the end. Then, whilst I come back into my body, just before I sink onto the ground, and the vision disappears as suddenly as it arrived, I "hear": "This is the renewal time of the feminine. She must thrive and shine in all her colors."

Exhausted and elated, I understood that the feminine is indeed multicolored and that she cannot thrive within the narrow parameters of societies that are dominated by patriarchal structures and masculine ways of thinking and being. She cannot thrive living from the outwardly focused, rational thinking mind-head alone, without being able to understand the language and messages of her body and without the ecstatic of the soul. For the feminine to thrive, we need to activate all of our energy centers, ranging from the wild, life-giving and sustaining energy of the sexual center and the womb, to the compassionate and loving heart, to the expansion into the fields through the crown. Trance dance helps us to express ourselves physically, clear the energetic blocks and contaminations, heal the wounds, and soar beyond the limits of our *thinking minds,* embodying vision and connection with the wider fields.

The feminine is in both men and women, and the call to regenerate it is a collective one, aimed at both. Nevertheless, it is in my experience a call still mainly acknowledged by women who begin to understand that they cannot thrive in the wrong garden. They feel the longing to access, reclaim, embody, and express the feminine aspects of the whole, to bring to the fore what the world so desperately needs: the connection to nature and the deep psyche, the embodiment of the sacred, the instinctual wisdom of the heart, the nurturing love for all of life, and an expanded, ecstatic consciousness that is embodied. Or, as the ecstatically dancing Korean shaman, Hiah Park remarks: "It is not gender that makes a woman superior but, rather, her access to the feminine principles of spirituality which makes her an essential bridge between this world and the states of bliss" (Haft 1992).

# 9

# She Who Births

## *The Psychedelic Nature of Procreation*

### Alana Bliss

The loud undulating tones of the crystal bowl sang throughout the room as my contractions surged. I breathed and toned with the bowl, the pain softened, and waves of endorphins washed over me. I danced the pain away, spiraling my hips and stomping my feet. I could feel the waves of pain coming as my womb, abdomen, and back began to tighten. I knew there was nothing I could do to stop it and I needed to face the waves rather than fight or try to run out of my body awareness and into tension. I stood my ground mentally and breathed into them. My partner massaged me, grounding me to fully feel my body, and I relaxed, transforming intensity into a soothing wash of endorphins. I was coping with the pain, riding the waves, and opening. My midwife recommended I sit on the birthing stool. I hesitated for a moment, afraid that I might hurt my baby if I sat on the hard wooden surface. My midwife reminded me that the baby was safe, and I could relax.

Pain seared through me for a moment before I surrendered into the waves of pleasure and relief that washed over me. It was then that I saw Her, glistening and beautiful. In awe, I witnessed a fluid stream of consciousness flow into the room and merge with me. I saw Her energy in my mind's eye, right there, as real as anyone else in the room. This gorgeous stream of feminine strength held within it every woman and animal that has or ever would give birth, and everyone that was birthing with me in that moment. I was engulfed in a profound feeling of support and belonging, held by the Great Mother: She Who Births. This presence flowed like a river. Images and a felt presence of countless mothers poured through me and danced with me through my surges. I was not alone. My courage surged, and I was able to birth my first baby boy into a pool of warm water in my home.

## The Sanctity of the Birth Field

Birth is sacred. It is a powerful rite of passage that pushes the initiates into a realm beyond the mundane, a place where reality shifts and perception is heightened, even altered. A laboring woman becomes a center point for an energy field generated from within her and stretching out around her. This is the birth field. Mother, father, baby, and their birth support team are all engulfed by this powerful field. This sacred birth chamber has been seen throughout history as a place of both life and death, entrance and exit to life. This is reflected by many goddesses through time as well as various cultures that are associated with childbirth but are also associated with death. Imagine that there is a veil that separates life from that which is not in physical form. Generally, that veil is thick, hard to penetrate. However, when birth occurs, the veil thins, so that new life can enter. This occurs when a woman's own body creates a toroidal field—twin vortexes that resemble a three-dimensional ring that spins life into the greater world. This field generates a powerful energy and pulls consciousness into hyperpresence.

Many cultures throughout time believed that there are supportive beings who are present when this field is generated. To the ancient Egyptians a goddess called Meskhenet watched over and protected a woman giving birth. In Greece it was Eileithyia, to the Romans Lucina, to the Yoruba of Africa she was Yemoja, in Ireland she was Bridget, and on and on. There are as many names for the Great Mother as there are cultures on the planet. When these goddesses were present, the energy of the space was touched by her, supported and nurtured by her, and sacred. In honoring this, women throughout history have communed with the Divine Feminine and trusted in this powerful process.

## Hormonal Elixirs and Expanded States of Consciousness

When the birth field is generated and the continuum of the birth goddess becomes present, a woman can tap into states of consciousness that allow her to calm her body and her mind. This happens from a state of trust, wherein she allows her body's hormones to flow freely. A biological dance begins inside a pregnant mother's body when her baby is ready to enter the world. The process of birthing is initiated by a protein being released from the baby's lungs, which results in a cascade of other biochemical reactions. Progesterone and estrogen flow into the mother's bloodstream and increase her uterine receptive sites for oxytocin, a hormone that stimulates contractions while also relieving pain.

Oxytocin could be considered a love or touch hormone because it is present during sexual activity, orgasm, birth, and breastfeeding. It increases when we are touched. Oxytocin helps us to forget ourselves, our challenges of individual self, and fall into a sweet feeling of bliss, given that it triggers the release of serotonin and dopamine. This creates a feeling of dissociation with ourselves and our stories. Oxytocin is released every three to five minutes once labor begins and begins to flood the body, creating a heightened state of intimacy and trust that can deepen the loving bonds between partners and with the baby after it emerges.

As this occurs, another hormone is released that increases the feeling of love—phenylethylamine (PEA). Some consider this to be the hormone most associated with falling in love because it elevates mood, mental activity, attention, motivation, alertness, creativity, awareness, energy, stamina, physical activity, pleasurable feelings, sexuality, and sensory perceptions. It also amplifies the strength and effectiveness of other neurotransmitters in the brain, such as dopamine (for a feeling of well-being and pleasure) and serotonin (better emotional mood and impulse control). We feel loved and euphoric when this hormone is secreted, which is Mother Nature's way of showing us that, as we procreate, we are loved.

We are also supported by our bodies during birth in that the body floods with endorphins. Endorphins relieve pain by attaching to pain receptors in nerve cells, thereby blocking them and blunting the sensation of pain. They give a sensation of euphoria, as expressed in the feeling of a runner's high. Endorphins also stimulate the secretion of prolactin, a relaxing and mothering hormone that regulates milk production and gives the initiate a boost toward enjoyment of mothering. One specific endorphin is beta-endorphin, which is an opiate that acts to restore homeostasis in the body, stimulate dopamine, and produce a feeling of pleasure. Beta-endorphin is similar to both morphine and heroin and pushes a laboring mother into an altered state, known to many midwives as "laborland."

Throughout this process the body also secretes catecholamines, which are considered the fight-or-flight hormones: adrenaline and noradrenaline. These hormones give the body the extra power it needs during labor, assisting in the tremendous effort that the body is going through. They are for protection, and the body needs them to assist in working hard.

However, these hormones can also cause the body to become anxious and distressed, thus leading to the mind and muscles working inefficiently and redirecting blood and oxygen from the uterus to the vital organs of the mother—the brain, heart, and kidneys. For this reason, it is a laboring initiate's work to keep a calm mind and steady breathing. Fear increases these hormones, and they can overpower all the hormones that are working to ease the pain.

Last, the most underexamined biochemical that many people

believe is released during labor is dimethyltryptamine (DMT), otherwise known as the spirit molecule (Strassman 2001). DMT is a psychedelic substance produced in the pineal gland that is released during birth, orgasm, and at death. DMT peaks during birth, both for the baby and mother, and is also released in smaller amounts at the beginning of REM sleep, lucid dreaming, and meditation. DMT is produced in the fetus as early as the forty-ninth day of gestation. DMT gives a sense of connection with everything—a sense of cosmic unity. It has been described as the most intense psychedelic experience known to humanity, causing visions and an out-of-body experience in many people who use it. Amazonian tribes have been using a plant mixture known as ayahuasca for over five thousand years in ceremony to access the DMT experience. They have developed a cosmological belief system around it.

## Forever a Mother, Forever a Father

A birthing woman has access in her own body to a plethora of hormones and endorphins that give her the power to go through the biggest biological initiation of her life. She can experience a powerful transformation, and in a way face her own death, to be reborn into motherhood. A birthing mother has quite a journey to go through, and nature has supported her in this process. On the one hand, she will need to release the maiden, the young and carefree part of herself that is not responsible for anyone but herself. The maiden is a grown child, a flower beautiful and vibrant, attractive and fleeting. This part of her will step back and, in a way, die forever, because she will forever be a mother after birthing a child. Even if the baby is raised by someone else, she has crossed a threshold, and undergone an initiation. The mother is born of the intense and profound journey of labor, ripening into the fruit phase of her life. She must learn to control her mind, relax her body, and cultivate her strength. The mother is born, just as the baby is born, just as a father is born in the process of birth.

The father has a subtler journey, but just as the mother, he too must transform. After he plants his seed, nurtures his partner through pregnancy, and holds loving space for her in labor, he transforms into a protector. Before, he was only responsible for himself, but once a child is born, he begins the strengthening journey from young man into father. A father who has supported the birth of his children can become a compassionate protector. Although he doesn't feel the hormonal rushes in the same way the initiate mother does, nor does he feel the pain, he is challenged to watch the mother face her pain and at times he can feel helpless. However, he can help his beloved by massaging her, kissing her, speaking loving words, giving her nourishment, and holding strong, loving space. He can help her release her fears and guide her back to her strength. This is the role of the masculine in labor. He doesn't experience the psychedelic euphoria that she feels, but he can support her in going deeper into it; massaging pleasure out of pain. The masculine is vital in the process, a grounded boundary to protect against danger, a cell wall holding firm the birthing field.

Meanwhile, the mother initiate faces her fears, dives into her hormonal flow, and moves through the pain. Her body floods her with psychedelic, euphoric hormones and endorphins for easing her pain, giving her strength, and assisting in her opening. The safer she feels, the calmer she can become, the more she can handle the intensity rushes, and the more vivid her perception becomes. Time stands still, and the breath becomes the steady wave of her reality. She can dance with her body's natural grace and cast fear from her mind. She is all set up for it. Inside of her there is a biological system of support. If she has worked on processing her fear prior to the labor and is able to surrender, the birth can be the greatest high and most transformational experience of her life.

## Birth's Imprint on the Psyche

Nature's wisdom is phenomenal. As humans we are mimicking and experimenting with what is natural. Birth is a perfect example of this. Within the process of birth, a mother and baby feel oxytocin, PEA, dopamine, serotonin, and even DMT. Each of us felt these sensations as we were being born, even if there was an overabundance of catechol-amines or stress hormones. We all have felt the euphoria of hormonal pleasure and in a way are searching to feel it again—whether that is in the form of falling in love, eating foods that stimulate it, chasing happiness, or ingesting substances that offer an altered state. Our mothers' bodies offered us these feelings, both while she was pregnant with us and in our births. Our births have a lasting imprint on our limbic system, which controls our emotions. When there is trauma there, we seek to soothe it, even unconsciously. Also, the imprint of our birth plays a huge part in the formation of our personalities and our perceptions of the larger world around us.

The manner by which we are brought into the world creates an imprint, like a first impression, which tells us whether we are safe or in danger, loved or discarded, supported or abandoned (Grof 1985). When our mothers are afraid of feeling pain, we too are afraid of feeling it, and we resist it. If our umbilical cord is cut before we have learned to breathe, we are depleted of vital blood and nutrients and we feel panic, fear, and disconnection in our first moments. Unfortunately, the modern birthing industry has neglected the sacred in the birth chamber, and many of us are born in a state of fear or disempowerment. When this happens the euphoric dance of hormones is replaced with man-made drugs that disturb this process. The graceful and empowering dance of birth becomes a medicalized and drugged emergency. We then begin to crave the feeling of connection and love that the hormones of natural childbirth offer. We begin to long for the bond that was broken when we were born. Perhaps this is a reason so many people are dependent on substances for happiness. Even when we have been born in a supportive and nurturing environment, we may long for the feelings of our birth. Perhaps we are reminded of them when taking mind-altering substances.

There is an amazing similarity between the hormonal release of birth and those of many mind-altering drugs. One common thread throughout many psychedelic substances and birth is increased levels of dopamine and serotonin. These are feel-good-reward neurotransmitters that are increased when ingesting opiates, cocaine, MDMA, LSD, psilocybin, or DMT. According to a 2014 paper by Giovanni Petri published in the *Journal of the Royal Society Interface*, an effect of psilocybin mushrooms on the brain is the increased communication between different regions, a hyperconnection that occurs by binding to the same receptors in the brain as the neurotransmitter serotonin.

## Reclaiming Our Psychedelic Nature

Being that serotonin secretion is triggered by oxytocin release and is strengthened by PEA, I would argue that the brain of a birthing woman becomes more connected the deeper into labor she goes. This gives her a subtle psychedelic feeling, not to mention that potential of the DMT release. Psychedelic substances such as MDMA, LSD, marijuana, and DMT all release neurotransmitters that shift the mind, emotions, and perception, and offer a feeling of connection. As these neurotransmitters are also released during labor, we could infer that giving birth naturally is a psychedelic experience.

The journey of giving birth, just like a psychedelic medicine journey, is all about being able to flow with the experience. In a medicine journey, a substance is taken that stimulates hormonal and endorphin secretions, and then an experience happens. The person on the journey has two choices: to flow with what comes or to fight it. When the initiate flows with the experience, it can be empowering, insightful, fun, and pleasurable. However, if the person on the medicine journey fights the feelings, or tries to hold onto the state of sobriety or normality, then the journey can become very frightening, damaging, or even traumatic. It comes down to flexibility, fluidity, and trust. By their very nature psychedelics expand consciousness, shift awareness, and give a new point of view. Rigidity is broken by an expanding consciousness.

This is the same with birth. The birthing woman has the same choice: to flow with her sensations or to fight them. She can become fluid and move with the pain, allowing the hormonal wash to ease the pain, or she can hold on to a fear of the pain, clenching down and flooding her body with stress hormones, or catecholamines. The biggest difference between birth and the intake of psychotropic substances is that at the end of labor there is a whole new being, and there is a pain that marks the passage toward transformation and strength. Birth is a biologically stimulated, ancient, body intelligence that, when a woman can allow the dissociation of her consciousness to occur, can result in an orgasmic experience. The same hormones present in orgasm flood through her body at this time. She can let go of the riverbank of control and swim with the current, directing herself around dangers by being soft and flexible. She can allow herself to feel the pleasure in the pauses between contractions. This renews her and, as she relaxes into these sensations, she releases even more of these hormones.

Imagine a woman in a forest, fluidly riding the waves of her labor. She is spiraling her hips, allowing herself to fall deeper and deeper into a felt awareness, dissociated from the world around her, from her own solidity. She moans and tones to the sounds of sensation pulsing through her as she opens. Suddenly, she becomes aware that there is a mountain lion watching her. She feels fear; it jerks her into full presence. She becomes ultra-aware of her surroundings. She picks up a stick and screams, hitting it against the ground. The mountain lion runs away. She hardly notices that her labor has stopped. She feels no rushes, the euphoric sensation is gone, and the softened light has shifted to sharp details. She scans the forest, looking for any signs of danger. Once she knows she is temporarily safe, she heads back to her village. She knows that once she feels fully safe, she will reenter "laborland" again. This is the natural purpose of fear. It is protective.

One challenge with the human mind is that thoughts can have the same effect on the body that our actual environment can have on us. This same woman in the forest might only have imagined that there was a mountain lion stalking her, and she would have experienced the same physiological effect. In this way, fear can trick us. Unfortunately, modern Western women have inherited generations of fear surrounding childbirth, rooted in the savage practice of burning witches and midwives from medieval times to the seventeenth century. There was a great disconnect that taught women to distrust their bodies and fear the flesh. Women were taught that birth pain was punishment for Eve's original sin and that their sexuality itself was sinful. Birth is sexual and it is sensual. When allowed to be fluid without fear, it can be pleasurable. This is our "birth rite," the gift from our bodies and nature. We are by nature psychedelic; by nature sensual. However, with this repression and collective birth trauma, women have become afraid of birth itself. This fear restricts the body's flow of hormones and endorphins and fills us with stress hormones, causing birth complications because we are fighting our bodies during the entirety of our labor.

The time has come to take back our births and feel the inherent pleasure that our bodies offer us, both in our sexual and birthing lives. As our hormonal rivers flow through us uninhibited, we free ourselves from a kind of oppression—oppression by fear of our natural selves. As we allow ourselves this freedom, we will find that we are inherently psychedelic. Our bodies secrete pleasurable liquids when we meditate, when we dream, when we make love, and when we procreate. This is amazing. This is the next liberation: allowing ourselves to fully feel ourselves and gift that freedom to our children as we birth them into the world. This is the time to remember all the goddesses who have been honored in the sacred birth chamber throughout the planet. As we honor our connection with Earth and the Great Mother, this is the time to follow our roots back to a place where we honored our bodies. After centuries of disconnection the time has come again to honor the sacred design of our body's innate intelligence, to birth without fear, unafraid of pain but also unafraid of orgasm and pleasure. The Divine Feminine is the path to reconnect with nature. May we remember how to see beyond what our eyes perceive and know that our sensations and intuition are just as true.

# 10

# Rebirth of an Ancient Calling

## *The Modern Medicine Woman*

### Shonagh Home

Looking back, my experiences as a little girl revealed the path I am on today, though it took another thirty-five years to get me here. As a child I was intimately connected with the fairy realms, searching my garden for their presence, which I felt very palpably. At the age of six, I used to sit beneath the boughs of one of the many evergreen trees that bordered the convent school I attended. On one such occasion I performed my first ritual, in which I brought a dear friend to my secret place where we pricked our fingers and mixed our blood together, declaring our bond as "Indian sisters." How I knew to do that I do not know. I was a very imaginative and perceptive child and even had the ability to sense events before they happened. I later called these "confirmations" because I knew when the information came in there was no arguing or bargaining, and events always unfolded just like I imagined them.

With no mentor to follow on the shamanic path, I eventually became somewhat assimilated into the societal construct. All but gone today are the elder healers and seers who once held the respect of their communities and initiated the young.

However, as the pendulum has clearly swung far to one side it is now beginning to arc in the opposite direction. Growing numbers of people today are seeking greater meaning in their lives through the exploration of shamanic practices that include the use of psychoactive plants and fungi. Many are turning to the few cultures remaining that have preserved their connection with the shamanic mysteries, in the hopes of receiving guidance and initiation.

On my path as a visionary medicine woman I have come into connection with extraordinary women who walk to the beat of their own drum, indifferent to the pressures of societal conditioning. Over the years I have put forth recorded talks and interviews that have inspired folks to contact me for mentorship or to share their own experiences. The path we walk is a very old one, and women have been drawn to it for millennia. That this path entails the use of psychoactive plants and fungi makes it, on one hand, a threat to our strategically designed modern industrial society and, on the other, an absolute necessity as a potential pathway for the restoration of internal healing and balance that so many people are seeking today.

## Borka

I had heard about Borka Cafuk through a woman who takes small groups to Borka's healing sanctuary in Peru. On her website I was fascinated to read that in addition to her work with ayahuasca, Borka specialized in energetic disorders like entity possession, an ancient shamanic art I wanted to learn more about. We emailed back and forth and decided to record a conversation for Psychedelic Salon, a website I collaborate with.

Borka is a Croatian native who has embraced the traditional role of visionary shamanic medicine woman. She began as an environmental journalist in Eastern Europe. She explains that before she found ayahuasca she was always trying to find herself. She tried Shotokan, qigong, and meditation, but they did not fill the void she felt within. As fate would have it, Borka discovered the work of visionary ayahuasca artist, Paolo Amaringo, which ultimately led her to an ayahuasca ceremony in Spain. There she was told by the spirit of the medicine to travel to the Amazon. She resisted initially but eventually answered the call and began an apprenticeship with a shaman that dramatically changed the course of her life.

During her first ayahuasca ceremony with the shaman, another participant went into a violent tailspin, and a spirit entity that was attached to him attacked Borka. The experience was harrowing, and Borka explains that she was fighting for her very soul. The shaman eventually removed the entity, and it was then that she was told that her medicine path was to assist people who were suffering from entity possession. This was out of the question, in her mind, and she returned home, only to be plagued by fear and anxiety.

It was at that time that she became aware of spirit possession in the general populace. Borka recalled using the public transportation system and becoming aware of others around her who were carrying parasitic energies. She eventually realized that her path was to alleviate the suffering caused by parasitic energies that attach themselves to people through trauma, drug and alcohol abuse, depression, and other means. This seems strange to twenty-first-century minds that have been steered away from their own indigenous beliefs, but on the entheogenic path, more is revealed, and more is understood.

Borka told me, "There is an important moment on this planet when decisions are to be made—whether we are going to walk on the path of light, whether we will evolve and change what is going on around the world, or we will walk on the path of darkness and destroy ourselves and everything going on around us." In seeing the darkness held within others, Borka made a conscious decision to walk the path of light and use ayahuasca as an aid to help those struggling in the darkness.

Borka went on to open the Yanapuma Healing and Educational Center in Peru, where she works as resident medicine woman with clients who come from all over the world to heal emotional, mental, and spiritual imbalances. She possesses extensive knowledge of local healing plants and how to prepare and administer them. When she travels home to Croatia, Borka runs a small center called Durga's Sanctuary, a place of respite, ceremony, and healing.

## Julieta

Very few indigenous medicine women can be found in our modern world today. In Oaxaca, Mexico, the art of mushroom shamanism is still practiced by certain women, one of whom is Doña Julieta Casimiro, an elder from Huatla de Jimenez and a member of the International Council of Thirteen Indigenous Grandmothers. She is known as a wise woman or *chota chine*, which means "one who knows." I have admired Doña Julieta for several years and have listened with great interest to the few interviews she has given.

Born in 1936, she married at seventeen and was initiated into the path of the mushrooms or *niños santos* (little saints) by her mother-in-law, a Mazatec healer and midwife who led mushroom ceremonies. Julieta took them with her mother-in-law and learned how to work with the power of the mushrooms, combined with the power of God, the Lady of Guadalupe, and other cosmological presences that lend their healing powers to the ceremony. This is a tradition that has been passed down through elders in her community for thousands of years.

Julieta explains, "Because we don't have money for doctors, we heal ourselves with the mushrooms." She makes it clear that the "little saints" are not drugs. "They are natural mind, because only the *niños santos* know about the Mother Earth and how to heal us. They spring from the earth and in working with them one is working with nature, with the Mother herself." She goes on to explain how the mushrooms work: "They study us. They're scientists, those little people. They clean you and they come from the Mother Earth. This will not hurt you, quite the contrary. It will go in your whole body and analyze what you need. It will go to where a person is sick inside the body or over the body or on either side. . . . You can be healed, little by little."

On working in the capacity of a medicine woman Julieta says:

> I believe that in order to dedicate oneself to this profession one must
> be very brave, very honest, and very humble. One's heart must be
> clean for things to turn out well. The guide should offer a genuine
> security, trust, affection, love, and acceptance, because this is the
> most important moment and the patient must benefit from it. It's
> the moment when the spirit finds itself at the highest point; it's the
> moment of encounter with God. . . . It's at this moment that she
> must use her entire being. . . . This is the ideal moment to show her
> power, her strength, her desire to achieve what has been proposed
> according to the case.

Julieta's daughters work alongside her, having been trained by
their mother for many years in order to carry the knowledge and pass
it to their own children. For them, the "little saints" impart tremendous love, light, happiness, and hope. For us, these women carry an
unbroken lineage that serves to illuminate and inspire our own sacred
relationship with the "little saints" and other psychoactive offerings
found in nature.

Over the past five years I have also come to know two very exceptional
women. As practicing psychotherapists, they incorporate the mushroom
into their professional practices. For obvious reasons, their real names
and locations will be left unsaid. Their past experience and training differs widely, yet each professes to be in a kind of sacred or heightened
relationship with the fungi teachers. Each woman speaks of having felt
"called" to her respective entheogenic path, and both feel that psychotherapy is a perfect channel for a medicine woman of today. "We have
to work with what we've got," says one, "and psychotherapy is an excellent avenue through which entheogens can reach the people who need
them the most."

## Beth

One therapist, "Beth," contacted me after hearing a recorded talk I gave in Seattle. She asked if we could meet in person to discuss her work and "compare notes." When we met, Beth told me she had worked for a number of years with a spiritual teacher as a means to clear early childhood trauma that held her back in relationships. Upon turning forty, she was compelled to take mushrooms, which she hadn't taken since college. Her teacher agreed, suggesting that psilocybin might serve to offer further insight and possible closure.

Beth went on to describe a candlelit ritual in which she prepared a peaceful space and ate the mushrooms at night, lying down, eyes closed. Her experience revealed a number of areas within her life that required more than just superficial attention. She was shown how she'd been using her therapeutic practice as a diversion away from her own deep-seated pain, which she had "managed" but not healed. She was shown the initial trauma as a kind of "geometry" that energetically permeated her life moving forward, and she saw how it had affected her body, resulting in an autoimmune disorder that had plagued her for years. The autoimmune disorder, she realized, served as a kind of shield from intimacy, which had been an issue for far too long.

The experience inspired her to create a consistent ritual practice with the mushroom where she would "go in" on a lighter dose with specific questions regarding her physical and emotional concerns and receive insights not only regarding how to regain physical and emotional balance but also on the deeper reasons that contained the necessary teachings behind such challenges. This dedicated endeavor eventually inspired Beth to bring this same experience to carefully chosen clients whom she felt were ready for it.

For these sessions she works out of a ritual space separate from her office. She explains that "A separate ritual space imparts a sense of entering a kind of temple." Beth feels this lends a heightened sense that something very special and unique is about to occur, and it invites the client to leave the conventional self behind and enter a far deeper state of being. Says Beth, "We're going beyond the therapist's couch and into the etheric planes where answers can be found."

Beth described her process to me. Her client arrives in the early afternoon and is given a specified dose of mushrooms. The next five hours are spent lying down with a soft pad over the eyes while Beth is present to guide if needed. After the session, follow-up takes place back in the office when her client returns for his or her weekly session and engages the essential process of integration. She has had success with clients who not only suffer from depression and/or anxiety but also those who have been grappling with issues similar to her own. Beth states that all the clients she has worked with in this way have received relief in some form, along with tremendous insights. All have unanimously declared that they are better-off for the experience.

## Sarah

It was at a full moon ceremony for women where I met "Sarah," who, after hearing me speak candidly about the work I do, privately confessed to me her own complicity in similar endeavors. Sarah had had a series of "solo initiations" wherein she engaged a number of different psychotropic substances over the course of her life. She said she prefers the mushroom because it is a natural substance from the earth and thus less likely to be corrupted. She also uses cannabis at certain times, particularly when spending time in nature.

An interest in counseling had eventually led Beth to a career as a psychotherapist in a large city. She has read prolifically on the effects of psilocybin for mental/emotional health and has little patience waiting for the government to catch up with the times and make these substances legal. Like Beth, she makes the mushroom available to certain clients whom she feels could turn a corner in their development after one or more sessions on the medicine.

Sarah explained that she conducts these sessions in her office. She and her client discuss dosage, and the session begins with her client lying down with padding over the eyes and soft music playing in the background. Like Beth, Sarah acts as guide, engaging in conversation if needed, but primarily acting as sentry while her client travels the inner layers of consciousness. She is careful not to get overly involved in her client's journey, as she feels it is important that they receive as much direct insight as possible. She has had excellent success with these sessions and praises the mushroom for its ability to confer tremendous illumination when used intentionally under the right circumstances.

I asked both Sarah and Beth if they felt there was a tutelary spirit or spirits within the mushrooms, and I was answered with a resounding affirmative. Both women have a distinct sense of a guiding teacher presence that they feel informs their work, and both feel they made that acquaintance through their personal medicine journeys. Each has what they describe as a profound spiritual connection to the Divine, and both distinguish themselves from the conventional psychotherapeutic model in that they see the spiritual component as an intrinsic element of the human experience and one that must be included in the container of psychotherapy. Neither Sarah nor Beth carry medicine traditions passed down through their family lines, yet each has taken her cues directly from the mushroom teachers and has formed an effective, safe, and beautiful modality through which to assist their clients. Neither woman advocates the use of antidepressants but rather sees psilocybin as a potent ingredient within a thoughtfully composed program of therapy to restore their client's well-being.

Herein lies an important consideration. Psychedelics present a problem for the multibillion-dollar pharmaceutical industry, which has enjoyed vast profits through the administration of antidepressant drugs. David E. Nichols, cofounder of the Heffter Research Institute, has this to say: "Many people also ask, 'Aren't drug companies interested in psychedelic medicine?' The answer, unfortunately, is no. Psychedelic medicines have been around so long that they are no longer patentable, and they work after one or sometimes two treatments. There is no money to be made with a non-patentable drug that is given only once or twice in a lifetime. Typical drug treatments are given daily and the treatment can last years, or even a lifetime." While there is hope that psilocybin will be made legal for therapeutic use in the future, the pharmaceutical industry will not likely support that scenario. However, as more people begin to turn from antidepressants to safer alternatives, it is going to be harder to ignore the promise that psilocybin holds for initiating profound illumination and self-awareness.

## Uma

Uma is an herbalist and steward of botanicals that include rare psychoactive species. Over the course of her life she has studied with master herbalists who have deftly guided her on the medicine path. She has a heartfelt connection to the spirits of the plants and intuits their needs with great care and wisdom. She speaks of the profundity of intentional connection to the botanical world, saying, "Living harmoniously with plants is a divine dance."

In her travels to Central and South America, Uma sought out rare plant medicines for propagation in order for them to become more widely available. The cuttings were taken to specific locations that were designed for their cultivation. Some of the plants collected were psychoactive. Those specimens were propagated and redistributed to specific areas that Uma determined would be safe for their unimpeded growth. Rescuing rare plants and psychoactive medicines from the ravages of industrialization has become her sacred activism. She is in partnership with Mother Earth and has committed herself to protecting and saving Earth's precious botanicals as a moral duty to the planet. Uma shares her knowledge through mentorship and sometimes offers talks on her work where she will present some of the psychoactive plants she lovingly tends.

Many of the psychoactive plants Uma grows are largely unfamiliar to the general public. Like her ancient medicine sisters before her, she grows them expertly and has cultivated a close kinship with the spirit teacher within each plant. Those fortunate souls who know her are given the opportunity to learn how to grow, propagate, and steward these sacred plant beings. Uma shares her expert knowledge not only on cultivation but also on the preparation of those psychoactive botanicals for ritual and communion with the plant teacher. Her wealth of botanical knowledge, wisdom, and experience makes Uma a kind of living national treasure.

## My Own Journey

My own sacred work with the mushroom has profoundly informed my shamanic therapy practice and prompted me to write a book, *Love and Spirit Medicine*, that is a woman's detailed telling of a year of dedicated monthly immersions into the mushroom's vast, mysterious realms. It was only after many years of shamanic study that I was called to the mushroom, and it was nature that initiated me, as I had no shaman to guide my experience. My first journey took place within the mossy cathedral of the Olympic National Rain Forest. After a stirring communication with Mother Earth, I apprenticed myself to the mushroom teachers for the next year, each month venturing into the dark of night to lie by the trees and fall into a deep trance state. Over that year I came into an extraordinary connection with nature spirits. Most notably, one presented in the form of a white owl. The ancient lord of the forest, Pan, who was known as Cernunnos to my ancient Celtic ancestors, also came to me. They became tutelary spirits and began informing my therapeutic work and making themselves known through uncanny, synchronistic events.

A few months into my "training" I was shocked to find I had the ability to go into shamanic mediumship and channel teaching spirits. This is probably the most misunderstood form of shamanry and one of the oldest. It calls to mind the ancient oracles who imbibed a psychoactive inebriant that took them into ecstatic states wherein they could connect with the unseen worlds and share messages. This was primarily the domain of women such as the oracles of ancient Greece, the priestesses of Ix Chel on the island of Cuzamil, and the vǫlva—the seeresses of the Norse traditions in whose graves were found henbane seeds, which produce a hallucinogenic smoke when burned. Still today in the Mazatec tradition it is the job of the *curandera* to transmit the messages by chant or song, thus embodying the ancient practice of mediumship under the influence of the sacred mushroom.

Barbara Tedlock, in her book *The Woman in the Shaman's Body,* writes that "Shamans are seers, oracles, and oral poets, and their artistic language creates a healing path for their patients" (2005, 150). Furthermore, Tedlock points out an interesting difference in style between male and female mushroom shamans. In describing the ritual work of a gifted couple, Irene Piñeda de Figueroa and Roman Estrada, she points to Irene's chants and discourse on the mushroom, describing her chants as, "emphasizing birth and agricultural growth, she sang of medicine, sweetness, and goodwill. She frequently repeated the words, *freshness, tenderness,* and *happiness*" (151). Tedlock wrote that Irene spoke of "searching, questioning, releasing, untying, and disentangling. Instead of calling upon a masculine deity or meteorological force for help in her divining, Irene spoke directly to the hallucinogenic mushrooms, requesting their aid in the cure of the sickness" (152). Tedlock described Roman's technique as involving chants that "affirmed his sacred role as mediator between human and elemental powers that determine a person's future. . . . As he confronted danger and promised to vanquish it by allying himself with the forces of nature he did battle with external political and social causes of illness, using bold, aggressive words such as *danger* and *fear*" (152).

This is a striking difference and calls to mind the ancient role of women as gatherers of the plants, nurturers of their communities, and midwives in both birth and death, while men assumed the roles of hunters and warriors and protectors of their communities.

Both Irene and Roman are mediums gifted with the power of the mushroom, and each takes on what seemed to be very natural and effortless aspects of their respective sexes. Irene clearly expresses decidedly feminine traits of nurturing, cooperation, and compassion in her ritual work, while Roman's role holds the more masculine aspects of battling, aggression, and force. The two complement each other in their shamanic practice. They are not the only example in Tedlock's book of male and female shamans who worked in a naturally harmonic way together.

In today's world that is spellbound to the seductive wonders of technology and industry, the modern medicine woman casts her own spell. Hers is a spell that leads the suffering out of despair. Hers is a spell that calls back the wisdom ways of working with the earth, in harmony with nature's laws. Hers is a spell that connects twenty-first-century people with a numinous magic they have long forgotten.

These extraordinary women are growing in number. May the spirits of the ancient wisdom keepers fill our hearts and minds with inspiration, curiosity, and courage as we traverse the mysterious realms of nature's visionary offerings. May we lend our support to the extraordinary women who walk this ancient path.

## PART 4
# Psychedelic Feminine Principles

# 11

# The Embodiment of Feminine Qualities in the Psychedelic Self

## The Realm of Mystery and Potential

### Kathleen Harrison

## Awareness Embodied

Through my lifetime of psychedelic experiences, I have learned two great lessons that can be put into simple aphorisms. The first is "Be here now," which is the essence of what many have learned, but it cannot be remembered too often. It is so fundamental a perception of awareness itself, and it is so wonderfully succinct, that one can write it inside one's own forehead and it would be right there to remind us whenever we forget.

Psychedelics not only offer that guiding principle to us, they also help us understand what it means. We can feel it in these states and remember how it feels in our cells, and then carry that awareness with us in quotidian life. We owe thanks to that storied old seeker Ram Dass for renewing this ancient guideline as a modern meme for our subculture. He was inspired to be here now, and to remind us too, by virtue of his LSD experiences, as well as by his other spiritual explorations.

The second helpful tip, a profound tip at that, although harder yet to decipher, is that "Nothing is as it appears to be." This is not glib. I have learned this truth, not only by examining this concept while on psychedelics but also by living and working with native peoples—people whose belief systems have evolved and been sustained for many centuries. These are people who seem to understand and negotiate with the very nature of illusion. These are cultures that have sustained active and continuing animistic beliefs, cultures that practice shamanism and educate their children through stories and hands-on experience with nature. Some of them use psychedelic species of plants or mushrooms, some don't. They all seem to grasp the reality of illusions much better than our "Western," materially oriented cultures do. In the deeply grounded awareness that everything is an illusion, one understands that everything may change from what it appears to be now to something else, at any moment. Everything. It's actually a fine rule to live by. It is one version of the principle of uncertainty.

## Nothing Is as It Appears to Be

My approach here has two themes: the perception of feminine or gendered personas in psychedelic species, and its parallel, the embodiment of feminine qualities in the psychedelic self. The conscious experience of these feminine qualities is as significant to the contemporary seeker as are those beings, or perceived personas, to the original cultures in which they arose.

What is a feminine quality? For example, I was walking around Greenwich, here in London, this morning. I saw a woman very properly dressed, an official looking woman, apparently walking briskly to work. She carried a smart leather purse, and on the outside of the purse was carefully printed: "Accept Mystery."

I laughed at the ironic humor, and thought, *Well that's really great, and very feminine, what I would call a feminine way of understanding reality, allowing for something to remain undefined, yet possible.* No matter the setting and structure, there is mystery in it, or nearby. The recognition of mystery acts as a balance to the authoritative, the quantitative, and the taxonomic, which demand to know: What is it, how can we talk about it, can we put it into words, can we define what it is, can we nail it down, then move on to the next thing? That approach is more masculine, a perspective that we generally assume is more "real." Yet we are dogged by the question, and the misunderstanding, of what is real and what is not real. We are too often imprisoned by the insistence on definition, on the structure of the expected. The distinction is undeniably tricky, because knowing and the pursuit of knowledge are human tendencies, not masculine or feminine, not male or female. The search for knowledge is not gendered. In our world view, what we accept, what we hold, and all that we unconsciously reject can be experienced as having qualities of the masculine or the feminine. Every one of us embodies both.

It's important to realize how we each hold within us the masculine and the feminine elements—these well-met opposites are swirling, dancing arm-in-arm, or sometimes in battle. But they are both always within every single one of us. So, this theme isn't about men and women, it is about the masculine and feminine principles and how they manifest in both our inner lives and our outer lives. Here we can also refer to the psychedelic species themselves, their essential characters, and the way they seem to manifest as feminine or masculine, only less often as androgynous or of flickering gender. These gendered qualities in a species, or in a brewed *medicina,* are generally recognized by the entire culture that has a long-term relationship with their visionary or ritual sacrament.

Later I want to circle back around to the visionary species, and to address these qualities in them as well as in us. For now, let us swim through this topic, exploring thought, seeing what drifts into our view.

## Awakening to Animism

I am what I call a functional animist. I function as though everything is alive and aware. One of my main awakenings in life was a quarter of a century ago when I was on my second long fieldwork period in the Amazon, in the early 1990s. A concordance of events happened that caused me to viscerally awaken to the reality of the animated world. I stopped wondering if I had been sensing something, and I actually really knew what it meant—that everything is alive, everything is talking and listening to everything else, and every species is a being. That was a realization, like many I've had over the years, which did not explicitly come to me during a psychedelic experience. Instead it was influenced by the combination of my frequent exposure to psychedelic perception, which had been ongoing for twenty-five years at that point, and my exposure to others who lived fully in the awareness of the multispecies, many-spirited conversation around them. These others were indigenous people—people who still had roots in nature and a long tradition of living in the midst of a constellation of familiar species.

These accumulated insights combined to give me a deeply felt sensibility to the living, breathing essence of what is sentient around us. A very dear old indigenous woman whom I was working with pointed out to me a small trailside plant with which I was forming a casual familiarity. As I was passing it, then bent down to touch it, she told me that clearly that plant was speaking to me, and that I had heard it, was pulled to its tiny whispers, to listen more closely. That's why I had leaned over to touch that succulent little herb on a log, right there in the middle of the Amazon forest—a forest filled with giant, showy spectacles and not insignificant thorns, venom, and other potential dangers.

I leaned in, touched the diminutive whisperer, and said hello. Then I stood up and said aloud, in shock and electric delight, "It's all one grand conversation! I can hardly believe it took me this long to recognize that." The old indigenous woman and I proceeded to have intuitive adventures in that shared awareness during our weeks of botany in the jungle. I felt that I was floating in a feminine way of knowing in a sea of potential experience that ranged from leaf-filled dreams to making dinner.

So this is the template: We are one being, our species—the *human* being. And each of those other species out there, which we have carefully classified and given our own names to, is also a being. Each species is a being, so hold that concept, and imagine the conversation between *all* of these species. Any individual member of the species may be the voice of that species, revealing the perspective of that species. All of these species-beings are in a very long conversation together.

When I really understood that, it was ground shaking for me. And I thought, *How could I have been psychedelic for decades and an ethnobotanist almost as long, in the Amazon, Mexico, the Pacific, and elsewhere in the world as well . . . How could I have spent all this time studying worldviews, plants and people, philosophy, and yet not have really understood in my blood, in my bones, the animated nature of the world?* That's when I truly got it. I am very grateful for that moment and for how it has guided me to be aware, in that way, ever since.

Functionally, I wondered *What does it mean to be an animist—or whatever term you want to use for that awareness—in our modern times?* Now I think that being an animist gives us a deeper, more actively engaged relationship with everything. When we are aware in that way of the aliveness that is around us then we want to take care of it. This is a feminine response, yet anyone can have it. It's a relationship, therefore our attention and capacity to care is activated. We become better stewards of the world. Our distant ancestors, from whichever background we've originated, had this sense, for all of human history. This is the vitalizing neural network of this worldview. Everything is alive, and everything is engaged in a relationship with everything else. I'm a small part of that network. Together, we are part of what nourishes it, just as it nourishes us. We all have a duty to look out for one another, and for our home. This is your feminine awareness speaking, whomever you are, however your culture has defined and shaped you.

That kind of awakened stewardship is so needed in the world now, in our growing awareness that things are tipping, have already tipped, way out of balance. And given that the basis of health itself is balance, our job is to tip it back to equilibrium as much as we can. Each of us can do this in our individual lives and address it together in our collective lives. I feel that it is very much the job of psychedelic people to seek balance and to help bring its resonance to the world around us. We in the contemporary psychedelic subculture are among the mobile, mingled, and relatively privileged people of the world. We have now been granted decades of dwelling in and exploring these extraordinary states of mind—and we have embraced relative discretion and the resilient underground in order to do this as safely as possible.

We've also made sacrifices to learn in this way. We feel largely outside the dominant culture, but we know that what we do, what we say, what we experience, and what we put out there in those psychedelic moments—whether they're ceremonial gatherings, or with individuals seeking insight—we know that that is medicine for the planet, not only for us. And we know that our conscious action is dropping a little more light, a little more heart, a little more connection with the ancient and the unconscious, and it's carrying a prayer for the future. We are able to embody that awareness, and to acknowledge the sense of collective responsibility that comes with such a gift. So of course, we're not only seeking to heal our own individual wounds, but to heal and rebalance the whole picture.

On the grand scale, this kind of awareness is of the flow of life and energy through time and space. The flow of being. On the personal or collective level, this awareness can guide your choices of what to do here in this lifetime, in your brief moment of incarnation. What is the droplet of good energy, action, or caring that you are adding to the mix?

## Vessels of Transformation

This quality of awareness that I am describing is a feminine one, or what we associate as feminine. Put most simply, as mythologists might tell us, or archetypal psychologists might say, the realm of the potential is the feminine element, while the realm of manifestation is the masculine. These are the classic ways of identifying the masculine-feminine dance. Being able to receive without measuring, just to hold, to embrace awareness—that's a feminine quality. It involves paying sustained, open attention to the possible. Our psychedelic investigations train us for this, if we care to let them. This awareness of which I am speaking is not purely passive. Rather, it's an active, awake awareness.

How does one put a sunrise into words?

How many of us, in our psychedelic seeking, in our three-dimensional daily seeking as well, think we know what we're looking for? We are hunting for something, someone, scanning beyond the here and now, which is where "just being" begins. As that tiny, aged, native Amazonian woman told me way back when, "People from your place come here, looking for something. They always think they know what they want, so therefore they miss what's all around them, they don't hear what's whispering to each of them." This is one of the big lessons I've received: it's the listening, it's the being receptive to the murmuring of the universe; that is where the real wisdom is. You may then be ready to notice what wells up; something that you didn't even know to look for: an insight, an observation, something that lies beyond what your logical mind could have guessed at. Hidden wonders.

Then you can review your insight, ground yourself, send down your roots. Conscious grounding is a great, fundamental art of being, one that we've largely lost. It's a feminine quality, like putting one's home in order. We need to relearn it, individually and collectively. We need to relearn it in order to be able to appreciate and even to witness this unbidden information that comes to us from the world.

You know that every ceremony or medicine gathering is a vessel that is created. The circle is a vessel, the village maloca is a vessel, the little safe haven you make for yourself in your own private journey spot is a vessel. That cleansed vessel is receptive, encircling, inviting insight, allowing transformation. The principle of creating this feminine container while we go through these experiences creates a vessel that surrounds us so we are safe and we are contained during the vulnerable stage of opening up.

We are able to see that the top of the vessel is open and that's where the transmission occurs, that's where the light comes in, that's where we send up our own sparkling fountain. It's where we send our questions and where we send our thanks. It is where we send our prayers, or whatever you call that conversation with What Is. The vertical openness within that surrounded, buffered vessel; that's the opening where we receive the blessings that come down.

Many of us have intuitively learned to create for ourselves some version of the ancient vessel when we're getting ready to trip. It may be alone, or with a few friends, in a chosen space that has been cleansed, smudged, and symbolically marked. A special space and a delineated moment in time, cleared and cleansed so that it acts as a vessel for receiving light, for exploring, for holding and generating the classic gifts that heal the world: love and light, mystery and reflection, sorrow and reckoning, and certainly gratitude. That's ceremony. That's a feminine phenomenon.

There is never only one way to be, nor is there only one right way to do a psychedelic, or to ingest an entheogen, or to pray with a plant. There are various modes of experience to which some of us humans are so drawn. Let me share with you one such variation. I recently made a pilgrimage to one of the final Grateful Dead concerts, in 2015, and there must have been around eighty thousand people at each show in that short, poignant series. While there, in that state of mind, awash in the music that felt like a cross between a celebration, an exploration, and a supplication, I thought about that concept of the vessel. I felt again the container, vast this time, holding so many people in a shared altered state, in ceremony, which is what it was. Of course, I was entrained to feel it. I used to go to Dead shows a lot when I was young, in the 1970s and 1980s, so back then I understood the principle: that tens of thousands of people on LSD or mushrooms, all together, vibrating exactly the same way to rhythmic sound and poetry, is clearly a marvelous, transformative, shamanic experience. A stadium filled with the positive resonance of so many hearts and minds can be a vessel for transformation.

In this final show of the survivors of that unique team, the awareness of created ceremony was so moving to me. It was marvelous to feel that even twenty years after the old wizard Jerry Garcia died, everyone can get together and embody that same awareness with that very same meme, with those sounds as they are now inscribed in the sky, with the help of our blessed medicines coursing through our perceptions. It has been a truly marvelous phenomenon for my lucky generation of now-elders to feel both the masculine and feminine elements woven into magical performance, a co-creation, as any excellent ceremony in human history would be.

And so, I want to thank the people of music, both music makers and music lovers too, who have crafted this ancient form into something vast and flexible for the twentieth century and beyond. It's a gift we received with the birth of rock and roll. Thank you. This music and these events in our culture have been a male-dominated model, but they are in part a feminine process. I'm really hesitating to use the word *channel,* as my rational self does not use that word to explain the reception of knowledge or creativity. Yet allowing oneself to receive energy, filter it a little bit, flavor it with one's own skill and insight, then put it out again in another form—that is what good healers do, that is what fine musicians and artists do, that hopefully is what impromptu speakers like me do too—be receptive, carry people along, offer it onward.

The intention to receive in order to share is feminine, but we are each the masculine and the feminine. Just as the yin and yang represents everything, who wants to live in an entirely yin or an entirely yang world? First of all, it's not possible, and second, it wouldn't be in balance, so how do we balance those aspects? How do we value the yin qualities that tend to be pushed to the background or undervalued by the yangsters?

## Corazón: Heart Means Courage

Among those feminine qualities that psychedelics can help us embody, we would include intellect—heart-centered intellect. We think of intellect as being rooted in the mind, in the brain actually, a kind of masculine toolbox for analyzing and organizing. We all have that, but we also have more than that. The feminine aspect of that analytic gift might be discernment, which brings us back to telling the difference between useful illusion, what is often called reality, and illusion that is not so useful. We discern which way to go when the path forks, or whether that eager person who is standing very nearby is all that he or she claims to be. We must use our discerning skills often in the pursuit of knowledge that comes to us in unsanctioned and sometimes risky ways. We must also use our discerning mind when power is totally sanctioned. Discernment and intuition can work together, checking the environment and even checking each other. It's like an invisible, animated world of shifting types of awareness, hopefully working toward well-being, a balanced way of carrying and sharing our gifts. That's psychedelic. We learn that on this path—we learn how to walk with our feet on the ground and our head in the clouds. If we don't learn that way of being, we often find ourselves lost.

Many indigenous people talk about there being two brains—one brain in the head that names things and remembers things, that solves problems and all of those important functions. And yet they also say there is actually a more central brain in the heart, the other brain, which senses things unseen, which is in fact the seat of awareness.

I think we modern humans have lost the recognition that this is how we humans work, and by having lost this, we are shut off from the root of our own awareness. Awareness is not something we catalog in the brain. We need to be able to remember that our awareness is centered in the heart, with the brilliant brain in service to this kind of awareness. Then we get a whole magnificent toolbox, or a medicine bag, or a mending basket in which to do our work in this world.

One of the feminine qualities that is really beautiful and important to remember is that of courage, and by that I mean risk-taking—a way of diving into the area of risk that exists between what's known and the unknown, between the dark and the light. I think it comes (and now

I will refer to women in particular), I think it comes very much from our relationship to birth, to the experience of birthing. It comes to us as caregivers, as those who help others through the narrow places that present the risk of life and death. It may come from those experiences that bridge the twin reality of giving birth and of dying and taking care of other beings in these transitions as well as going through them ourselves. It comes with the female constitution, this embodiment of potential and response, but the courage and assessment are accessible to all.

I would say that I am a person who is comfortable with risk and that is what has gotten me to this point in life, although the trail has led me both uphill and down, in and out of trouble. I'm also a mother, a grandmother, and a passionate teacher, so I know from experience what it means to nurture and protect. Like others in these fields, I examine the landscape of shamanic descent, share folktales of transformative moments wherein people enter an unknown place, undergo risk, change form, and come out standing on their feet, at least as good as they went in the day before. That is the impulse to take care of the world, which is a feminine impulse as well. Embrace that quality when you find it in yourself, for the world needs us to remember how to take care of it.

## Nature Presents Character

Let's talk about the plants for a moment. If we listen to the longtime human experts in using some of these species, we see that the species are often (but not always) defined as deities or beings, teachers, or spirits. We have many different names for them, and the sense of a particular kind of mind behind each one. These appear in many psychoactive plant experiences, in psilocybin mushroom experiences, and sometimes even with LSD.

The emotions they bring may include compassion, a feminine quality, wherever it may arise. We each feel compassion to different degrees, or we turn it on and off. Or we are afraid to let it show, but it may be awakened in a psychedelic experience, so you find that in your mind's eye, you are putting yourself in someone else's shoes. Your heart goes out to them, as we say.

Another emotional dimension these plants can open us up to is sorrow, which may include mourning and accepting the loss of something or someone beloved. Accepting that sorrow is part of our journey. There is a lot of suffering all around us, and there will be a lot more suffering before this whole drama is over. I find that part of every big experience is just letting myself feel that, the weeping for the world. It's part of our job to be aware in that way, to let our selves feel it. You know, even in the old LSD days before we had ayahuasca and mushrooms and all of these things, I always knew that at some point in the trip would come the sad but sweet waterfall of tears. It would just wash me clean. It would wash and rinse everything that I was sorrowing for; it would be a little bit of the invisible help that I could give to the world, to weep for it. Acknowledge the pain, send compassion, and let that go. I encourage you, male or female, to allow that quality to come forth and realize that it's one of the jobs of conscious people to feel this. It's not all joy and not all reason by any means, and that's okay; that's actually how life is.

One more archetypal activity that comes naturally in psychedelic feminine awareness is mending. I use that word because late in each trip, whatever the medicine or the setting, I realize that I am beginning to think about people I know, or causes that I identify with, or troubles that I have witnessed. I then realize *Oh, there's something I can do for that person.* Or I might realize that *Now I understand why that person is like that and has that habit,* and *What can I say that has never been said to them, that might help them feel better?*

That's when I pick up my mending basket and start stitching those holes and darning those socks. Symbolically, energetically. I just send a little prayer of mending out in each of those directions that I notice. Don't you catalogue those people who are closest to you when you are well into a meditative journey? And perhaps you think about where that medicine came from, that miraculous gift of an experience that found you. You really truly pray that the person who made it possible isn't doing time for making or delivering true medicine. Sometimes in fact they are paying that price of freedom, or of fear. So that's part of the really honest regard of the world. We can do it in that virtual way, we can do it as activists—and we should—but we can also do it in these experiences, because we are very powerful in these experiences. Our brief power is mysterious. And yet, we know that what love we send out in those moments is very potent; it helps. After all this time, I still really believe that's true. So please, let's keep doing that.

Different species have different personas associated with them in our projections. Cultural recognition of plant spirits or plant teachers constitutes a broad and fascinating terrain of study. Many contemporary Western people refer to ayahuasca as Mama Aya, or variations on that idea of the Great Mother. But for many cultures in the Amazon, ayahuasca, the brew of components, the matrix from which the experience arises, is not considered female. The vine in the brew (*Banisteriopsis caapi*) is often considered androgynous, or even masculine, as it represents the force. And the brew's leaf component (most often *Psychotria viridis*) is usually considered female, representing light. But overall, ayahuasca is considered to be a blend of these things, each being essential. I think that our own Euro-descended cultures are so disconnected and hungry that we are desperate for a cosmic grandmother to hold us.

Maybe that's why folks say that ayahuasca is female; why we have adopted that in this subculture. In these still early days of incorporating animistic sentiments into mechanistic culture, we have a tendency to call all things with recognized spirit female. We are still understandably awkward with an animistic concept and language that had been forgotten for centuries. And we assume the goodness of plants too. In the indigenous view, there are many energetic forms. The feminine and masculine are woven and spun together in intricate ways, and goodness or pure intentions are never assumed. The animated world is more ambiguous than that. Nothing is what it appears to be.

Last, I'd like to recognize the woman warrior side of femininity.

Back in what I call the "good-old-LSD days" (life was so much simpler when there were not so many kinds of psychedelics!), I was, among many other things, a tarot card reader. Of course, I pondered and invoked each of the archetypal suits in the tarot universe—the wands, the discs, the cups, and the swords—but the persona whom I identified with was the Queen of Swords, who has the refined and always-available skill and inclination to cut through illusion. It's a precise, beautiful, powerful, and startling skill. That's the clarity of mind, the immediate presence of clear mind, which is also a very significant feminine quality.

There is a way in which true clarity, seeing what is and what is not presented in a situation, the art of spontaneous discernment, can be recognized as a fundamentally feminine quality. This is saying what needs to be said, straight to the heart of things. This invokes the image of the circle of women elders, who were for so many generations the ultimate council of wise advice in innumerable cultures around the world. May we grow again to recognize the value of that kind of voice, that experience-based wisdom, the feminine insight translated into action. We have it in us yet. We could turn to that voice again, each in our own way, as well as together.

We can embody the psychedelic-trained perspective that we honor here, acknowledge that it has been shaped and tested by the joys and sorrows of daily life. We are being trained by the plants, the fungi, and some other marvelous molecules to see what truly is. We are able to find the place in ourselves—the feminine awareness, the psychedelic voice— that knows how to be present, to speak up, to discern, and to help. Shall we then? No time like the present.

# 12

# Toward a Radical Uncertainty

## *Into the Darkness*

### Anna Luke

In the spirit of radical uncertainty, this talk* is not going to offer any answers. It's more a series of questions that emerged from a concentrated period of ayahuasca use in Peru. Broadly I want to talk about how darkness and uncertainty have been deeply undervalued by our patriarchal culture, which favors that which can be measured and seen. I want to look at how plant-based spirit medicines might offer us a much-needed bridge back to a degree of reverence for darkness, and to look at how being able to tolerate uncertainty might be an increasingly urgent social and environmental need.

So, let me start with a confession—I have been very afraid of the dark. As a child I used to sleep with the lights on, and before bed would check behind things, around things, and underneath things, because

---

*The following essay is a transcript of a talk I gave at the Breaking Convention Conference, at Greenwich University in London in the summer of 2015. In the intervening years the world feels as though it has become a more uncertain place than at any point during my lifetime, and the need for us to cultivate the capacity to sit with the unknown feels more vital and urgent than ever.

the darkness held . . . well, I didn't know. That was the problem. In the dark our fantasies assume their most frightening forms—it's potent just to say those four words *afraid of the dark*. The dark holds our most archetypal fears, our nightmares; it's the wood in which we lose our way, the night in which our demons find us.

As I grew up I thought I'd given up being afraid of the dark, but when, in March of last year, I found myself lying on a mat in the middle of the Peruvian jungle, having taken a very strong dose of ayahuasca, I realized that I hadn't—quite the opposite, in fact. I was absolutely terrified.

I was at the Temple of the Way of Light outside Iquitos. I'd gone there to seek help with a health issue, one I'd been battling with for about five years. As I went into my first ceremony I held my intention really tightly—I was going to gain insight; I was going to find the key that would unlock my health—but what actually happened was that I became overwhelmed by terror. At various points this terror reached operatic proportions. During an epic thunderstorm I became convinced that a jaguar had come into the maloca and was prowling around—it came and sat behind my head and growled at me. I left the maloca and went back to my *tambo* and lay there in abject fear; a fear that didn't cease for days.

As the ceremonies progressed, however, I began to gain some distance from this fear, and I began to see that a lot of it wasn't even mine. It had been handed down from my parents, from their parents—a sort of twisted intergenerational baton in the relay of life. I'd imbibed it in the womb, and as a child, I'd absorbed it from the society around me.

As I reached the end of these ceremonies I was shown myself sitting underneath these three words: *I don't know.*

The medicine told me that I needed to sit underneath those three words, meditate underneath those three words, and learn to tolerate uncertainty. It also told me "Don't come back—don't take any more medicine, until you have sat with this."

When I emerged from the Amazon I began to try to integrate some of these experiences, and to think about how tolerating uncertainty might be important not just for me, but in a wider social and environmental context.

Let's think a little bit about darkness. It's very difficult to find ourselves in darkness nowadays. If we live in a city as most of us on the planet do, we've got a twenty-four-hour culture: it's strip-lit and light-polluted—the stars have gone out in our skies. As city dwellers we are not going to experience darkness unless we actively seek it out. I'd even go so far as to say it's become a luxury item—people pay a lot of money to go to places where there's no electricity.

I looked in the *Oxford Thesaurus of English,* that great arbiter of language, for the phrase *in the dark,* and found the following definitions: *unaware, uninformed, oblivious, ignorant, unenlightened, unacquainted.* So we can see that this shunning of darkness is encoded at the level of language. Not one of these phrases suggests that it might be anything other than an unfruitful, unprofitable, unworthwhile place in which to dwell.

And how easy is it for us to admit to being in the dark, to admit that we don't know something? I don't know about you but I, particularly professionally, find it very difficult . . . the ego struggles. Instead of admitting our ignorance, we hedge, we bluff, we retreat behind our defenses. Or we feign certainty, we shout louder, in the hope that no one will see the fear behind our eyes.

So why all this need for certainty? Where did it come from?

In scientific terms I think it goes back to the Enlightenment at the very least. The clue is in the name: a movement that literally sought to bring light to the darkness of not knowing. I believe that in the process it gendered that darkness. Francis Bacon, the founder of the scientific method—you may well know this quote—declared that nature must be "tortured—put on the rack—until she gives up her secrets."

With the inauguration of the scientific method, we culturally entered an inexorable trajectory: linear progress—or an idea of progress—out of the dark, away from superstition, toward a point where everything would be understood in the clear light of scientific inquiry.

I'm very interested in the high summer of this idea of progress, which was, I believe, in Britain at least, the late Victorian and early Edwardian era. In my other life I'm a novelist, and at the moment I'm writing a novel set in 1911. In 1911 one of the things that was all the rage was eugenics—broadly the idea that we can breed better humans. There's positive eugenics, which is that the best people are encouraged to breed. And then there's negative eugenics, which is the idea that the people that "shouldn't" breed are prevented from doing so.

The founder of the eugenics movement was a chap called Francis Galton, who was first cousin to Charles Darwin. Galton was infatuated by the arguments in *On the Origin of Species* and wanted to apply them to the human race. He died early in 1911 and his obituary in *The Eugenics Review* stated that he had a "great appetite for mensuration" (vol. 1, 1–9).

Now me being me, I read this as a "great appetite for *menstruation.*" And I thought *Hey! That's a great thing for a late Victorian patriarch to be into! Maybe he's not so bad after all!* But oh no, *mensuration* is, as you probably all know, "the act of measuring."

It struck me, though, that mensuration and menstruation can be thought of as opposite poles: one is the preserve of the patriarch who carries a slide rule in his pocket at all times, while the other— menstruation—is cyclical and runs by a clock of its own. It also reaches toward the infinite; it's the home and birthplace of our consciousness.

The eugenicists had an absolute mania for mensuration. You can laugh at their excesses, but their other work remains hugely influential. Galton gathered the vital statistics of thousands of British citizens, wanting to prove that the so-called higher classes were genetically superior, and in the process founded the science of psychometrics. Galton was also an explorer. As a young man he went to Namibia, mapping its wilderness triumphantly and paving the way for the colonization that would follow in his wake. Galton's protégé Karl Pearson—you could find him measuring the skulls of Cambridge undergraduates to prove that bigger skulls meant bigger brains—is the father of statistical analysis, a hugely influential field today.

So mensuration is intimately tied to power and patriarchy. And if it's tied to power, then who suffers most when things are measured? Well I would argue that it's those whose subjectivity is decreed to be less important: it's women, it's indigenous people, it's animals, it's plants, it's the land. In fact, I'd go so far as to say that in almost every instance attempts by a dominant culture to measure and taxonomize—to make certain—lead to exploitation. Take the *Doomsday Book*. William the Conqueror comes to Britain, wants to find out what he's got, and the *Doomsday Book* kicks off the enclosure movement that lasts for centuries, impoverishes the rural poor, and eventually sends them into the factories.

It's not just land. Why was the measurement of time so important? Well, because of power; because of trade, empire, domination, dominion. Jay Griffiths wrote a fantastic book entitled *Pip Pip: A Sideways Look at Time*. In it she calls the Greenwich Observatory a "spectacular erection, a Palace to Patriarchy" (2000, 147) and she noted how the language of empire was encoded in the way time was talked of. Thus was the main clock at Greenwich the "master clock," with "slave clocks" elsewhere in London. There's also a plaque here in Greenwich that commemorates the victims of the slave trade. It acknowledges Greenwich's role in that, saying it was to "enrich England for centuries and correspondingly destabilize and impoverish Africa." Mean time indeed.

Rebecca Solnit, a writer I admire very much, has written extensively about the concept of uncertainty and writes that "Ultimately the destruction of the earth is due in part, perhaps in large part, to a failure of the imagination, or to its eclipse by systems of accounting that can't count what matters, the revolt against this destruction is a revolt of the imagination, of pleasures money can't buy and corporations can't command, of being producers rather than consumers of meaning, of the slow, the meandering, the digressive, the exploratory, the numinous, the uncertain" (2014, 105).

So how to find our way back to uncertainty? Because we don't want our imaginations to fail us—not now. The world needs our imaginations more than ever.

The ancient Greeks had a word for uncertainty—for being in the dark. They called it *aporia*. I love this term. It's quite new to me, but as far as I'm aware it speaks of a doubt about what to do or say. However, it's far from a negative doubt—it's a profoundly generative state of being. *"The true philosophical Aporia . . . is always fertile . . . it breaks with the logic of identity and pertains to the logic of the intermediary"* (Kofman 1988, 7). This, to me, speaks to the psychedelic experience, which is a liminal zone where the calcified ego—the "logic of identity"—breaks down, and where we can find something new, in an "intermediary" space. To me too, the logic of the intermediary suggests saying "I don't know"—because *I don't know* is, by its very nature, a mediating phrase; it builds a bridge, it lets down the drawbridge of our defenses. In Plato's *Meno,* Socrates describes the "purgative" effect of reducing someone to aporia, or not knowing. He may not be speaking of literal purgatives, but ayahuasca literally had a purgative effect on me. In the process of physical purging in the jungle, I felt as though I was also purging my overwhelming need for certainty, bringing me to a state of aporia.

In Aristotle's *Metaphysics* (trans. 1998), aporia plays a role in the enquiry. He says: "With a view to the science we are seeking, it is necessary we should first review the things about which we need to be puzzled" (995, aporia 24).

Wouldn't it be wonderful if today's science, which more than ever seems to be dominated by this aggressively fundamentalist agenda—when biologist and parapsychologist Rupert Sheldrake's Wikipedia page is desecrated by skeptics on a regular basis—wouldn't it be wonderful if science started from a place of true agnosticism, of puzzlement, openness, and mystery?

There is, of course, always a deeper level of knowing that's available to us, and it does not take plant medicines to get there. It's available to all of us, at all times, and beyond our ego's need to shore itself up with knowledge. It's a knowledge that is rooted in the body—or at least doesn't feel the need to separate the body from the mind or the heart. But this sort of knowing cannot be approached head-on—its true nature is always wrapped up in mystery.

I think *mystery* is such a gorgeous word—made to be whispered in a forest at night. John Keats, the English poet, liked a mystery. On a walk in 1817 he coined the term *negative capability,* saying in a famous letter that this was when someone was "Capable of being in uncertainties, mysteries, doubts, without any irritable reaching after fact or reason" (Keats 1899, 277). I think there is medicine in that phrase, and it seems to me that he is also speaking to one of the most valuable experiences of plant spirit medicine, which is to invite us to partake of mystery, a mystery which, by its nature, depends on the dark.

In Peru as I lay there in the dark, the shamans came to us one by one, and sang to us, and as they sang they helped me release my fear. And it's my understanding that they depend on darkness to do their work; they depend on darkness to be able to see, to be able to sing the body and its systems back into alignment.

I want to speak a little bit about language and mystery here, though ultimately we are talking about something for which there are no words; something essentially beyond language. As Maria Papaspyrou said, language itself is a patriarchal principle. It tends toward clarification of utterance. But perhaps what we need is something different, a bit *tricksier,* a little more elastic than that.

During the last century there were various attempts to deconstruct language—to make it more porous, more liminal, more responsive. Luce Irigaray, the French feminist and critical theorist, went so far as to say that language itself has to change if women are going to have their own subjectivity that is recognized at a cultural level; that inclusion of women in the current forms of language just doesn't work.

I'd go further. I think our ecological, spiritual crisis is also a crisis of language, and we need to acknowledge that language is utterly limited when it comes to extending a subject position to animals, to plants, to all living matter. A strong medicine ceremony though, especially taken in nature, can show us that a tree, a stone, a river, has its own language—has a subject position as real and as valuable as our own.

I don't mean to suggest that psychedelics are the only way to approach this, but this reciprocity of relationship seems to be taken for granted in cultures with a long psychedelic tradition. I've been privileged to come to know a little about Wixaritari culture in Mexico in the last few years, and they have an intact peyote tradition reaching back millennia. They are animists. They accept that we are in dialogue and dynamic relationship with the natural world. Peyote—taken as a sacrament—allows them to communicate with the deer, the Grandfather Fire, the Father Sun, and also to listen, to learn to listen to what the fire wants, to what the river wants, to what the mountain wants, and to make offerings as a result. Peyote is the intermediary, but this is no po-faced reverence. The Wixaritari have a playful element even when things are at their most sacred. When they go on their pilgrimage to collect their peyote they change the meaning of nouns, so the sun becomes the sky, and the moon becomes the president.

This is a trickster spirit at work; this is language that refuses certainty and refuses to be pinned down. It is a language that accepts no hierarchies of meaning; in fact it subverts them in a fertile act of disruption. And this trickster spirit too seems to be important in the defense of the essential mystery of the numinous. Indeed, the Wixaritari adopted the Christ figure as a symbol of reverence at the time of Los Christeros, a murderous Catholic sect. On the surface it may have appeared that they were buying into the Christian propaganda machine, but far from it. It actually cast a net of protection around them; a smokescreen that kept their traditions intact. They knew well the benefits of disguise, since what can't be seen can't be counted, can't even be said to exist. I think this was how they wanted it for a very long time, but now they are reaching out—similar to other groups like the Kogi in Columbia, and I think we need to listen to what they have to say.

A question that's come up for me is that I wonder if increasingly in the psychedelic community we are ourselves in danger of falling prey to an urge to taxonomize, to prove, to make certain. People say things like: "How many elves did you have in your DMT trip? How many praying mantises? Hey! Perhaps we can put them through this statistical program and come up with . . . something."

And though in so many ways I celebrate the psychedelic renaissance, it troubles me a little to think that these sacraments are only now getting traction in the scientific community because they can be *seen* to exist as medicines, because modern science can measure their effects. But that's a whole other talk.

To conclude, this is a call to heed the importance of that which cannot be measured—that which refuses certainty, or absolute meaning—to the trickster! That which says no to the slide rule and "up yours" to the rulers. This is a call to the dark tides of menstruation rather than the clinical exactness of mensuration; a call to the slippery, elliptical, wet, delicious, beating heart of the darkness. This darkness is not of the grave, but of the generative darkness of the womb.

# 13

# The Bioethics of Psychedelic Guides

## Issues of Safety and Abuses of Power in Ceremonies with Psychoactive Substances

### Eleonora Molnar

This essay is concerned with issues of safety and the abuse of power, primarily by people who claim to be shamans, neo-shamans, healers, and wisdom keepers in ceremonies involving nonordinary states of consciousness.

Ceremonial settings and use of psychoactive substances can hold great promise for healing and transformation. However, such potential goes hand in hand with the potential for harm. The practice of ceremonies and the interest in the healing potential of psychoactive substances has been spreading internationally. Westerners who use ayahuasca, iboga, peyote, and psilocybin in search of *authentic* and ritualistic experiences open themselves up to abuses of power by shamans and neo-shamans. Such potential predators can take sexual, physical, and psychological advantage of participants, with female participants particularly vulnerable to this kind of maltreatment. While not all self-described ceremonial guides are abusive in their behavior toward ceremony participants, safety matters and precautions are important and relevant to all who participate in such explorations. Some of these ceremonies are of questionable legitimacy, authenticity, and participant safety.

According to the *Collins Dictionary of Biology* (2005) bioethics refers to the "study of the ethical issues relating to biological, medical and other scientific research and applications. Bioethics considers the perceived risks and benefits of the technologies involved, and their impact on society." Bioethical concerns need to be considered in regulating the behavior of guides. During ceremonies, guides need to be responsible for ensuring a safe container for the exploration of nonordinary states of consciousness and the healing process.

There are four basic bioethical principles that, if followed regularly, would make ceremonies that use psychoactive substances safer. These four principles are: respect for autonomy, beneficence, nonmaleficence, and justice (Beauchamp and Childress 2001). Respect for autonomy refers to the patient being able to choose or refuse treatment. Beneficence refers to doing what is in the patient's best interest. Nonmaleficence refers to, above all, doing no harm. Justice refers to the allocation of health resources with emphasis on fairness and equality. The word *patient* could be interchanged with the one who has sought guidance regarding the therapeutic use of psychoactive substances.

For centuries and across myriad spiritual traditions, stories of gurus, priests, and teachers taking advantage of their students, subjects, and believers prevail. Archetypal power dynamics have been the basis of such abuses throughout history. The mythos surrounding nonordinary states of consciousness, in addition to indiscriminate power ascribed to guides who are sometimes called shamans or neo-shamans, can leave ceremony participants too vulnerable, open, and receptive to resist the suggestions of their guides.

Perhaps because of this mythos or because of the indiscriminate power ascribed to guides, ceremony participants may feel disempowered to question abusive behaviors. Once people experience a nonordinary state or a mystical experience, they often romanticize the benefits while minimizing the risks. *Enchantment* is the state of being under a spell or being charmed by a guide, the medicine, or parts of an indigenous culture that suit one's Western idealization (one's cultural paradigm). When enchantment is combined with unethical behavior on the part of a guide, participants are highly vulnerable to abuses of power.

The *Merriam-Webster* online dictionary defines *safety* as "the condition of being safe from undergoing or causing hurt, injury or loss." Although some guides and retreat centers have done due diligence with respect to safety, there are many others that have not. Safety here can refer to a number of variables including mental and emotional wellness, physical and medical safety, preparation and integration support, and the beneficent intentions of the guides and others involved.

There can be risk for participants, most often women, to be harmed by guides who lack personal integrity and who do not subscribe to basic bioethical principles during or after ceremonies. In the custom of wise-women, community builders, healers, artists, academics, and visionaries, it is our collective responsibility to maintain an ongoing dialogue in our communities to empower and inform each other regarding how potential risks can be minimized and managed. This essay is one means to that end.

## Cultural Appropriation and the Commodification of Traditional Indigenous Practices

In addition to safety considerations, any discussion of ceremonies, guides, and substances necessarily leads to the topics of cultural appropriation and the commodification of traditional indigenous practices; they are synonymous for several reasons. Historically, ayahuasca and iboga, as well as peyote and *Psilocybe* mushrooms were used within the context of indigenous traditions and rituals in their geographic place of origin within the Amazon, Africa, and Mexico, respectively. Indigenous belief systems, with built-in cultural norms and corresponding economic systems, provided a protective container for ceremony participants (Dobkin De Rios 1990; Peluso 2016). Even though sorcery was used by some guides (in line with traditional practices), the safety of ceremony participants was oftentimes provided by family and friends who accompanied the participant (Fotiou 2010 article; Peluso 2014). Overall, Western cultural paradigms of indigenous shamanistic rituals are tainted by a lack of understanding of the social, economic, and environmental contexts in which they are germane.

Contemporary global consumption and neo-ceremonial use often disregard the cosmovision and culture that are necessary wholes in understanding the context of healing, spirituality, and protection in which these experiences are frequently sought. It could be argued that the modern use of these substances is a reenactment of the colonial mind-set, which exemplifies taking only parts of a culture that are useful, and disregarding the intelligence and practicality of the whole. Indeed, giving reverence to the entire cosmovision of these cultures would be inconvenient for the purposes of modern guides. Gaining proficiency in an ancient healing method can take a lifetime, yet guides or centers often present themselves as experts after a training period of just a few years, if not months. Furthermore, contemporary uses of traditional plant medicines contribute to the large-scale commodification of indigenous beliefs and rituals. Certainly, the area of cultural appropriation requires further exploration within the contemporary Western use of traditional indigenous plant medicines.

## Basic Cautions

Of primary importance is that one does not know what psychoactive substances were used during a ceremony unless one prepares the concoction oneself or completely trusts the maker of it. In many cases in North America, it is not possible to know who made an ayahuasca brew because it happened in another region of the world, possibly where the plants were grown, in places such as Peru, Hawaii, and Costa Rica. There appear to be multiple admixture variations, made using different ayahuasca brewing processes. Some brewers will add scopolamine or other additives to the concoction, which may give it properties that are not purposefully sought. Almost every plant-based brew of psychoactive substances is prepared differently each time because the substances may be grown in a different place, under different conditions, or harvested at different times of the plant's life cycle, alongside many other variables. Participants need to keep this in mind as well as inform themselves of the various possible admixtures and their properties.

As well, one does not know the intention of the guide(s) if one is meeting them for the first time and then ingesting some psychoactive substance. There is high vulnerability when one is in a nonordinary state of consciousness and in unfamiliar surroundings. It is commonly assumed that the guide is credible and trustworthy and should be listened to, as they are thought to have extensive experience with the substance and the ritual. Yet when the guide does not subscribe to basic bioethics, nor knows who made the brew and what is in it, a variety of predicaments can result.

The reader might be familiar with the popular phenomenon of "I want to be a shaman." Oftentimes, ceremony participants will take on the messianic zest of wanting to become a guide, open a church, move to the Amazon, or otherwise materialize the visions presented to them during their experience. This phenomenon of enchantment has resulted in a number of self-proclaimed shamans, neo-shamans, guides, and healers who are not well trained, don't grasp the responsibility implicit in their vocation, and may develop an ego that is generally not responsive to tips for improvement.

In traditional indigenous cultures, there are several routes to becoming a guide, and these routes are necessarily tied to the cosmovision of the culture (Walsh 2007). What we currently have in the West is a system of self-proclaimed guides and limited proficiency assessment other than by trial, which has its inherent risks. It is notable that ceremony participants themselves often do not know what proficiency looks like from an indigenous point of view.

## Why Abuse Goes Unreported

Abuses of power in ceremonial settings often go unreported, providing a fragmented sense of the scale of such events in communities. There are many reasons for such underreporting. One reason why victims fail to report crimes of a sexual nature is that they fear reprisals from the guide that may be physical, emotional, or psychic in nature.

There are also occasions where the guide that has abused them may only be identified as "Poncho" or "Steve," without a known legal first or last name or address, making it more difficult to accurately report them to the authorities. Often the guide conducts sexual transgressions in private, leaving other ceremony participants unaware of what has taken place, as they were not mentally or physically present at that time.

However, there have been occasions where ceremony participants have known about a transgression that took place yet have vilified the victim instead of the perpetrator. Targeting victims, who have already been traumatized by the abuse, can retraumatize them as well as impede them from reporting the incident(s) to the authorities. The participants involved in such a travesty value their future experiences with that guide above all and want to safeguard their subsequent access. Due to the underground and illegal nature of ceremonies, there is often pressure on the victim not to report. In some cases, ceremony participants will ask the victim to recant their story of abuse because they believe it will increase negative publicity for the plant medicine and the attending guide and his or her teacher lineage. And there are also times when recovering from the trauma needs to be prioritized before the difficult and emotionally demanding process of reporting can begin.

## Grassroots Community Involvement

Most recently, grassroots community involvement has emerged, predominantly online, when matters of violation need to be addressed. Information about abuses of power and lack of safety with certain guides or facilities was not easily or widely shared in the past owing to the different locations that guides traveled to. However, with today's online interconnectivity this is changing.

For example, due to the coalescing community dialogue about safety, it came to light that one particular guide had a long history of alleged abuses. Although a number of people had experienced abuse by the guide in question, it was difficult to access firsthand reports, yet the condemning message from the community was very clear. A collective letter was written to the followers and supporters of the guide and to the ayahuasca community to raise collective awareness and concern about the actions of this guide (Ayahuasca Community Awareness Center 2013).

On another such occasion it had been suggested by North Americans that there could be a certification labeling program for ayahuasca and other retreat centers for Westerners seeking experiences in South America (Multidisciplinary Association for Psychedelic Studies, n.d.). These programs would be akin to organic food certification and product labeling/certification programs that show the consumer an icon to prove that the food is indeed organic and accredited. Although this could be a great idea in principle, this approach for produce and other products may not be well suited to psychoactive substances in principle; psychoactive experiences thus far have not commercialized equally in North and South America, nor do they operate above ground with many of the requirements necessary to partake in a labeling scheme. In addition, there is potential for this labeling scheme to negatively affect ayahuasca communities by creating more power imbalances within the economic structures of indigenous groups, as well as other perceived negative implications. A group of concerned researchers were vocal in expressing their collective consternation when the Ethnobotanical Stewardship Council, a nonprofit organization, communicated that it was embarking on the development of a labeling program (Brian et al. 2014). The labeling program did not come to fruition, and since then the Ethnobotanical Stewardship Council has dissolved.

Another such occurrence was the case of Alberto Varela, a businessman who falsely stated that he and his organization, Ayahuasca International, were endorsed by the highest traditional authority of the Cofán people of Columbia: Taita Querubín Queta Alvarado. Varela ostensibly lied to create a sense of authenticity for his business activities regarding ayahuasca tourism. Subsequently, the Cofán people discredited his false claims (Putumayo 2015).

Respect for autonomy, by the person being guided, provides an ethical conundrum because forays into nonordinary states can see full mental faculties ebbing and flowing; decision-making can become quite relative. For example, a previously firm decision by a participant can easily change when one is in a nonordinary state and when one's thoughts and priorities are being contemplated and prioritized. Furthermore, it may not be clear to the participant or the guide whether or not the participant is able to choose or refuse treatment due to their fluent mental state. The beneficence of the guide is of utmost importance as they are ultimately responsible for the well-being of the participant during the nonordinary state of consciousness and until the participant regains their full mental faculties. This is why, in my opinion, it's crucial for the guide's helpers and the facility hosts to be sober while others are not; a safe container needs to be maintained. The basic bioethical principles are mutually self-supporting, and it is imperative to give them credence.

Men can be just as vulnerable as women when attending ceremonies that are held by inexperienced guides, or guides that lack ethics and integrity. There are also cases where men can pay for a guide who offers services for sexual healing that add further risks. There have been cases of men hiring a female intimacy coach to guide them through an experience with psychoactive substances and provide *sensual awakening services.* Sometimes these services are advertised as sexual initiations and a lesson in the erotic capacity of plant teachers. Certainly in such cases, there is a fine line between therapy and solicitation. Respect for autonomy could be challenging in the case of giving or withdrawing consent for previously agreed upon touching or sex during the course of the experience. Perhaps if men were offering the same service for women, there would be more critical discussion of this underground practice.

Furthermore, there seems to be some confusion about whether sexual activity and nonordinary states of consciousness are compatible. The anthropologist Daniela Peluso (2014) writes that it is likely a New Age belief that ayahuasca and sex can be used to facilitate healing. She points out that the combination was never included in traditional indigenous practices. Mathematics and philosophy graduate Lisa Bieberman (1967), also a student of Timothy Leary, has a cautionary point about sex and LSD wherein she understands the urge to engage sexually while under the influence of the substance as a way of cutting the psychedelic experience off. She says that people who want to somehow dissociate from the experience try to draw others into a sexual exchange in their attempts to soothe themselves. She argues against such acting out and advises that the real power and pleasure of a psychedelic experience is to be found in a state of *being* rather than *doing.*

Some communities, such as churches, communes, and regular ceremonial groups may be safer than a drop-in group that is unknown to the participant. However, such communities need to be especially mindful not to exhibit cultish behaviors that some underground religious groups tend to demonstrate. These behaviors may include compliance with the group, dependence on a leader, devaluing the outsider, and avoiding dissent (Deikman 1994). In 2008, it came to light that a leader (a *padrinho*) in the Santo Daime church was engaging in sexual contact with female *daimistas.* This was a problematic issue for the church and was difficult to resolve. Sexual abuse within the power structures of religion is an ancient theme; one must look no further than the Catholic Church as well as First Nations residential schools to find epidemics of sexual, physical, and psychological abuse toward both men and women, or indeed young boys and girls.

Some believe that the medicine or psychoactive substance will do the work that the participant requires despite the role or intentions of the guide. It is true that the participants have a central role in their experience and that once a substance is imbibed, there is a lot of inner work to be done.

## Considerations for the Future

While this essay has presented examples of how to address abuses of power and safety considerations, it is worth mentioning that some retreat centers, clinics, churches, and guides maintain bioethical standards and do excellent work. In this, I am referring to places with guides that get to know participants, focus time and attention on preparation and integration, document medical history, and do test doses before administering a flood dose (e.g., with ibogaine). When traditional plant medicines such as peyote, iboga, and ayahuasca are taken within a spiritual/religious context (Native American Church, Bwiti culture, Santo Daime), the kinds of safety considerations discussed here may not arise as frequently as they do for commercial clinics and secular treatment centers. The context of an experience in a spiritual or religious setting is significantly different for indigenous guides (or nonindigenous guides who try to replicate indigenous rituals) who may conduct ceremonies in a traditional way, and some regular participants might be acquainted with one another, which is a protective factor. In any case, it is fair to say that some guides offer a valuable service, exhibit exemplary methods, and employ successful models for others to emulate.

In response to expressed concerns over safety of ceremonial spaces, the Women's Visionary Congress published, on its website, a document with safety tips for those participating in ceremonies that use psychoactive substances (Oak 2015). The suggestions offered are useful; however, even by following prudent safety practices one cannot avoid *all* potential risks. If one opts to use a guide during the ceremony, I believe it is best to be acquainted with and establish trust with this person in advance in order to promote safety. Ideally, the guide would be familiar with the personal history and worldview of the participant(s).

The only way to limit risk entirely and absolutely safeguard oneself from potential harm by guides would be by not engaging in ceremonies with psychoactive substances, especially with people one doesn't know. However, if one is compelled to do so, it is wise to undertake due diligence in learning about the guide(s) and the place where the ceremony is being held, and to have a safety plan that addresses a number of possible scenarios. I liken my advice to parachuting out of a plane: one risks death as well as the reward of the experience if one lives to tell about it. If one is not willing to risk life or injury, do not jump out of a plane. While this absolutist ethos is not popular, it can perhaps save one from potential abuse. Ultimately, one must trust one's own inner guide as to what is appropriate. When a considered decision has been taken to attend a ceremony, a first line of safety is bringing a sober friend to be one's chaperone. This person is entrusted to stay with the participant and assist with what is needed before, during, and after a state of nonordinary consciousness is experienced. This person would take on the role of offering support and oversight that may not be available through the guide(s).

Perhaps Lisa Bieberman's (1967) idea of psychedelic info centers will become a reality in the future. It would be progressive to have legitimate facilities where one could seek legal, safe, therapeutic, spiritual, and/or recreational experiences with psychoactive substances. With MDMA phase III clinical trials underway, this could be a not-so-distant reality (Philipps 2016). These centers could operate through the lenses of public (possibly primary) health and psychotherapeutic provision frameworks under the jurisdiction of laws in North America and elsewhere. These models would involve "the regulation of psychedelics, which includes governance, supervision, set and setting controls, youth access, supply control, demand limitation, and evaluation" (Haden, Emerson, and Tupper 2016, 243).

This proposal would differ greatly from what currently transpires in South America in the vein of drug tourism and in the drug underground in North America. Haden et al. "propose establishing a Psychoactive Substance Commission (PSC), which would have government-delegated authority to regulate psychedelics and other currently illegal drugs (e.g., cannabis, opioids, cocaine), and potentially also alcohol and tobacco" (246). In addition, they suggest the establishment of a "College of Psychedelic Supervisors."

The function of the college would be to establish, monitor, and enforce standards of practice among its registrants. The college would be administered by individuals who had training and experience in psychedelic supervision, including indigenous, spiritual, and medical practitioners. It would be tasked with granting licenses for new supervisors, dealing with complaints (e.g., psychological or sexual abuse) and developing and implementing best practices. This college would be responsible for licensing facilities or environments where psychedelics are administered, including inspection and certification to ensure that best-practice requirements have been met. It would develop regulations, performance standards, procedures, guidelines, and accreditation criteria, which would be used to structure appropriate environments, and to ensure the delivery of high-quality, safe psychedelic administration and supervision (247).

Perhaps the Psychoactive Substance Commission and the College of Psychedelic Supervisors is exactly what is needed to allow psychoactive drugs to be legitimately used for healing and religious practice in North America and elsewhere. Although a regulated approach is useful for advancing practice and research regarding the therapeutic use of psychedelics, it does not guarantee that abuses of power will not occur in those settings.

In tandem with the discussion about the abuse of power and sexual predation, as well as with discussions about emotional and psychic predation, there are arguments that any suggestions about how to keep women safe from predators is akin to victim blaming (Ross 2017). Any discussion regarding emotional or physical harm needs to stand firmly on the clear premise that any act of violation, be it physical or emotional, is never the fault of the victim; the full and absolute responsibility always rests with the perpetrator. It is always the violating agency of the perpetrator that should be scrutinized. Feminist research indicates that political and economic systems need restructuring in order to change social norms regarding gender, sexuality, and violence. Yet, while we collectively work at these systemic changes, we need to engage in primary prevention. There is a fine line in addressing these topics, and they can be interpreted in many different ways. Ultimately, we need to address such issues as a unified community that speaks out on matters of abuse, and engage with these issues from whatever perspective is helpful. The issues around abuses of power in ceremonies that use psychoactive substances are complex and sensitive, and instances of trauma carry enormous charge and can affect the individual, as well as the collective. We need to work toward operating from a centered place within ourselves, a place where we can access our sensitivity, compassion, and responsibility for addressing such matters and for supporting each other. To achieve this, it would behoove us to embrace our own vulnerability in the face of life's challenges and offer it in service to each other.

This essay has been a foray into the many issues regarding the abuses of power and participant safety in the particular context of neo-ceremonies that use psychoactive substances. We have an ethical obligation to share what we know, especially if it can raise awareness in the community and mitigate potential harm to others. As more participants become aware of these issues, there will be higher standards of care expected of guides, and, hopefully, ceremonies can become safer for participants everywhere.

～

**PART 5**

De-gendering
Psychedelics

# 14

# De-essentializing Notions of the Feminine in Psychedelic Research

## Western Women, Ayahuasca, and Possibilities for Transformation

### Lorna Olivia O'Dowd

*Feminism is tremendously underestimated, viewed in the present context primarily as a woman's concern. The understanding has not yet percolated throughout society that the advancement of women is a program vitally connected to the survival of human beings as a species. The reason for this is simply that institutions take on the character of the atoms which compose them, and what we are most menaced by in the twentieth century are dehumanized institutions. . . . I see feminism not as a kind of war between the sexes or any of these stereotypic images, but as actually a kind of effort to shift the ratios of our emphasis that is expressed through our institutions.*

TERENCE MCKENNA (2010)

This paper explores the role of feminism in Western ayahuasca culture and asks how opening up a space for discussing what is meant by "feminine" within that culture might help to address gender imbalances and power relations in psychedelic discourse. "Western ayahuasca culture" refers to the Western appropriation of indigenous healing practices with the use of the visionary brew ayahuasca.

It might seem paradoxical to begin this essay with an old quote from Terence McKenna, a dominant masculine voice that could arguably be set apart from subordinated female voices in the field. Thinking through McKenna's ideas raises questions about why a relatively sparse body of female scholarship can be found in the domain of psychedelic studies and whether illuminating women's narratives specifically could help shift cultural perspectives. "Divine" and "sacred" feminine tropes prevail in New Age discourses, which seem to be shaped by oppositional patriarchal structures, setting ideas of femininity apart from masculinity in fixed gendered hierarchical systems of thought. By analyzing the ways in which women are positioned and theorized in Western ayahuasca research, the discussion in this chapter seeks to expose some of the ways in which foundational notions of femininity can be broken down and played around with, creating space for pluralities and differences.

In digital stories of ayahuasca experiences told by women in different online spaces (Robinson 2015; Serbonich 2016; Short 2016) we find a growing literature about Western women's engagement with "ayahuasca tourism" and "healing," which offer interesting counternarratives to the idea of masculine hegemony. But it is not my intention to reproduce the binary oppositional logic of demarcating men from women. Rather, following McKenna's notion that feminism is not a war between the sexes but instead a project that can open up a debate about institutional power relations, this essay explores the intersections between concepts of femininity in psychedelic literature and possibilities for emancipation from gender and identity constraints. It is hoped that by exposing some of the "essentializing" (fixed, foundational, and fundamentalist) ideas about the feminine and its connection to notions of mystery, divinity, and fear of the unknown, we might create a dialogue for dismantling some of these fixed gender categories. In this, we pave a way for multiplicity and pluralism, allowing new or alternative subject positions and potentialities for transformation to emerge.

## Notions of the "Feminine" in Western Ayahuasca Culture

What is the place of the "feminine" within Western discourses of the ayahuasca experience? And is there anything unique about constructions of Western women's ayahuasca use as distinguished from men? First of all, it is important to note that such gendered categories are vague and demand deconstruction. To look at the question of the "feminine" more closely, it is helpful as a starting point to contextualize it within dominant Western discourses of nature and ecofeminism because of the cultural links between femininity and birth, roots, and the natural world.

The idea that "nature" is rooted in a feminine gendered identity has long been part of the Western cultural imagination. Ideas about the mysteries of "Mother Nature" and the healing powers of "Mother Earth" are set apart from the notion of "Father Sky," relating cultural constructs of femininity to the natural, irrational, and hidden, while masculinity is associated with rationality, visibility, and status. The psychoanalytic tradition of joining together understandings of the masculine with the phallus and castration anxiety has led to the Freudian "riddle of the nature of femininity." Femininity is conceptualized as the unexplored and enigmatic "dark continent." The governing system of patriarchy is organized by its suppression of femininity, and Western culture might be demarcated by its melancholic character, fixed by repression and repetition compulsion, and arising from an inability to mourn the lost primary object of the mother.

In *The Undead Mother,* psychoanalyst Christina Wieland argues that the Western cultural denial of maternal power has created a disconnected society of production, consumption, subjugation, and destruction. In our desire to control our environment and block out suffering, we have become haunted by the lost object of the mother and live with the constant threat of her revenge. This has led to a split culture of denial, dominated by a "masculine psychic structure that is founded on a psychic murder, the murder of the early mother, and the subsequent elevation of the father to custodian of the psyche" (Wieland 2002, 9). The "undead mother" lives on as an unspeakable ghostly presence.

One response to the denial of the feminine subject has been put forward by the movement of ecofeminism, a philosophical and political movement that interprets feminist and ecological issues in relation to male societal domination. The American ecofeminist philosopher and historian of science Carolyn Merchant writes about this in *The Death of Nature,* in which she levels criticism at the scientific era of Enlightenment, which gave rise to an ethos of breaking down and atomizing nature. According to Merchant, in man's quest for dominion over his environment, Mother Nature's mysteries have been exposed and the natural world reduced to a series of objects. In her words, "The female earth was central to organic cosmology that was undermined by the Scientific Revolution and the rise of a market-oriented culture" (1990, xx).

Merchant explains that prior to the scientific culture of measurability and control, "the root metaphor binding together the self, society and the cosmos was that of an organism" (1). In this interconnected system, the human body was not elevated to the individualized position it has come to occupy within the Western "culture of self." Rather it was understood as being part of a community, interdependent with nature. In Merchant's ideology then, gender has been separated into two spheres, with the repressed "natural" feminine standing as a counter-narrative to the patriarchal culture, which now seems to be reaching its limits.

The patriarchy is then constituted by male domination and operates through practices of rule—subjugation, subordination, and submission. Discourses and norms have emerged, founded on binary oppositional principles of collusion and manipulation, master and slave, and any possibility for transformation would involve a difficult process of naming the problem of the denial of femininity and integrating it into our unbalanced world. Following Merchant, McKenna and Eisler name this potential for transformation in terms of mystery, creativity, and chaos—principles they relate to the archetypal feminine. "Early in prehistory," McKenna said, "there was a religion which was a celebration of the feminine" (McKenna and Eisler 1988). Eisler's book *The Chalice and the Blade* first provided a foundation for McKenna's ideas about primitive goddess culture, to which he added that the goddess religion had a distinctive psychedelic character—an environment of boundary dissolution, erotic connection, and community. In McKenna's descriptions of this primordial culture in which femininity was elevated, the breakdown of borders and sensual interrelationality is associated with the essentialized feminine principles of mystery and chaos. What psychedelics can open us up to, McKenna (1998) argues, is a "lost continent of the human mind," the Gaian mind of higher consciousness—an intelligent force that reveals our interrelatedness with all life forms. Indeed, throughout psychedelic discourse we find notions of boundaries collapsing to reveal spaces of liminality and new potentialities.

However, static ideas around femininity still proliferate, as evidenced by literature on women's experiences of using ayahuasca, where we find multiple narratives of people embarking on a quest or journey, seeking self-transformation rooted in dissatisfaction with Western materialist society and its detachment from the nonhuman world. The rebirther and avatar master Javier Regueiro writes in *Ayahuasca: Soul Medicine of the Amazon Jungle* about the repression of the female principle linked to nature. This raises questions about what the "female principle" is, widening the space for exploring the very notion of "selfhood" and making trouble for the idea that an essential human "self" even exists. Regueiro's text consists of a number of totalizing claims about women's experiences with ayahuasca, which can each be unpacked and thought through.

First, Regueiro's work follows the pattern of prevailing New Age and Western shamanic discourses of reproducing gendered dichotomies.

"Masculine energies" are linked to the rational scientific mind while the "female principle" is fixed to an ancient identity connected with nature and the sacred. Female potentiality is thus limited from the outset by universalizing notions of fragility, divinity, and the natural. According to Regueiro's descriptions, women have been reluctant to engage with consciousness-altering plants, but ayahuasca can benefit women hugely as it "powerfully reconnects them to a realm they have been dispossessed of for far too long" (2014, 180).

If we consider the millennia of patriarchy that has dominated the social, cultural, and political world, then the notion of a dispossessed realm carries some weight. And yet it becomes complicated when, following Regueiro's work, we think in terms of the opposing relationship between "male and female energies." What are these "energies" and how do they conflict? Rather than grappling with these questions, binaries emerge in Regueiro's text—of shadow and light, the physical and emotional, spirit and matter—which naturalize notions of femininity and masculinity and speak to the healing potential of indigenous practices within a reductive gendered framework.

As Regueiro argues, we are faced with a necessity for people "to reconcile and reunite the masculine and the feminine within themselves, thus regaining and embodying the consciousness of Divine Androgyny. Balancing these two energies and fully respecting their expressions wherever they manifest is the task ahead for all human beings" (184). While the focus here is on processes of balancing and integration, the neat model of bringing together binaries to transcend them seems to overlook the messier, chaotic, or unknowable constructs, which do not fit within the fixed system of oppositional categories.

In her anthropological doctoral thesis "From Medicine Men to Day Trippers: Shamanic Tourism in Iquitos, Peru," Evgenia Fotiou studied Western cultural constructions, fantasies, and experiences of ayahuasca in the context of shamanic tourism in Iquitos, Peru. Fotiou notes that the ritualized experience of ayahuasca can break through dominant cultural beliefs, cultivating processes of self-transformation and facilitating healing. She writes that the desire for transformation "stems from the belief that cultural conditioning in the West teaches rationality, materialism, and disbelief in spiritual reality, something that creates a void" (2010, 132). Links can be made here with McKenna (1988; 1998) and his view of the primitive goddess psychedelic culture, celebration of the feminine, and so on. When McKenna identifies with feminism, he is not simply arguing for women's equality within the patriarchal system, but rather aligns with an ideal that radically opposes and reforms this repressive system.

Signifying the growing popularity of ayahuasca within Western culture and its widespread interest among women, a number of women's retreats (Wilmer 2016) have been set up that offer ritualistic practices of "containment, transformation and emergence," reflecting processes of "renewal and rebirth" in their life cycle. An account of a women's ayahuasca retreat in Peru, for instance, promises "an opportunity to enter the sacred space of the divine feminine" (see Ayahuasca Foundation in the bibliography), through healing journeys of "exploration and self-discovery." Foundational concepts of "reawakening" the "Divine Feminine" and the restorative properties of ayahuasca are given further credence by the notion that ayahuasca has commonly become known as a "female plant" in Western culture. Constructions of "Mother Ayahuasca" permeate dominant Western discourse even though, as Fotiou articulates in her thesis, the feminization of the plant is a phenomenon that has largely been appropriated by Western outsiders. In Fotiou's view, the feminine and motherly characteristics that have been attributed to ayahuasca have become associated with the notion that the plant spirit opens up pathways to more highly intuitive states and a connection with nature and the sacred, qualities that are prevalently deemed "feminine" in Western dualistic philosophy.

Fotiou goes on to comment that ethnographic and anthropological accounts of Amazonian societies have also told stories of fixed binary oppositional gender roles, which are distorted by the Western lenses through which they are read. In traditional Amazonian shamanism, the majority of shamans were men; drinking ayahuasca gave them courage and insight, which they needed for survival in their roles as warriors (Fotiou 2010). Accordingly, there is a suggestion that women did not drink ayahuasca because they were not so actively involved in hunting. None of these reports are fully corroborated, however, given that these are accounts that have been passed down through oral tradition and are only told here as a result of indigenous people's contact with Western culture. The ethnographic history notwithstanding, the relationship between ayahuasca and femininity in recent popular Western narrative remains mostly unchallenged.

A further link between ayahuasca and the feminine experience, which Fotiou picks up on, is the notion of sexism in indigenous shamanic practices, ascribed to the prohibition of women from ceremonies while menstruating. This has been borne out in my own research wherein Western women attending ayahuasca ceremonies in the Amazon have leveled similar charges against certain shamanic lineages there. According to Fotiou's study, women are excluded from ceremony at certain times in their cycle because they are more visible to spirits during menstruation, leaving them vulnerable to attack or rejection. As one of the shamans Fotiou worked with said, "the medicine spirits don't like gore, they don't really like blood, they don't like all the things that are traditionally, typically human" (146). In this way, the splitting of women from men is rooted in biological and transpersonal concerns, based on indigenous beliefs and experiences of working with spirits and their interaction with bodily fluids.

Even so, the notion that sexism is grounded in Amazonian shamanism proliferates in much Western discourse and has given rise to reactionary practices of honoring the "Sacred Feminine" and caring for "female energy" as though it exists as an essentialized life force, set apart from the governing masculine ideal. This paradigmatic dichotomy demands critique on the basis that it produces a totalizing picture of the "feminine," which is problematized by queer theory, transnarratives, and feminist scholarship, which regard gender as performative and a production of state apparatus. This is highlighted in *Being Different: The Autobiography of Jane Fry* (1974), on the sociological life history of a transsexual: "Our system is set up to make the unusual usual." The structures of maleness and femaleness are created and performed within a matrix of power in which we are all implicated.

As the American philosopher and gender theorist Judith Butler argues in *Gender Trouble,* gender is "the discursive/cultural means by which 'sexed nature' or 'a natural sex' is produced and established as pre-discursive, prior to culture, a politically neutral surface on which culture acts" (1990, 10). That culture acts upon us and creates our gender makes trouble for the notion that gender is chosen, "or that gender is a role, or that gender is a construction that one puts on, as one puts on clothes in the morning, that there is a 'one' who is prior to this gender, a one who goes to the wardrobe of gender and decides with deliberation which gender it will be today" (Butler 1993, 21). This loops back to the question "What is woman?"

## De-essentializing Femininity—
## Multiplicity and Possibilities
## for Transformation

In his seminal book *The Cosmic Serpent,* the Canadian anthropologist Jeremy Narby writes about the symbol of the snake in mythology, relating it to creation, causality, and timelessness. The representation of the visible snake is a manifestation of the "Great Invisible Serpent," twin to itself, defined as "a primary old god found at the beginning of all cosmogonies, before monotheism and reason toppled it" (1998, 66). Stories of patriarchal gods going into battle and defeating the cosmic serpent figure as important tropes in mythology, but as Narby wrote: "These patriarchal and exclusively masculine gods are incomplete as far as nature is concerned. DNA, like the cosmic serpent, is neither masculine nor feminine, even though its creatures are either one or the other, or both. Gaia, the Greek earth goddess, is as incomplete as Zeus. Like him, she is the result of the rational gaze, which separates before thinking, and is incapable of grasping the androgynous and double nature of the vital principle" (1998, 67).

The implications of this, he writes, are threefold: to begin, Western scientific materialism has severed ties with the serpent (DNA), the roots of the vital life principle. Second, since shamans are aligned with the origins of knowledge, they communicate with DNA, the life force, which is itself nonbinary. And finally, the part of humanity that detached itself from the serpent brought to light its material existence in the laboratories of molecular science some three thousand years after the original split, when monotheism and reason dislodged the serpent. Returning to earlier descriptions of the "undead mother" (Wieland 2002), it might be tempting to reproduce notions of the original split as related to our detachment from the mother. The initial passage out of the mother's womb signifies the infant's entrance into the world of dualism, a binary oppositional system comprising two essentialized parts—man and woman, night and day, good and evil, and so on. But this is a reductive worldview.

As Narby says, shamans using ayahuasca gain access to knowledge of the life principle through their visions. Quoting Reichel-Dolmatoff: "When [shamans] say their knowledge comes from beings they see in their hallucinations, their words mean exactly what they say" (Narby 1998, 68). Shamanic knowledge then belongs in the realm of the mysterious—outside of language, time, or space. Awareness comes from an unnameable place between worlds and beyond good and evil, woman and man, and other dualities, in connection with DNA, the origins of knowledge, the life principle itself. Narby's theory is based on the idea that both DNA and nature are "minded" (145), a notion that undermines the rationalistic and fragmented contemporary model of molecular biology.

What this means in relation to Western notions of the feminine is that oppositional constructions are rooted in Western rationalism, and this logic is dismantled when we communicate directly with DNA, opening up other possibilities about the relationality of being. Beyond the binary structures of masculinity and femininity, pluralities therefore emerge that subvert fixed categories and create pathways into transdimensional spaces and possibilities for integration.

It is at this point that we might go beyond the question of what the feminine is, and ask instead what it could be. This shift in focus moves us away from the project of naming and fixing identities and stories to the possibilities inherent in experimentation. As the late Gilles Deleuze, professor of philosophy at the University of Paris, writes in *A Thousand Plateaus: Capitalism and Schizophrenia:* "The self is only a threshold, a door, a becoming between two multiplicities" (1987, 275). Taking this thread further, we can venture into the realm of new materialism and nonhuman subjectivities; the interdependencies between all matter and the implications for rethinking ourselves and our world. American political theorist and philosopher Jane Bennett (2009) writes about this in her book *Vibrant Matter: A Political Ecology of Things,* in which she posits a reconstruction of matter as an active and affective constituent of political life, which has become overshadowed by human subjectivity.

Dissolving the subject-object binary and boundary by breaking the "habit of parsing the world into dull matter (it, things) and vibrant life (us, beings)," the "vitality of matter" (vii) emerges in a space where we can "begin to experience the relationship between persons and other materialities more horizontally" (10). Shifting from vertical to horizontal forms of relationality compounds the critique of subject-object dualism; hierarchical gendered categories are dismantled, making way for a new kind of ethics.

So long as the human subject remains isolated from other species through discursive and institutionalized dualism, it seems that gendered binaries will continue to be reproduced. Further attempts to create pathways for thinking about horizontality and multiplicity have been made by theorists of the "posthuman," a concept that has emerged from interdisciplinary spheres of art, philosophy, and literature. Prominent feminist scholar and author Donna Haraway takes up the question of the posthuman in her book *When Species Meet,* which raises questions about what happens when species meet and become companion species in techno-culture.

Beginning with the avowal, "we have never been human," Haraway reminds us that only about 10 percent of cells in the human body contain human genomes, while the other 90 percent are filled with the genomes of bacteria, fungi, protists, and so on. "I am vastly out-numbered by my tiny companions," she says, "better put, I become an adult human being in company with these tiny messmates. To be one is always to become with many." She continues by saying that the lives we encounter around us are "at the same time creatures of imagined pos-sibility and creatures of fierce and ordinary reality" (2007, 4).

These entangled dimensions suggest that we are always constituted in intra- and inter-action; the "partners do not precede the meeting; species of all kinds, living and not, are consequent on a subject- and object-shaping dance of encounters" (4). Applying Haraway's work to the question of Western women's experiences of psychedelic transforma-tion, the question is no longer a gendered one that speaks to origins and fixed identities. Instead it becomes a question of who and what we are, and what the possibilities for transformation may be. Again, these ideas broaden out our understanding of the complex web of interrelationality and connection to life outside the category of the human.

Destabilizing gendered identities can therefore create a space for reimagining the problem of what it is to be human, possibilities of the multiple and open-ended change. I will end here with a quote from the French philosopher Jacques Derrida's (2002) work "The Animal That Therefore I Am," in which he explores the boundaries of what we call human and animal. Inventing the idiom "limitrophy" to define the project, "Not just because it will concern what sprouts or grows at the limit, around the limit, by maintaining the limit, but also what feeds the limit, generates it, raises, and complicates it. Everything I'll say will consist, certainly not in effacing the limit, but in multiplying its fig-ures, in complicating, thickening, delinearizing, folding, and dividing the line precisely by making it increase and multiply." It is this play on multiplicity that is useful for thinking critically about psychedelic discourse that at once goes beyond notions of everyday human experience into altered states of consciousness. At the same time, it reproduces pathologizing gendered binaries about what it means to be a woman or a man. Overall, the totality of this work has emerged from the question of the ways in which notions of femininity are figured in Western psychedelic discourse (especially related to ayahuasca), and how an exploration of the category of the feminine can open up possibilities for personal transformation. As I have argued, framing femininity as a stable category should be problematized on many levels. Pigeonholing the notion of "femininity" against generalizing notions of the normalized "masculine" fails to lay out the particular nuances and complexities of sexual or gender difference and otherness.

Psychedelic research, and particularly indigenous shamanic practices of psychoactive plant use, offer a way of disrupting binaries, which have become naturalized and assimilated into the norm. The implications for Western women (and men) are numerous. Resisting universalizing patriarchal logic, multiple possibilities emerge about the question of what we are and what we can be. The mutability and fluidity of emerging subject positions challenges reductive systems of thought, unsettling ideas about naturalized identities and reminding us that, in the words of the renowned political theorist Hannah Arendt "Inside we are all alike" (1978, 34–35).

# 15

# The Feminine Enshadowed

## The Role of Psychedelics in Deconstructing the Gender Binary

### Cameron Adams
### and Timothy Davis

Ethnographic research on psychedelics forums conducted between 2010 and 2014 by the lead author (Adams 2011, 2012, 2013; Adams, King, and Waldstein 2011) shows that it is common to associate a feminine spirit with psychedelic substances; even, perhaps, the Jungian archetype of the Sacred Feminine. A perusal of cross-cultural materials seems to support the feminine nature of psychedelic plants. However, the concept of the feminine cross-culturally is inconsistent except that it contrasts with that which is masculine, and vice versa. This undermines the concept of a unified feminine archetype and rather suggests a situation where we find multiple femininities.

## The Feminine Cross-Culturally and Its Link to Psychedelics

One facet shared by these femininities is, as we argue, that they constitute one possible means to access the Jungian shadow and further depths of the psyche owing to their socially defined hierarchical position. Instead of being an autochthonous psychic given, the perception of a feminine nature to psychedelics is a perceptual artifact of cognitive and cultural filters. The psychedelic experience lays bare these filters; the masculine/feminine contrast is an echo of the contrast between the socially promoted normal waking state of consciousness and downplayed altered states of consciousness.

Cosmopolitan reports of psychedelic use invoke nurturing, love, and an approach to balance. For example, psychotherapeutic effects include alleviating emotional imbalances, dealing with end-of-life anxiety, working with interpersonal relations, and exploring the inner realm, intrapsychic structures, and spiritual development. These experiences lead to a heightened feeling of well-being through a sense of unconditional love and acceptance. These are commonly achieved through an increased sense of interconnection with earth and cosmos, a focus on nature, and an acknowledgment of the beauty of all things (e.g., Alper, Lotsof, and Kaplan 2008; Griffiths et al. 2006, 2011; Grob et al. 2011; Halpern et al. 2005; Osmond 1957; Schmid, Jungaberle, and Verres 2010). Adams's (2013) research participants tended to associate such experiences with feminine qualities. This is further reinforced by the use of the personal pronoun *she* when referring to certain psychedelic substances, in particular plant-based psychedelics such as ayahuasca and *Salvia divinorum,* among others.

However, in Amazonian contexts, where psychedelic substances are also considered to be feminine, the typical motifs include, but are not limited to, creating the structures of reality, undertaking supernatural warfare, divining criminal and/or antisocial acts, or entering the spirit world to negotiate with spirits on behalf of the living (Eliade 1964; Dobkin de Rios 1993). While these realms of action are attributed to the feminine in these cultures, in cosmopolitan cultures these actions would seem quite masculine. The contrast between these experiences of femininity is due to culturally defined gender roles and begs us to evaluate what is meant by "the feminine," and why these divergent motifs are applied to ostensibly the same entity or phenomenon engendered by psychedelic experiences.

## Defining Gender Identities

From an ethnographic perspective, Sherry Ortner (1974) argues that women are subjugated in all societies. She attributes this subjugation to the biological facts of reproduction, which limit the action of women. Men, on the other hand, are free to apply themselves to the elaboration of the arts, technology, and religion—in short, cultural activities. Because of this, Ortner claims that it is universal that males are associated with culture, and females with nature.

Following Ortner, Gilmore (1990) further develops the nature/culture aspect of gender identity. However, in this model, women are chthonic, natural beings with vague and expansive identities, but the cultural endeavors of men require that they constantly act in order to (re)define themselves. These acts hone an increasingly narrow and well-defined male identity.

In reviewing the sexual division of labor cross-culturally, Goody (1969) and Goody and Buckley (1973) find that with the exception of the biological facts of reproduction, childbirth, and breastfeeding there are no hard-and-fast universals as to what men or women do. Likewise, Moore notes that the cultural fluidity of women's roles between cultures, "make it impossible to assert a commonality based on shared membership in a universal category 'woman'" (1994, 9), leading Loftsdóttir to remark that "the sign 'woman' [is] characterized by diversity rather than singularity" (2002, 306). Throughout the world, one can find women who, as mandated by culture, engage in all of the activities deemed either feminine or masculine in cosmopolitan culture. The classic example of this is among the Chambri (formerly Tchambuli) of Papua New Guinea who display diametrically opposed gender roles to those of European influenced societies (Meade 1963).

The same, as an obvious corollary, can be said of "man" (Gutmann

1997). In fact, in the review of the anthropology of masculinity, Gutmann makes clear the fact that the only universal aspect of femininity and masculinity is that they are co-created. In the context of masculine hegemony, this co-creation encourages a definition of the feminine as that which is unmasculine regardless of the wide variety of specifics encountered throughout the world.

Becker (2011) argues that the human ability of abstract and future thought gives us an awareness of our own mortality and ignites in us a fundamental terror of death. The masculine endeavors of civilization and culture follow as "immortality projects": meaningful symbolic systems and structures of belief applied to becoming eternal. The most fundamental immortality project is that of identifying children as carrying on the symbolic self after death. According to Christ (2016) the primordial identity was based upon private property, so it was necessary for men to trace their biological sons, who would inherit. Female sexuality was violently controlled to guarantee paternity and thus became "property" deemed to be of less value than males.

In striving to deny death we idealize the symbolic self and its immortality projects. In this, the body, our physicality, and anything associated with it becomes associated with our mortality and finitude. Menstruation, being a reminder of female corporeality, reiterates female embodiment in a way that does not occur in males. The female closeness to the body serves as a reminder of impermanence, mortality, and death, which arouse existential anxiety and dread. Meanwhile, male embodiment is lessened, putting the accent upon apparent transcendence of the body and, therefore, of death. In terms of value then, that which is disembodied becomes elevated while that which is closer to the body becomes devalued (Becker 2011).

Moreover, the female association with the corporeal body, and therefore nature, serves as a reminder of mortality and leads to the enshadowing of femininity itself, or the culturally sanctioned performative behaviors and normative presentation of female bodies (Butler 2006). Due to the female association with mortality there is an attempt, as in death, to control and dominate women. Seeing women as merely mortal rather than transcendent reiterates the ascendency of males and legitimizes female oppression. These attitudes are often internalized by both males and females alike, widening the gulf between them and reiterating their symbolic associations and therefore power relations (Goldenberg 1993).

This masculinist bias in culture and spiritualization is reinforced by religion through modeling appropriate moods and motivations that exemplify cultural ideals, or more pointedly, the "ideal man" (Geertz 1966). Anything else is repressed via models of sin and transgression. Yet, among these excluded aspects, there are some that must be tolerated as they are important to the functioning of society. These are relegated to women who are not held to the same standards of social discourse as men (Harris 1997). Moreover, they are these facets of human activity that act as a sociocultural bridge into the collective shadow as defined by the unique cultural expectations of each individual society.

## The Power of the Feminine

The power of culture and its transcendence is shown in the exclusion of women from men's ritual activities, not because they are unworthy, but, in some cases, because it is feared that if women have access to ritual and its paraphernalia, they will take social ascendancy (Gregor 1985; Murphy and Murphy 1985; Hays 1988). Further, occasional postmenopausal women in cultures as far-flung as Mississippian pre-Columbian, Zimbabwean, and modern cosmopolitan, are able to achieve the status of "honorary men" (Cheater 1986; Sullivan 2001). This allows them access to the full spectrum of masculine and feminine action for that community, but only as long as they don't undermine patriarchal ascendance (Longwe 1998). In fact, this transgendered boundary crossing seems to be an important source of power as exemplified by the practice of transvestism by shamanic practitioners that is found in many of the world's tribal cultures (Eliade 1964).

The exclusion of the feminine here is not a statement of powerlessness, but instead an acknowledgment of the incredible power potential of the feminine that, for men to maintain status, must be tamed. Likewise, shamanic techniques of ecstasy (Eliade 1964)—in the case under discussion here, psychedelics—provide the means to cross over the shadow bridge without drowning in the dark depths. It matters not what the specifics of "masculine" or "feminine" within any given culture may be.

As we dip into the collective shadow that manifests as feminine, it shows us what we value as a society through the stark relief of presenting what we dismiss. The psychedelic feminine is a bridge to the shadow from which the arbitrary boundaries of culture can be perceived, and normality and rationality redefined. In this context, the feminine acts as a redresser of social imbalance.

Nobody is born gendered as masculine or feminine. These are categories loosely draped upon the biological fact of sex and are both culturally contextual and fluid. Nor do feminine and masculine constitute a firm binary; some cultures have multiple genders (see Herdt 1996 for multiple examples). These identities are developed through a lifelong developmental and socialization process that, by necessity, excises aspects of the whole person to fit within the narrow categories defined by the society into which one is born. The psychedelic experience allows us to review that process and to see the rules of society as arbitrary and malleable. Instead of merely accepting culture as inscribed in stone, one can begin to analyze it at an abstract level. In so doing, one sees how that which is excised could be, instead, integrated as perfectly acceptable aspects of the self, which become valuable in changing contexts, creating paths toward greater integration and wholeness.

The boundary crossing between the symbolic realm of cultural action and the embodied realms of nature calls to mind the powerful transvestism of shamanic practice. Though transvestism may ultimately unify both masculine and feminine traits, cultural biases tend to highlight the feminizing of the masculine rather than the other way around.

Rationality and emotion are never actually separated, for both are grounded in bodily experience, arguing that there is always a corporeal ground of experience and cognition that moves us away from a denigration of physicality, the body, and by extension—the feminine.

What we are really doing here is destabilizing the idea of a monolithic "feminine." "Feminine" is a complex concept that on the world stage has only a very small set of shared characteristics: body parts and reproductive roles. Beyond this, the feminine is vast, changeable, and contextually construed most effectively by its contrast with the similarly complex and contextual masculine. When we hear or read people describing psychedelics as feminine spirits, we naturally envisage our own model of femininity. Yet, we must be very careful about our assumptions. The feminine is unpredictable, dangerous, and erotic, not because of any innate quality but because it is the manifestation of what we have culturally enshadowed; that which is acceptable for some persons in some contexts but downplayed and devalued in general. It titillates and threatens destruction, but what it titillates and destroys is merely the patriarchal definition of idealized culture.

What one experiences as entities in the psychedelic experience, or by extension other altered states of consciousness, and to which some might ascribe an archetypal aspect, may not be as well defined as they appear. As the similarities and differences between aliens, fairies, elves, and angels attest (Brown 2008), it is clear that anomalous experience, particularly that of numinous quality, is cloaked in the cultural trappings of the observer. This is not to argue the ontological status of such entities. Rather, it is to make clear that as we enter a state of loosened associations, which makes such experiences increasingly likely, one is nevertheless obligated to process these experiences or encounters through their cognitive and cultural filters. In a way, it is an opportunity to see these filters in and of themselves. These are the *delic* manifestations of *psychedelic*. By critically assessing the manifested mind-soul, one may experience it as whole, or at least the possibility of its wholeness. Spiritual, psychological, and physical healing can be occasioned in this state of mystical awareness and may be attributed to the entities that are encountered. These entities, as manifested in the shadowy spaces of the psyche, may likewise be attributed to the feminine.

**PART 6**

In Service of Vision

# 16
# Creating Portals into Other Worlds

*Sharing My Visionary Symbolism*

## Martina Hoffmann

For as long as I can remember, I've been drawn to the creative process, and it has remained the most important and central force in my life. From the first childhood drawings to my current work as a full-time artist, the levels of joy, the satisfaction and connection I experience while making art, and the sense of being in the presence of a mysterious higher force have remained the same.

## A Preponderance for Expanded Consciousness

I feel that I also have a natural predisposition toward experiencing realities and worlds beyond "consensus reality," an easy access to expanded states of consciousness. This may be a rather common occurrence with only children, like me, who spend much time in a quiet atmosphere that allows them to pay closer attention to the subtleties in life. These subtleties include changes of light, sound, and energy in nature. Coupled with this was my indulgence in daydreaming, hypnogogic states, and so on. However, anyone can experience such expanded states of awareness, given favorable conditions and the time and space to pay attention to them in order to recognize them as such. Throughout human history there are innumerable accounts of people experiencing such extraordinary states and visions in fairy tales, legends, and myths. Often, they are described as occurring in the dream state, the hypnagogic state, in ascetic practices, during fasting, with sleep deprivation, during or after traumatic events, or in shamanic drumming and chanting circles as well as in other shamanic practices.

Personally, I have great memories of many experiences of this kind in my early childhood. Some of these experiences include lucid dreaming, change of perception in daydreaming, and auditory and visual hallucinations brought on by migraine headaches. These are only a few, and I'm sure that all of them have shaped the way I perceive my world and create my reality today. This was possible through deploying them in the creative process. Growing up in Africa gave me an awareness of the effects of prolonged drumming, dancing, and singing that, I see now, was a firsthand, initial introduction to shamanism. At the same time, I experienced similar out-of-body experiences during church visits where extended listening to the majestic organ music took me into realms of great peace and calm.

Later in life, when I began traveling to South America, another dimension was added to experiencing such states of expanded consciousness through work with indigenous shamans and plant medicines. In this part of the world, psychoactive plant medicines are legal within the context of indigenous spiritual practice as well as with the Church of Santo Daime and União do Vegetal (UDV), which are Christian Spiritist religions, a blend of Christian and native spiritual practices. Here the plant teachers are considered sacraments. Working with them allowed me to achieve a deeper understanding, and to find meaning in and integrate my earlier extraordinary experiences. The plant teachers are powerful substances, which require a humble approach of careful physical and emotional preparation, proper set and setting, as well as the guidance of an experienced shaman.

Discovering the master plant teacher ayahuasca was a blessing in my life. It offered me a highly visual glimpse into the living universe and its structure, all the way down to its smallest particles, while giving me a perspective into the workings of the natural world. This greatly enriched my artistic toolbox and led me to investigate further creatively as well as express in my paintings how we exist and function within such a "universal matrix." A special feature of my experience with ayahuasca is the way it helps me understand my connection to nature and the interdependency of all life. This is a theme that is quite common in indigenous cultures worldwide, but often forgotten in Western societies. Unfortunately, this disconnection from nature is impacting the whole planet, as it is creating great damage to our global ecosystems and with it, has placed us in danger by challenging the very existence of all life on Mother Gaia.

## Illustrating My Inner Landscapes

Today I work mainly as a painter, and I hope to offer the viewer a detailed glimpse into my inner landscapes by using imagery inspired by everything I experience in life, including expanded states of consciousness. My works are explorations of the realms of the imagination, meditation, the dream state, and the shamanic worlds encountered with and without the help of a sacramental plant teacher. These "other" worlds are inhabited by animal and plant totems, archetypes, guides, angels, alien life-forms, and a visual language of sacred geometry, all of which have at some point or another found their way into my paintings.*

I feel that my work is well described by the term *visionary symbolism,* and I consider it to be decidedly feminine, for it places the "Universal Woman" within an intimate cosmos. Many of my paintings represent

---

*[Please see plates 6, 8, 9, and 10 of the color insert to see art by Martina Hoffmann.]

a central heroine in her quest for or experience of a higher truth and connection to the All. This deep connection to the Sacred Feminine has long been a central feature of my life as well as my work. My art, in fact, has been greatly influenced by the so-called Paleolithic goddess art expressed in cave paintings and pottery, as well as my own mother and the native women I encountered in Africa. My human inspirations very generously shared their gentle loving ways of integrating motherhood and physical grace, as well as the struggles countless women have endured throughout human history. Finally, this connection was also encouraged by my parents, who allowed me to grow up in an environment of love and support, fueled by the knowledge that the feminine has always held a very special place in human existence.

It has therefore been and remains my pleasure and honor to artistically portray feminine persistence and our ability to overcome and transform adversity into strength. My art often points to the undeniably central role of women in the spiritual life of their communities, as evidenced by their presence in indigenous creation stories. Women are always portrayed as lifegivers who ensure human continuation on this planet. As well, they have occupied the roles of powerful shamans, guardians, and keepers of the sacred mysteries throughout time. Furthermore, I feel the importance of showing the manifold physical beauty of women, the expression of which has been corrupted and often replaced by unhealthy stereotypes in today's Western culture.

My works transcribe my ecstatic experiences, together with my reflections on the nature of women, in a partially realistic style that marries the fantastic to the sacred. My personal creative method is a channeling process. Most of my paintings are not premeditated, nor presketched, but rather they unfold like an "oracle" while I let myself fall into deep meditative states and interact with the forms my canvas is presenting me. While painting, I become an open channel for any message or insight that wants to manifest on canvas. During this process, information comes through me spontaneously via auditory inputs, emotions, and in visual form. This is then transferred to the canvas by first laying down abstract, random forms that are further "trance-muted" into coherent imagery by my paintbrush.

In addition to holding great personal meaning to me, I feel that sharing my creative expression with my community and the human family at large is also of great importance because such visual information may contain valuable messages for all. It appears, in fact, that these creative visioning processes are very similar to those used by shamans in indigenous cultures and by the mystics and seers of older times. The primary role of the shaman has forever been one of seer and intermediary between this consensus reality and the spirit world. By using his or her ability to enter deep states of higher awareness, he or she retrieves information for his or her community. This may involve locating energies that create disharmony and disease for the tribe. The shaman may also potentially foresee future events and offer solutions to prevent harm to his community, resolve and harmonize conflicts, and aid in keeping peaceful relations between tribe members by generally offering inspiration and transformational tools. In this respect, we might consider today's true visionary artists as holding a neo-shamanic position, with the intention to reenliven and reenergize the communication between humans and spirit, which has remained dormant in Western culture for a long time.

Ultimately, I believe that many of us feel the call to reclaim our tribal roots, so we may reconnect with our indigenous brothers and sisters and thus rediscover together the awareness of a global human family. Incorporating this fundamental understanding of a truly shared planetary existence is a great necessity and, I believe, more pressing than any other contemporary human issue. I feel it is only through a unified consciousness and through the awareness of our fundamental oneness that we will be able to implement all required environmental changes necessary to save life on this planet. How and by which means, methods, or pathways we will ultimately reach this awareness should remain a personal choice and not be regulated by any external agents. Moreover, it appears that the ways to gain such higher awareness are infinite. I consider this state to be our birthright as well as an integral part of human existence, which our ancestors and sages of all ages believed as well.

## The Mission of Visionary Art

As an artist, I recognize the great power of the creative process in helping to forge connections to the spirit world and express levels of expanded awareness through art. The question arises: What is the mission of art and of visionary art in particular? As my late husband, Robert Venosa, used to say: "It creates the future, everything we see, besides the natural world was first envisioned and then designed by a visionary . . . artist." Visionary artists create maps and symbols reflecting consciousness and the subtler and intuitive insights into existence. To what extent the viewers will be able to experience this will depend on their ability to allow the energy of a piece of art to enter their being. In other words, paintings can function as mirrors reflecting the onlooker's personal consciousness, given that we can only observe what our consciousness allows us to see via our individual filtering system. With finer introspection, we may surrender and gain access to the deeper layers of a piece of art, in which case a painting may also function as a portal. In this, it opens gateways into the realms of the transpersonal, the extraordinary, helping us to understand universal existence and thereby allowing us to connect with "the other side." This deeper level of understanding might be greatly potentiated by an ability to enter higher states of awareness, a possibility, which, I believe, is available to anyone who really desires to discover it.

One of the most profound messages that expanded states of awareness has allowed me to catch a glimpse of is: "if we allow it, there is no limitation to form and content." This holds tremendous potential for us to create and transform our lives at will, and it encourages us to leave behind old paradigms of separation, victimhood, and social conditioning. Ultimately, I see one of the roles of the artist as the proactive visionary, seeding awareness of the mystical experience, and spreading the message that it is our birthright to become conscious of our connection to the universe and its multidimensional realities.

My work is an attempt to portray energy, love, and spirit as unifying forces beyond the confines of cultural and religious differences. By embracing our oneness as a global family, by becoming aware of the interdependency of all life on the planet and its interconnectedness with the universe at large, we have a chance to heal and transform the current state of disconnection. In this pursuit, art appears as a tool for transformation and offers us the opportunity to create a reality as beautiful, healthy, and strong as our imagination can see.

# 17

# Eggstatic Creations

## Remembering Our Feminine Core

### Amanda Sage

*As I step through the doorway of infinite possibilities, I*
*take a deep breath.*
*I ask for guidance and consider my role as creator.*
*Then I begin to move and allow feeling to lead the way.*
*Prayers manifest and I hold an intention that acts as*
*my guiding light.*
*My intention is to contribute to the good, the healthy,*
*the wise, the vibrant in this world and I find*
*myself re-membering.*
*The result is a painting, the record of an inner journey.*

## Remembering the Mother

The prayer, which is now a painting, is infused with life energy, and it goes into the world to inform.

Through the act of creating I awaken to natural law, as I am witness to the fact of the matter, which is changing constantly before my eyes.

When I look at my creations, they appear so female, filled with organic, natural motion. They are peaceful, soothing, and sometimes confronting. Symbolic subjects such as eggs, women, and yoni-shaped portals create infinite, timeless references of adoration for the mother.

When I look into the world it seems that so much has been forgotten, and a sorrowful fog of trauma lingers, keeping the illusion of separation dominant and overbearing.

It is time to transcend this suffering and remember who we are as individuals, and as a collective, so we can alter the course of generational trauma.

Such healing can be triggered through witnessing the face of the Holy Mother in myriad ways, such as mindfulness practice, meditation, art, dreams, near-death experiences, and psychedelic journeys.

Most controversial is still the psychedelic experience, even though it has been practiced as a holy ritual longer than can be remembered.

The use of sacred concoctions to stimulate this dying unto oneself and provoke the experience of oneness is vast in origin and practice.

If the psychedelic experience is there to show us this deeper truth and layer of reality, then why has it not been celebrated as a rite of passage for every human interested in such concepts as they come into maturity?

Why is it not accepted as therapy, and a medicine, in this experience of being human?

Thousands of years later, we are now living in times where a great remembering is happening, a fractaling mycelium web is connecting billions of people directly to each other in ways never seen before.

Daily stories of unity, alignment, and harmony are surfacing, in opposition to the screaming walls of war and chaos.

Many of us are direct live witnesses of this tension, this journey of rebirth, with our smart devices, recording and disseminating information more independently and immediately than ever before.

I see no choice after seeing what I have seen, but to be one of Her children on the front lines of Her revolution, of the Divine Mother being remembered and celebrated as the Divine Father steps beside her, into harmonic union.

I often feel compelled to paint energetic weaving lines, as this dance of polarities is not in competition, it is not seeing ourselves as separate, but rather as unique individual awarenesses that are experiencing the majesty of existence.

I am proud to be among those that have experienced these states of consciousness, which have brought me to my knees as I have witnessed the truth that the world is alive and not dead, and there I too have come alive.

I felt deep waves of remembering flood through me during my first deep psychedelic moment.

This experience opened a new kind of sight that bridged the tools of rendering skills with a more spectral multiverse that I was certain existed and had vague memory of.

After training my eyes to see what was in front of me and as honestly as possible represent it on canvas, a kind of split became apparent—a disconnection between my perceived inner and outer realms.

It was through altered states that I was able to open these channels, let go of the dominant mind, and allow an intuitive state to guide me.

I used the practiced hand and eye to study these new realms and realized they were not so very different from what I remember seeing as a child.

Once I had the tools to paint anything, I wanted to create paintings that became objects of power that could alter our states of mind.

This is when I began to really create work that was authentic.

There is a fierce kind of nurturing tone to the art I see spilling from my fingertips.

The images are often of women serenely regal and noble, sometimes filled with rage, or with an air of deep knowing.

Somehow timeless and personal, I find myself in all of them. Some of them are self-portraits, and all of them archetypes, ancestors, sisters.

Through their portraits I seek answers that lead to more questions. They open portals and weave stories as I do my best to listen to their tales.

They are messengers, and I gaze into their faces asking for guidance.

I see my paintings as tools for transformation in that they are here to encourage and remind us to remember and come back together again.

In this way, they have a sacred and benevolent mission to uplift our hearts and remind us of the intricate, magical truth that exists within us and in every moment and every thing.

# INNER TRADITIONS
## BEAR &COMPANY

**Inner Traditions • Bear &Company**

P.O. Box 388

Rochester, VT 05767-0388

U.S.A.

# PLEASE SEND US THIS CARD TO RECEIVE OUR LATEST CATALOG FREE OF CHARGE.

Book in which this card was found _____

❏ Check here to receive our catalog via e-mail.

| Company _____ |
| ❏ Send me wholesale information |

Name _____

Address _____

City _____ State _____ Zip _____ Country _____

E-mail address _____

**Please check area(s) of interest to receive related announcements via e-mail:**

❏ Health          ❏ Self-help          ❏ Science/Nature      ❏ Shamanism

❏ Ancient Mysteries  ❏ New Age/Spirituality  ❏ Visionary Plants    ❏ Martial Arts

❏ Spanish Language   ❏ Sexuality/Tantra    ❏ Family and Youth    ❏ Religion/Philosophy

**Please send a catalog to my friend:**

Name _____ Company _____

Address _____ Phone _____

City _____ State _____ Zip _____ Country _____

Order at 1-800-246-8648 • Fax (802) 767-3726

E-mail: customerservice@InnerTraditions.com • Web site: www.InnerTraditions.com

I will explore four of my paintings, accompanied with poems and short descriptions that I have written to accompany the visual experiences. May they further illustrate and translate what I have attempted to convey in these words.

### Ana Suromai

*The veil is lifted,*
*as a scream shatters the matrix.*

*All of existence stands still*
*for a moment.*

*Then, Birth*
*Revolution*

*An ecstatic cosmic symphony rejoices,*
*Heart blasting*
*Light healing*
*Life giving,*
*Truth.*

*All is revealed,*
*A new world is born.*

The act of revealing publicly the hidden core of womanhood initiates a process of change that operates on a world scale, as well as on an individual level. It is said that the evil-averting gesture of women collectively exposing their genitalia has the power to shame and defeat an advancing army.

Derived from the Greek word *anasuromai,* meaning "to lift the skirt," also known as *anasyrma* or plural, *anasyrmata,* this symbolic act is found in mythologies of ancient Egypt, Greece, Persia, Ireland, Africa, Indonesia, and Japan. "At some point in human history, female genitalia were considered potent enough to be used as the catalyst for bringing the earth and all life back from the brink of destruction" (Blackledge 2003, 23).

In 2005, after reading *The Story of V: A Natural History of Female Sexuality* (Blackledge 2003), I immediately knew I needed to paint this. Chills ran throughout my body as I realized the task ahead would be life changing. As I began this life-size self-portrait, it was unavoidable to question what I would lift my skirt for, and that this painting would have to illustrate this. It took me six years to finish it, as this story took the time it needed to reveal itself.*

In the center between my legs sits the table of power. On the right side of the canvas are the "slaves to the system": identity, religion, industry, and so on. On the left are war and destruction. The full moon crescents my head, and my face is one of rage as I lay a bright and potentiated egg onto the table of power. This egg is the pure essence of life itself, and is blasting out electrical currents, connecting with the thirteen humans in the thirteen chairs as they sit in silence. Where this energy is striking the Earth, new life springs up between the leftover carcasses of civilization: shopping carts, oil barrels, car tires, trash bags, and plastic bottles among them. Metatron's cube floats in front of my heart as the most potent symbol of sacred geometry, clearly referring to the allegiance and guidance of life itself through the most powerful center of our organisms. A scarab representing immortality, resurrection, transformation, and protection is at my throat chakra, referring to the wisdom and knowledge of ancient civilizations. Behind me rise two rainbow-feathered serpents, great guardians and originators of our genome, which have been described as aeons as they watch over this moment of ultimatum, stepping in as guides and support for this great moment of awakening.

---

*[Please see plate 11 of the color insert for the image *Ana Suromai* by Amanda Sage.]

## Limbic Resonance

*I see you seeing me,*
*seeing me seeing you.*
*Our prayers are entwined.*

*We resonate with HER,*
*life giving, honoring, nurturing.*

*We re-member, that*
*Everything is Alive,*

*We are Peace.*

The power of prayer is a potent and vital force between all peoples. Though something still mysterious, the measure of our focused intention has proven undeniable.

The painting *Limbic Resonance* originated from a transdimensional experience of meeting a dear friend, Cheri Rae, for the first time. I saw and felt a holographic mirror of myself in different stages of life, reflected by her presence. Her friendship has inspired me to go deeper into the medicine of my craft and push the boundaries of active prayer.*

As with many of my paintings, there is an initial flash of inspiration that seeds the image, and as it grows it becomes so much more than I could have initially imagined. This painting has become not just a portrait of the two of us in prayer for the awakening of a new Earth; it is a portrait of sisters bowing to each other as they recognize themselves in each other.

The flowering eyes symbolize the oneness shared between the two beings, and the flowers are from the San Pedro cactus, a sacred medicine plant that deepens our connection with the earth and each other.

---

*[Please see plate 12 of the color insert for the image *Limbic Resonance* by Amanda Sage.]

## A Waking Dream

*I am a Queen,*
*my crown is fearless and open.*
*My heart is a lotus flower*
*relentless in its beauty.*

*I am powerful*
*when I open my mouth,*
*and radiant when I speak.*

*I see the future in my dreams,*
*a circus celebration of life,*
*as ancient and celestial magic merge*
*to create new worlds.*

Painting is a form of active prayer if you include intention. The fruit of the practice then becomes a tool and invitation for anyone that views it to join in the prayer. Art is a form of magic; it distracts us from time as we know it and takes us into alternate possibilities while expanding our minds.*

When as creators we become more aligned with the responsibility bestowed on us, and we show up to the canvas with an open heart, the cosmos communes with us. It is, by far, one of the most ecstatic experiences I know to be in this kind of dance with creation itself.

## Arise

*It is Time,*
*to rise above the horizon limiting our imaginations.*
*It is Time,*
*to open the heart and allow it to guide.*
*It is Time,*

---

*[Please see plate 13 of the color insert for the image *A Waking Dream* by Amanda Sage.]

*to burn beyond concepts and trauma through conscious*
*focus.*

*I salute myself, my mission and planet Earth.*
*I am reporting to duty, and you all are my witness.*
*I feel the burning of the crown of thorns as the fall of*
*man into sin transmutes into freedom.*
*I see the light grid of hearts connecting into an ever-*
*changing life web*
*sparking consciousness as we see our reflections in the*
*stars.*
*This is what I see.*
*I am transparent, I am unafraid, I am you.*

Have you ever really looked into your own eyes in a mirror for an extended length of time without judgment? And then asked yourself who you really are? What you really believe? We are practically owned by our image, name, and occupation, and suffer under these imaginary constructs of personality as we make excuses that we don't have time to ask such questions.*

Self-portraiture is a very direct way to dive into these inner realms and heal them. It also helps manifest our hopes, dreams, and desires by spending focused time painting them into existence. We have to look into our own eyes and see love, beauty, and purpose in order to embody those qualities in the world.

I believe that going straight to the source and questioning our truth is a powerful way toward self-realization. This is the source where our lives are becoming an extension of our truth.

---

*[Please see plate 14 of the color insert for the image *Arise* by Amanda Sage.]

## Active Intentional Creating

We live in an era of incredible potential, where the veil of separation between us is thinning and the truth of the matter is being revealed. There is nowhere to hide as we are confronted with global issues, and there is no time to waste in doing our part as valuable members of our communities and stewards of the land we live on.

Each one of us has a part to play in this grand story of life. It is not our responsibility to *fix the world,* though we can have great influence by finding our joy and contributing to the good in this world.

I believe that we are all artists, constantly adding to the creation of the masterpiece that has no end and no beginning. What I've found as an active intentional creator is that the way is rarely ever easy, and often one can get lost. It is in these dark moments when we think we have lost our way that we are forced to our knees and remember to ask for help, surrendering to life's guidance.

These are moments that bring revelation and rebirth, humbling our narrow perspectives of what we think is important as we flower into new frontiers full of potential never before seen.

Plate 1. *Chaos Order Secret Writing* by Allyson Grey.

Plate 2. *New Beginnings* by Amanda Sage.

Plate 3. *Timeless Keepers* by Autumn Skye.

Plate 4. *Angels of Our Nature* by Heidi Taillefer.

Plate 5. *Eve* by Hannah Faith Yata.

Plate 6. *Universal Mother* by Martina Hoffmann.

Plate 7. *Deep Dreaming* by Stuart Griggs.

Plate 8. *Alien Life Form* by Martina Hoffmann.

Plate 9. *Alien Ascension* by Martina Hoffmann.

Plate 10. *Caught in the Web* by Martina Hoffmann.

Plate 11. *Ana Suromai* by Amanda Sage.

Plate 12. *Limbic Resonance* by Amanda Sage.

Plate 13. *A Waking Dream* by Amanda Sage.

Plate 14. *Arise* by Amanda Sage.

Plate 15. *The Rise of Sachamama* by Jessica Perlstein.

Plate 16. *Light Work* by Autumn Skye.

# 18

# Feminine Flowers of Consciousness Bloom

## Alana Bliss

*Mystic memories flow out of me like the blood of my red
flower cycling femininity.
We are the carriers of the seed, the sacred soil planting
future beings.
Womb reflections mirror the essence of creation, cosmic
seat of initiation spiralling procreation.
From within the fertility of cosmic seeds we find our
destiny ever unfolding perfectly.
Diving into deepening states of being, consciousness
expanding and contracting,
We commune with the Great Mother attracting nurturing
energy indefinitely,
We surf the waves of destiny.
We find flow enchanting, so we ride it like lightning
across the sky of infinite potentiality.
Yes, we are the women claiming femininity as sacredly as
the cross for Christianity,
Or the womb of Mother Mary,*

*Hailing a new era of sexuality where we are free to*
*understand our bodies and our minds.*
*No longer falling behind in an illusion defined by a people*
*in sensitivity decline.*
*Feminine power ignite as we shine this ancient energy inside.*
*Dancing between psychedelic states,*
*We contemplate our power and vow not to desecrate our mother.*
*Discover the altered state of our moontime,*
*Uncover the ecstatic orgasmic transcendent feelings of our*
*sexual shine.*
*Face death with courage and you will find that the soul is*
*beyond our concepts, undefined.*
*Surrender to the flow and know the essence of you,*
*Not sporadic nor chaotic,*
*Rather rhythmic and melodic,*
*This earth song is erotic and true.*
*Sensual energy flows through our bodies like rivers of bliss,*
*We tease consciousness with rocking hips,*
*Uniting through a kiss and feeling kundalini lift up from*
*root to crown.*
*We dismiss the taboo and drown out any fear of being*
*held down.*
*Astral body fortified,*
*Feel the third eye open wide and see the world behind the material.*
*Surreal yet potent,*
*Alive and not broken,*
*Energy bodies dancing unnoticed by most.*
*The divine feminine invokes a feeling provoked by a*
*sensual world.*
*No longer just girls,*
*Women rise to meet this psychedelic elation,*
*Honored by all of creation.*
*Matched by the masculine empowered and lovin' the balance.*

*No more malice, we got this.*
*Fall into the abyss and trust that you can fly,*
*Even through the dreamtime,*
*We are determined to thrive.*
*Close your eyes and see the truth behind your wondrous eyes.*
*Rise alive.*

# 19

# Reflections on the Gift of Blood

## Omolewa

**Blood Moon Woman**

*Crimson blood, my Sacred gift*
*Blessing from my foremothers*
*From the primordial womb and waters from which I came*
*Keeper of knowledge, wisdom, medicine, and ancient ritual*
*I stand proudly in my Bloodright, my Birthright*
*Moon Woman, waxing, waning, full, new*
*Shape-shifting Maiden, Mother, Crone*
*Creatress of the Divine masculine and feminine*
*Supernaturally equipped for life, death, and rebirth.*
*Anointed One, keeper of Ancient secrets*
*Nurturer of the young and old*
*There is Power in my Blood*
*Now I know why roses have thorns*

## Blessed Gift of the Blood Shamans

Shamanism. Every Wombman is a Shaman by Birthright. From our menarche or "first blood" we are given the gift of intuition, dreams, wisdom, and a divine connection to ourselves, our families, our communities (past, present, and future), and Mother Earth herself. The powers to transcend from one dimension to the next. Portals. Full of Power, Medicine, and Divinity. Our Sacred Moon Blood is a consistent reminder that we come from source. That same source energy that created the Heavens and the Earth. The Darkness and the Light. And everything that is of life, death, and transformation, we are. Holy, Sacred, and True, it is through us, the Goddess, where you are planted, rooted, watered, nourished, and birthed into being. Be ye baptized, healed, cleansed, and renewed through her sweet, sacred waters. Remembering that through our blood, you are a sacrificial offering. A Blessed Gift of the Blood Shamans.

**PART 7**

Feminist Psychedelic
Activism

# 20
# Creating a Community of Wisewomen

## The Women's Visionary Congress

### Annie Oak

*I'm not entirely sure where we crossed paths sister*
*but I know you when I see you.*
*Kindred spirit.*
*Woman of the plants and the pleasure gardens.*
*Healer, seer, witch, herbalist, storyteller, conjurer.*
*Defender of your tribe.*
*Nowadays we meet online.*
*And still there is that yearning*
*to be together in the physical world.*
*To gather and observe the seasons,*
*share ideas, drink tea, eat, dance,*
*mark rites of passage,*
*watch over each other as we dream,*
*hold space and vision our communities together.*

When I was young and scratching out a living in a big city far from home, books kept me company. But what I longed for most was a community of like-minded women willing to exchange ideas. My mother gathered with her book club each month, why not us? One winter during the nineties, a few of my women friends in Boston, Massachusetts, decided to read a book and meet to discuss it. We had shared interests in ritual, religious history, medicinal plants, and healing traditions of indigenous cultures. Before long we had assembled a bibliography of texts and spent Sunday afternoons talking about these books. Our reading list eventually included much-loved books such as *Plants of the Gods: Their Sacred, Healing, and Hallucinogenic Powers* (Schultes, Hofmann, and Ratsch 1979), *Maria Sabina: Her Life and Chants* (Estrada 1981), and *The Spiral Dance: A Rebirth of the Ancient Religion of the Goddess* (Starhawk 1979).

Immersed in these texts, it seemed only natural for our study group to expand our research by sampling the psychoactive plants and substances that inquisitive women like us had used for centuries. We embraced the Greek meaning of the word *psychedelic*, which means "to make visible or reveal one's soul or spirit." We explored the worlds inside the classic psychedelics that we then had access to: psilocybin, LSD, and mescaline. We created our own rituals to enter these experiences with due reverence, and moved beyond youthful experimentation.

One day, we received a message from an ethnobotanist and author who had contributed to books on our reading list. I offered her tea in my cold little apartment and she gave me two precious gifts; the first was a perfectly pressed datura flower, and the second was an invitation for a member of our group to join her for a private gathering of women in California who shared our interests.

None of us had much money, so we pooled what we could scrape together. I was the lucky one selected as our envoy. Off I went, with scanty information about where exactly I was to go; basically, I had nothing more than an address and a phone number. Driving north of the city, I arrived at a private home and found a group of more than two dozen women who had gathered to talk. Promising to protect the identities of those present, I sat and listened to women who had thirty or more years of experience working with the substances and states of consciousness that my study group was just then getting to know.

There they were! A community of psychedelic women fully living the meaning of the word *psychedelic,* manifesting their expanded awareness in alliance with plant and spirit allies. They talked fearlessly into the evening exploring topics seldom discussed publicly at the time. What was learned during psychedelic explorations that could be applied to one's life? Was it safe for women to use cannabis while pregnant? What new synthetic substances being produced in laboratories were worth investigating and which were best avoided? If the first waves of feminism were concerned with political enfranchisement, equal pay, and reproductive rights, here certainly was the logical extension of those freedoms—a woman's right to her own cognitive liberty.

And what did these women do with the insights they gained with this freedom? A great deal, as it turned out. They cultivated their spirituality. They built schools, gardens, businesses, and organizations. They grew their own food, raised gentle and intelligent children, and served their communities as healers, counselors, and teachers. They were good "psychedelic citizens." These women were also interested in other forms of altered states, not just those generated by psychoactive substances. They chronicled their dreams, meditated, prayed, created art, practiced yoga, and attended to their embodied wisdom.

Here was a flowering community, nourished and shaped by the social revolutions of the sixties, but arguably the spiritual descendants of the European midwives, herbalists, and wisewomen who had weathered centuries of persecution by the church. Their knowledge of medicinal plants connected them to a long tradition of witches and shamanic healers down through the centuries. Like their foremothers, they knew that courts and law enforcement or other authorities could target women like them for various forms of reprisal. They could be branded as unfit mothers and have their children taken away. They could lose their professional licenses and be driven from their jobs or professions.

This then was a largely private world, but also a joyful one. I felt lucky to be an invited guest and receive their trust. I made friends, listened, and received suggestions for further reading and study that I carried back to my frozen corner of New England. Back in our little study group, my cohorts and I warmed ourselves over those friendships for years. Walking into that room full of initiated women was a life-changing experience for all of us.

Fast forward to 2006: I had left Boston for San Francisco to join the great tide of tech workers who arrived in the first Internet bubble of the late nineties. I was working as a journalist, and I was in Basel, Switzerland, covering the one-hundredth birthday celebration of Albert Hofmann, the great Swiss chemist who first synthesized lysergic acid diethylamide, also known as LSD. The event was billed as the biggest psychedelic conference ever held. It was grand to see Hofmann honored in this way, but I was surprised to see that of the eighty-some speakers at the event, only four were women.

*How could this be?* Where were all the women speakers? Women had surely participated in—and benefited from—the profound psychological insights, spiritual renewal, and social transformations sparked by LSD and other psychedelics. Women priestesses, together with their male counterparts, conducted the Eleusinian Mysteries in Greece for *two thousand years,* dispensing a brew that contained the ergot fungi from which LSD is synthesized (Wasson, Hofmann, and Ruck 1978).

On the other side of the Atlantic Ocean, María Sabina and other great female *curanderas* of the Mazatec had used species of psilocybin mushrooms in their rituals for centuries (Rothenberg and Estrada 2003). Were the organizers of this conference disconnected from history and other psychedelic communities around the world? Had they been captured by some form of institutionalized European sexism? Was this a resurgence of a quantitative worldview that devalued qualitative forms of research and knowledge held by women? The answer wasn't clear, but there was much muttering in private rooms from female attendees who pointed out that women were significantly underrepresented at many other such gatherings. We came to the conclusion that if we wanted to hear from women in the psychedelic community it wasn't sufficient to complain or ask for permission to be included. We would need to hold our own events.

Returning to California, I decided to do what my parents had done for their church and tithe a portion of my income to support my own spiritual community. In 2007, I organized a gathering of women and our male allies at Wilbur Hot Springs north of San Francisco. Inspired by the gathering of women I had joined more than a decade earlier, I assembled a wish list of speakers, including the most interesting women I knew who worked with altered states. Other women stepped forward to help with the project, and we extended invitations to people of all genders who we thought might want to attend.

Given that many women in this community were more accustomed to private gatherings, there were safety concerns. Women had less money to defend themselves if they were targeted or harassed for sharing their ideas. If we were holding public discussions on these topics, were we putting participants and their families at risk? There were no assurances, but I remember setting aside money for a bail fund and legal expenses. Fortunately, the owner of Wilbur Hot Springs, Richard Miller, was a firm ally, and we felt safe in the embrace of the lovely old hotel in which we would hold our gathering, and its healing springs.

Twenty women accepted our invitation to speak, among them scientists and researchers, side by side with activists, priestesses, and artists. Speakers at that first gathering included ethnobotanist Kat Harrison, scholar Karen Vogel, and Amy Emerson, the director of clinical research at the Multidisciplinary Association for Psychedelic Studies (MAPS). Annie Mithoefer, who works together with her husband, Michael Mithoefer, presented information about their MAPS-sponsored study evaluating the therapeutic use of MDMA-assisted psychotherapy for treating PTSD, and the therapist June May Ruse discussed her work as well. Cynthia Palmer presented images and text from her excellent anthology of women writing on the drug experience, *Sisters of the Extreme* (2000), which she edited with her husband, the scholar Michael Horowitz. Fire and Earth Erowid, the founders of the Erowid Archive, took us through their remarkable collection of data describing the interactions between humans and psychoactive substances. Carolyn Garcia, also known as Mountain Girl, an original Merry Prankster and author of *The Primo Plant: Growing Sinsemilla Marijuana* (1977)—one of the first books on cannabis cultivation—offered her insights. Medical cannabis activists Revonda Colbert, Rosura Kenyon, and Mira Ingram brought us good news from the struggle for drug-law reform.

There were creative contributions from author and musician Adele Getty, writer Lizbeth Rymland who read from her book *Strange Evolutionary Flowers* (2006), erotic artist Annie Sprinkle who reflected eloquently about the impact of psychedelics on her films, photographs, and performance art. The artist Allyson Grey flew in from New York City to tell us about the creation of the Chapel of Sacred Mirrors in collaboration with her husband, the artist Alex Grey. Spiritual leader Wendy Grace offered us her wisdom, and Jennifer Dumpert led an *oneironauticum,* a group-dreaming event in which we consumed an *oneirogen*—a legal substance that promoted and enhanced our dreams. A high point of the weekend was the presence of author and therapist Ann Shulgin who worked with the psychoactive substances MDMA and 2C-B while they were still legal. Ann closed the weekend by taking questions. She did this with her husband, the revered psychedelic chemist Sasha Shulgin, with whom she had written the classic books *PiHKAL: A Chemical Love Story,* published in 1991, and its sequel *TiHKAL: The Continuation,* published in 1997.

Unlike other gatherings where psychedelics were discussed, we wanted to show that the work of one group did not detract from or reduce the credibility of another, but represented rather an entire community of inquiry and collective experience. By the end of that first gathering there was abundant enthusiasm for holding more such events. We realized that there was value in collecting and distributing the information presented by the speakers. We also saw how important it was to give accomplished women an opportunity—perhaps their first opportunity—to present their ideas and their research in a respectful and supportive environment.

I set to writing an application for a 501(c)(3) educational nonprofit organization and invited the two wisest women I knew to form a board of directors with me. These were Carolyn Garcia and Mariavittoria Mangini, a midwife and nurse practitioner who also served as the land manager for an admirably durable intentional community, the Hog Farm. We christened our new nonprofit the Women's Visionary Council (WVC), which was a homage to the Girl Scout Council. We had all been enthusiastic Girl Scouts, and we were now scouts of a different kind. We decided to make our gathering an annual event, known as the Women's Visionary Congress. Our mission was to present information about investigations into nonordinary forms of consciousness, preferencing the voices of women, and promoting the exchange of information across generations.

We wanted to promote our right to self-knowledge and new modes of healing that linked us to female wisdom keepers and traditional users of plant medicines throughout history. Given that many of us were experienced users of psychoactive agents, we resolved to present information about the potential challenges encountered in these states, possible risk-reduction strategies, and ethical issues surrounding the use of these substances. Most importantly, we wanted to create a community of women who shared our interests. We were, as far as we knew, the first nonprofit women's psychedelic organization in the world.

## Conversations with the Skeptics

After creating the WVC, those of us who organized the first gatherings were asked by some why we felt there was a need for an organization of psychonauts that focused on the work of women. After all, there were already groups that organized gatherings discussing similar topics, and there were already existing nonprofit organizations such as the Heffter Research Institute and the MAPS that conducted investigations into the therapeutic uses of psychoactive substances. As we had discovered in Basel, however, women often made up only a small portion of the invited speakers at such events and were underrepresented among the organizers. Despite the fact that women make up more than half the global population, and were a significant number of the subjects in studies and clinical trials sponsored by both groups, MAPS has no female board members, and Heffter has just one out of twelve. Additionally, both of these organizations focus primarily on quantitative research of drug-assisted therapies as regulated by U.S. government organizations.

The WVC is interested in both quantitative and qualitative research, the latter of which includes a larger number of female researchers. We also value equally traditional forms of knowledge held by different cultures. The WVC respects the work of other groups who conduct and present psychedelic research. MAPS assisted the WVC by serving as a fiscal sponsor for tax-deductible donations until the WVC received its own nonprofit status in 1998. But it was clear to us that there needed to be an organization that was not only run by women, but also presented findings from a feminine perspective and represented the entire breadth of the psychedelic community.

Other people have attempted to argue that women are not deeply attracted to, or commonly seek out, altered states of consciousness. The significant number of women who use alcohol and prescribed pharmacological substances refutes this argument. A report published by the *Journal of the American Medical Association* (Grant et al. 2017) noted that high-risk drinking among women increased in the prior year by close to 60 percent, and alcohol-use disorder increased by nearly 84 percent.

According to the 2011 "America's State of Mind Report" (Medco Health Solutions 2011), which analyzed prescription data from

2.5 million insured Americans from 2001 to 2010, 25 percent of American women take some form of medication for a mental health condition, compared to just 15 percent of men. The report reveals that the use of antidepressants is especially high among women, with over 20 percent of them taking a drug prescribed to treat depression. Antianxiety medications are used by 11 percent of middle-aged women—the largest group overall—and women's use of these medications is almost twice the rate of men.

Given that women are more likely to be poor, victims of violence and discrimination, and disproportionately affected by family-related stress, it is not surprising that many would seek relief in altered states offered by prescription pharmaceuticals. However, their repeated usage carries significant dependency and overdose risks. In 2014 there were one and a half times more deaths from drug overdose in the United States than from motor vehicle crashes (Rudd et al. 2016).

Given these bleak statistics, the medical and research communities acknowledge that current drug therapies to treat pain, stress, depression, anxiety, and drug dependency have serious flaws. As women who have experienced the benefits conferred by the judicious use of psychoactive agents, it comes as no surprise to us that an increasing number of women are drawn to potentially less dangerous and addictive psychoactive substances. These include cannabis, MDMA, psilocybin, ayahuasca, LSD, and other psychotropics, and they are now being studied as alternatives to prescription medications.

The acknowledgment that cannabis can be an effective medication has prompted the legalization of this plant in some U.S. states and countries around the world for both medical and recreational use. The embrace of cannabis as an alternative to alcohol for recreational purposes is especially important for women in light of recent research linking alcohol usage to breast cancer (Cancer Research U.K. 2007). Many women have quietly used cannabis for menstrual cramps. This specific medical use of this plant ally has been documented in the Chinese pharmacopeia since 1500 BCE (Stuart 1987).

## A Decade of Women's
## Congress Discussions

The WVC hosts a Woman's Visionary Congress every year, and in the decade since we organized our first congress in 2007, we have seen an explosion of interest in psychedelics and their potential for healing and spiritual growth. The WVC began to hold Women's Congresses at successively larger venues over the years. We raised funds to provide grants and scholarships to women of slender means and began organizing events throughout the United States and Canada. Together with local supporters, the WVC organized salons in Seattle, Washington; Santa Fe, New Mexico; and Vancouver, Canada. In the spring of 2016, the WVC held its first gathering in New York City, and three months later WVC members gathered north of San Francisco for the tenth annual Women's Congress.

The discussions that took place there illustrated the evolving interests and concerns of what is now an international community of thousands of fellow female psychonauts, friends, and allies. Researchers and healers who presented at the 2016 Women's Congress illustrated the ongoing integration of established and alternative therapies that make use of expanded consciousness. The rapid growth of retreat centers and gatherings offering ayahuasca has sparked conversations about the ethics and safety of psychedelic ceremonies.

Many WVC members and organizers have found ayahuasca experiences, and the use of other psychoactive substances in ritual settings, to be beneficial for healing and spiritual growth. But the steep increase in the number of such ceremonies around the world has sometimes resulted in abuses of power, which have arisen throughout history when unethical ceremonial leaders from various spiritual traditions exploit trusting participants. As one of the first women's organizations to take on this topic, the WVC now receives messages from people around the world seeking advice on how to confront shamans and other ceremonial leaders who sexually assault women under their care and guidance.

The WVC supports efforts to hold these people accountable for their actions and in 2014 published on its website a series of safety recommendations (Oak 2015) to help participants prepare for these ceremonies and reduce the potential for unsafe encounters. These safety tips reflect collective wisdom held by WVC members. They include useful recommendations for practicing self-care when exploring any altered state of consciousness—and encourage women to exercise their voice and seek support when they have concerns about the safety of their experiences in ceremonies. The safety recommendations also acknowledge ceremonial leaders whose actions reflect the highest degree of integrity and ethics.

Speaking out on behalf of the needs and interests of its community, the WVC has waded into other controversial discussions. In the summer of 2016, the WVC launched a series of risk-reduction workshops in response to the escalating rate of opioid overdoses. We also decided to provide often difficult to acquire information about how to prevent overdoses of other substances. Partnering with Gantt Galloway and the New Leaf Treatment Center in Lafayette, California, the WVC provided free training in the use of Naloxone, also known as Narcan, which can be administered to reverse a potentially fatal opioid overdose. We also offered training developed by the nonprofit Earth and Fire Erowid, whose mandate is to educate the public about psychoactive plants, drugs, technologies, and practices. The training involved helping to prevent overdose by accurately measuring liquids and powders. Using baking soda, we demonstrated how to properly operate a milligram scale and how to use commercially available reagent testing kits to test for the presence of psychoactive substances and potentially deadly adulterants. This training was provided to the public at no charge for maximum accessibility, and we gave away hundreds of free Naloxone kits.

We are keenly aware that our harm-reduction initiatives and the discussions we hold within and for our community are considered controversial by some people. In an effort to help preserve the privacy and anonymity of people visiting our website and attending our gatherings, the WVC developed a series of protocols for improving the privacy and security of our website and mailing lists. To help prevent visitors to our sites from being tracked or surveilled, we assembled a list of suggestions for best practices. Based on these, we have modified our use of Mail Chimp, PayPal, Google Services, and other widely used tools to make the information on these platforms more secure. With input from our friends who work in computer security, we collected a list of suggestions for additional resources that we posted on our website.

## The Evolution of the Women's Psychedelic Community

As we address the challenges and possibilities ahead, presented by the renaissance of psychedelic cultures around the world, many members of our community continue to find balance and strength through their connection with the divine forces of the natural world. We walk barefoot in our gardens and admire the resiliency of species and cultures that adapt to meet adversity. At the conclusion of the 2016 Women's Congress, Eda Zavala Lopez, a *curandera* in her Amazonian tribal community, offered a blessing that reminded us to approach healing plants and their traditional use among her people with reverence and respect. Botanist Jane Straight offered a living altar of medicinal plants from her garden to remind us that we are indeed descended from a long line of plant women.

Presentations by Sophia Buggs of Lady Buggs Farm, located in Youngstown, Ohio, and Maya Blow of Soul Flower Farm, located outside of San Francisco, sparked long discussions about stewarding land, nourishing our internal psycho-biomes, and reimagining our systems of food production. Out of these conversations sprang a WVC gathering in the fall of 2016 wherein we toured an urban farm, learned about the large-scale waste of cosmetically imperfect produce, and taught our members how to can applesauce and pickle vegetables as our thrifty grandmothers once had. Given that Sophia and Maya are both African

American women, their talks were an opportunity to reflect on our strong desire to receive wisdom from more women of color and those from different classes and cultural traditions outside of the predominantly white, middle-class members of psychedelic communities based in the United States and Europe. Kati Silva, a community leader who serves as WVC's program coordinator, has agreed to begin translating our website into Spanish. Reaching out to Latina women who speak Spanish is an essential part of our mission going forward.

At the close of 2016, the board of the Women's Visionary Council made a decision to temporarily suspend the annual Women's Congress in favor of smaller and more affordable events. With the rising costs of large conferences, we wanted to ensure that our gatherings were as inexpensive and accessible as possible to the thousands of people who are now part of our community. The WVC board and advisors now include Mariavittoria Mangini, Anne Tara Szostek, and elder emeriti Carolyn Garcia, Diana Slattery, and Denis Berry. Our reverence for the older ladies of our community prompted us to print our first WVC bumper stickers this year with an image of lightning striking mountaintops and the phrase "Don't Mess With Granny."

In 2017, the WVC launched a series of workshops that are representative of the evolving interests and needs of our members. As the legalization of recreational cannabis in California and other states has drawn increasing numbers of women to use that plant and form cannabis-related businesses, our first WVC event of 2017 was a daylong examination of the relationship between women and cannabis. Near the top of the agenda was a decades-old discussion about cannabis and pregnancy, which appeared on the front page of the *New York Times* (Saint Louis 2017) on the very day I wrote this sentence.

The WVC also presented a workshop at the Psychedelic Science Conference in Oakland, California, which examined the psychedelic roots of long-standing intentional communities including the Tennessee Farm, the Hog Farm, the Merry Pranksters, and the Brotherhood of Eternal Love, whose founding members Carol and Michael Randall told their stories at the 2015 Women's Congress. Members of these groups described how they preserved their ideals and offered lessons for surviving our present political turbulence in the United States, which is reminiscent of the cultural environment that these communities broke away from in the sixties. The WVC is now planning the next Women's Visionary Congress and practicing our own forms of resiliency. As elder members of the WVC community begin to complete their journeys in this world, young women are stepping up to carry forward the work of our psychedelic sisters and preserve our collective knowledge for future generations. It is our hope that this wisdom encompasses and reflects the experiences of women from all cultures and backgrounds who cultivate relationships with sacred plants and their right to various realms of consciousness.

# 21

# Beyond Psychological Patriarchy

## Plant Medicines and the Resurgence of Medical Eros

### Adam Aronovich

*Psychological patriarchy is the dynamic between those qualities deemed "masculine" and "feminine" in which half of our human traits are exalted while the other half is devalued. Both men and women participate in this tortured value system. Psychological patriarchy is a "dance of contempt," a perverse form of connection that replaces true intimacy with complex, covert layers of dominance and submission, collusion and manipulation. It is the unacknowledged paradigm of relationships that has suffused Western civilization generation after generation, deforming both sexes, and destroying the passionate bond between them.*

TERRENCE REAL (BELL HOOKS 2003, 32).

## Patriarchy and Psychiatry

Feminist and social activist bell hooks writes "patriarchy promotes insanity. It is at the root of the psychological ills troubling men in our nation" (2003, 30). And when we speak about *patriarchy*, writes hooks, we are not referring to male dominance over females alone but to an entire sociopolitical system in which psychological terrorism and violence are used to maintain dominance over those deemed inferior or weak. It is through these forms of psychological patriarchy that patriarchal thought is reproduced and perpetuated, not only by patriarchal men, but by everybody who participates, whether consciously or not, in institutions and organizations characterized by domination and power. These include most of the world's religions as well as our educational systems, family systems, and health care systems. This institutionalized violence is not fortuitous; it serves to reinforce a dominator model "in which the authority figure is deemed ruler over those without power and given the right to maintain that rule through practices of subjugation, subordination, and submission" (hooks 2003, 24).

Although the popular essentialization of qualities deemed "feminine" or "masculine" is problematic and controversial, on a symbolic level psychological patriarchy can be partially understood as the overarching historical subordination and subjugation of the body (female) to the mind (male), and the patriarchy's popular identifications with passion (female) and reason (male), and all of the human traits that this division entails. Women, seen as the personification of sensuality, have been feared and demonized for leading the rational mind astray, for tempting Adam with the fruits of irrational passion. Mind over body, in its iteration as reason over sensuality, is at the core of most of the world's patriarchal religions and spiritual systems and, since the Enlightenment, also of Western scientific epistemologies. The intuitive body has been robbed of its natural role as a channel through which we can make sense of the vast world around us and the private space *inside* us. Ayahuasca is one way of reconnecting with our bodies, our sensuality, and the continuum of interdependent experience that we share with the rest of the world.

As Victor Seidler observes, "Kant crucially established reason as an independent faculty which is separated from our emotions, feelings and desires, which can in no sense be genuine sources of knowledge" (1989, 7). Patriarchal systems thoroughly oppress women and they also oppress men by denying them the possibility of fully embodying their emotional selves. Most men learn to fear the irrationality of their physical bodies, always in opposition to the immaterial, abstract realm of thought. By glorifying logic and reason and subjugating passion, emotion, and intuition, patriarchy creates incomplete, immature, and emotionally crippled males whose only reference of masculinity is based on domination and subjugation of the weak and the irrational. This is a self-replicating and perpetuating pattern evident in our societies and their institutions.

One of the most damaging rules that patriarchal systems have in common, argues the founding father of the self-help movement, John Bradshaw, is blind obedience: "The repression of all emotions except fear; the destruction of individual willpower; and the repression of thinking whenever it departs from the authority figure's way of thinking" (hooks 2003, 23). Many elements of blind obedience are indeed foundational components of the hegemonic mental health care system founded on biological or neo-Kraepelinian psychiatry. In the modern biopsychiatric clinic, the narrative voices and qualitative experiences of the patients are often silenced and rendered irrelevant by the authoritarian medical gaze of the experts (Foucault 2007). Complex and meaningful subjective symptoms are usually reduced to a checklist of purportedly universally objective and observable signs of an underlying neuropsychiatric illness (Martinez-Hernaez 2000).

The dominant psychiatric culture, as an exemplary manifestation of patriarchy, represents the immature masculine; it often exerts force not to protect the weak, but to dominate and rule over them. There are countless historical examples of how psychiatry has pathologized, medicated, and forcefully committed individuals and collectives for political and ideological reasons. They range from the infamous *drapetomania,* a bogus medical condition that pathologized African American slaves who had a compulsion to run away from their white owners, to the *dysaethesia aethiopica*, the alleged mental disease that caused the same slaves to be lazy (Cartwright 1851). Other examples include the determination in diagnostic manuals that homosexuality was a mental illness (a determination that lasted well into the 1970s) or the diagnosis of *sluggish schizophrenia* pushed by Soviet psychiatrists. This latter diagnosis was often applied to political or religious dissidents who held a delusional belief that the Communist Party system was not the ideal form of government and that it might be preferable to live in a free or democratic society (Gershman 1984).

Psychiatry has been at the service of colonial regimes all over the world, disproportionately pathologizing and incarcerating dissident Maori populations in Aotearoa New Zealand (Cohen 2014) or nonsubmissive Malay communities in the Dutch East Indies. During the 1950s, exhausted and overworked American housewives were routinely prescribed habit-forming amphetamines by the medical establishment; whenever they became frustrated by the lack of career opportunities and self-fulfillment, they were prescribed benzodiazepines.

In present times, Brazilian psychiatry is pushing toward medicating children in isolated Amazonian communities via diagnoses of ADHD, particularly in the Karajá villages of the Araguaia River valley (Azevedo et al. 2010). ADHD is a very controversial diagnosis as it is. It becomes more controversial when it's deemed to be a product of an ethnopsychiatry—the Euro-American one—born out of a culture that glorifies productivity over sensuous play, that promotes competition over cooperation, and that praises children who submit blindly to authority. But these are not universal values, and the ethics of medicating children with powerful drugs in order to promote those values in other cultures are highly questionable. More than anything, the imposition of these diagnostic categories is a direct result of colonial subjugation and domination, a patriarchal dynamic that has affected indigenous communities for centuries. In so doing, it has supplanted their diversity of being and knowing with a homogenous set of sanctioned experiences and behaviors that serve the dominant cultures.

A culture of patriarchal domination and subjugation, exploitation and extraction, doesn't only affect the earth and the vulnerable collectives who are at the front lines of oppression, marginalization, and exclusion, and, in some cases, like in the case of indigenous peoples, ethnocide and epistemicide. It is a culture that also greatly affects the health of those privileged enough to enjoy the fruits of Western affluence. The participation in violent structures and institutions, whether explicit or implicit, requires a degree of alienation and the suppression of empathy and compassion, which inevitably creates emotional and mental distress.

When we talk about madness, or mental illness, we should not be talking only about reified diagnostic constructs that individualize mental suffering, but about the structural violence that creates so much alienation, loneliness, and disconnection in our highly individualistic, consumerist, colonialist, extractivist, and exploitative patriarchal cultures. So how can we reframe our current notions of mental illness and mental health to move beyond the excesses of psychological patriarchy, and incorporate a much more balanced approach in our health care systems, without disposing of the undeniable benefits that biopsychiatry has to offer?

## Reconnecting Medical Logos with Medical Eros

In "Un-forgetting Asclepius: An Erotics of Illness," scholar David B. Morris argues that "illness and medicine operate within an intrinsically erotic dimension" (2007, 419). For Morris, *medical logos* is the path of rational medicine springing from the Hippocratic tradition; the cold and hugely successful, evidence-based dominant model of Western biomedicine. In that sense, medical logos symbolizes the more *masculine* dimension of the healing arts.

Hippocrates, however, had a counterpart that has been all but forgotten in modern practice: the Greek god of the healing arts, Asclepius.

For Morris, the subordination of Asclepius the healing artist to Hippocrates the intellectual physician reflects the emphasis given by practitioners to the rational knowledge of disease—a historical process that has resulted in an overwhelming suppression of erotic medicine.

As we can learn from listening to the narratives of many patients and psychiatric survivors, overly rational medicine often entails experiences of impersonal, uncaring, and detached doctors. As well, it features the invalidation of lived experience, asymmetric power relations between expert and popular knowledge, marginalization, exclusion, and a whole lot of frustration with governmental and corporate bureaucracies. On the other hand, many of these narratives point toward the huge benefits of the healing that comes not from applying the tools and methods of a positivist science but from trying to understand human affliction in a much deeper, broader, embodied, interconnected, and interdependent way. Psychedelic medicines allow precisely this understanding of human affliction as a whole: they are erotic in the sense that they manifest embodied experience in its entirety. *Medical eros,* often invisibilized by patriarchal medical institutions, symbolizes the feminine (or perhaps feminist) dimension of the healing arts. But what does an *erotic medicine* mean?

Trying to explain what *eros* is, Morris rightly points out the futility and contradictions inherent to any attempt to reduce eros to either a concept or a set of social practices. Furthermore, he argues, reductive strategies to grasp eros in terms of logos have historically translated into efforts "to domesticate eros, to manage or to purify it, to separate good eros from bad eros" (Morris 2007, 420). This is akin to understanding the feminine through a masculine lens, reducing it to make it manageable for patriarchal consumption. Part of the power and medicine of eros, however, stems from its embracing "an unknowable dimension—a mystery at its heart—bottomless, disorderly, and uncontainable" (Morris, 2007, 420).

In Morris's use, eros is not reducible to its more popular sexual or even pornographic connotations: erogenous zones are not as important as the primeval arena of human consciousness—the inner, murky, and mysterious realms of subjective experience. Bataille says, "Human eroticism, differs from animal sexuality precisely in this, that it calls inner life into play" (Morris 2007, 421).

Like many enterprises and institutions that operate from and within the premises of psychological patriarchy, Western psychiatry tends to consider itself the global authority on normalcy and sanity. In this, it relegates other modalities of knowing and being in the world, and of experiencing and addressing mental affliction, to the realm of the local, the particular, the culture-bound. They are, at best, alternative or complementary curiosities that hold little weight within the dominant streams of the medical logos.

It was during the time that I spent working at the acute inpatient ward of the Mental Health Center of Beer-Sheva in Israel that I encountered the fascinating cultural dimensions of mental health for the first time and became aware of the inherent limitations of medical logos on one hand, and the latent power of medical eros on the other. In a social context where Ashkenazi, Oriental, and Ethiopian Jews, nomadic Arab Bedouins, and Russian immigrants coexist in similar proportions, a uniform, dry psychiatric diagnosis often encapsulates radically different experiences.

In the acute ward, it was a pretty common occurrence to come across Ethiopian patients who had been diagnosed with schizophrenia. Through conversation, I soon discovered that many of them in fact suffered from a very different affliction. They believed that they had been possessed by a malevolent demon called Zār. For the psychiatrists, however, it was all the same. These patients were given a standard diagnosis and treated with the same psychopharmaceuticals as everybody else. Doctors and caretakers ignored or dismissed the inherent complexities of a culture-bound syndrome—a category that is in itself revealing of the ethnocentricity of biopsychiatry—and the particular intricacies of being possessed by an evil spirit. Psychiatric logos fails to differentiate between very different complaints and very distinct subjective experiences by considering instances of *demon possession* as an objective sign of an underlying neuropsychiatric disease. The symptom is inevitably stripped of any intrinsic symbolic meaning, as the narrative of the person becomes redundant to the authority of the diagnostic manual.

However, as Asclepius would argue, subjective symptoms are hugely relevant for the patients' prognoses. Israeli researchers Arieli and Aychen (1996) have noted that when Zār possession is treated in its traditional context—through ritualized, communal exorcisms—the rates of remission and improvement are relatively high. Following a similar vein from a very different context, Kapferer writes about demonic illness in Sri Lanka: "Where the experience of suffering, realized as demonic attack, is rooted objectively in physical or mental or social disturbance, its comprehension as demonic transforms the meaning of the illness, and exposes it to all the potential significance of the demonic" (1983, 88).

This, of course, is the sheer force of medical eros at play. A community-based ritual exorcism brings into the equation the power of community, the power of empathy, the power of mutual care. It engages the group, and not only the individual, in a richly symbolic and significant act that allows the person the liminal space that is needed to heal and transform.

Back in the acute ward of Beer-Sheva's hospital, however, anti-psychotic treatment did very little for the Zār-possessed men. No number of pills is going to take care of demonic possession, simply because, in the cultures of the Horn of Africa, pharmaceutic treatment doesn't have the deep symbolic efficacy that a ritualized exorcism has. If we do an exercise in *reversed ethnocentrism,* as proposed by Martínez-Hernáez (2000), and instead of diagnosing Israeli-Ethiopian Zār sufferers with schizophrenia we attempted to impose a Zār diagnosis on the rest of the people in that same ward to whom spirit possession is irrelevant, the absurdity of treating symptoms as universally valid signs of allegedly objective psychopathologies becomes evident.

In line with the prevalent mythologies of Western science, bio-psychiatry, like all modern branches of Hippocratic medicine, rests on a "soma-centered, materialist, biological view of illness, in which doctors are first and foremost scientists of the body" (Morris 2007, 422). Yet these assumptions are not widely shared by other medical traditions, and even for the ancient Greek, Hippocrates is but one-half of their medical vision and practice. His complement and rival, Asclepius, was in charge of the mythical, spiritual, and religious aspects of the healing arts: "Asclepian medicine, as Aristides shows, is less about specific therapies than about dreams and about human possession by a godlike, immortal otherness. Although dreams in antiquity may be deceptive, they are not irrational but offer an alternative, even preferred, route to truth" (Morris 2007, 424).

Medical eros, as the symbolically feminine aspects of medicine, heals through opening windows to the transpersonal and the intuitive. It allows a much broader range of experience to be lived in a nonpathologizing way. Not only oneiric states but also hallucinations, delusions, and other nonordinary states of awareness are valued as important and legitimate channels of information about the world and our inner states. The primacy of firsthand, lived experience, however bizarre it may look to others, is not subordinated to dominant notions of what is normal and what is sane.

## Ayahuasca and the Erotic

The notion of Asclepian medicine seems to fit well with the sort of healing that the ritual, contextualized use of ayahuasca and other psychedelic substances and plant medicines bring. Its therapeutic power surpasses the parameters that medical logos can quantify. It pertains to a different domain of experience: it is inherently mysterious, irreducible to rational logics. The healing doesn't exclusively occur by the immediate agency of either Asclepius or the Amazonian healer. Instead, subject to Amazonian ontologies, the healer is but a conduit through which a "higher power" can penetrate the body and psyche of the afflicted. The real doctors are the plant, the spirits, the songs, the purge, the dream, the vision, the symbolic, the erotic.

Morris writes: "Asclepius belongs to the preliterate oral tradition. He represents body, emotion, and dream: all evoked by the totem snake (a reminder of the live snakes inhabiting the *asclepieia* or healing shrines)" (2007, 425). Perhaps it isn't fortuitous that the serpent is so deeply intertwined both with Asclepius and with many of the Amazonian ayahuasca traditions. Maybe it's just a happy coincidence. Be that as it may, Asclepius, his serpents, and the ritual consumption of ayahuasca and medical eros all enhance healing, partly through profound visionary states and dreams that have deeply personal and intimate meaning for the experiencer. These states, if left to the cold, sterile hands of medical logos, would likely be pathologized.

Furthermore, both Asclepius and ayahuasca often help us heal by allowing us to experience emotion and sensation as equally important to rational thought. They catalyze transformative processes by touching and tapping into the transpersonal, by opening and exposing us to the wondrous world beyond language, by presenting the isolated and alienated individual with the possibility of a world inhabited by interdependent layers of sentient, intelligent, communicative, expressive, and intentional plants, trees, animals, rivers, storms, and spirits. This is the full manifestation of an erotic medicine in harmony with a rational one, the masculine and feminine in harmonious union.

In short, these are the sort of experiences that are so often suppressed or invisibilized by rational medicine. And yet, it is important to remember that for the ancient Greek, Hippocrates and Asclepius were not antagonistic but complementary: "Although Hippocratic doctors and Asclepian priests often agreed in recommending identical regimens, the contrast could not be clearer: Hippocrates cured through reason and through empirical knowledge of the body, while Asclepius cured through dreams and through the personal contact with divine power" (Morris 2007, 422).

A better integration between Hippocratic and Asclepian medicine, of medical logos and medical eros, is one of the main challenges and opportunities that healers from all traditions, particularly the biomedical one, are presented with. It is evident that taking polarized stances, favoring one praxis over the other, will always fail to account for a substantial part of the picture by mystifying the diversity of therapeutic practices. Psychiatric logos has indeed developed many useful tools; psychopharmaceuticals sometimes save lives and are of priceless value for people who seek symptomatic relief. However, psychiatric logos has proved unable, for the most part, to reach the deep roots of affliction. Furthermore, as Abraham Maslow noted in the famous *law of the instrument,* "I suppose it is tempting, if the only tool you have is a hammer, to treat everything as if it were a nail" (1966, 15). But not everyone is a nail, and a misused hammer can cause much harm. A multiplicity of approaches and diversity of tools to treat each person according to their own ordering cosmology and world of meanings seems to be the right approach for reimagining a better approach to mental health.

Under the current domineering paradigm, the authoritarian medical logos leaves little room for the methods and approaches of its erotic counterpart. As we have argued throughout this chapter, this dynamic is but a reflection of a much wider and systemic repression of one polarity over the other, perpetuated and reproduced through the mechanisms of psychological patriarchy. In order for balance to come about, the masculine and the feminine must work in harmony. This seems to hold true for every dualistic conceptualization of the world, so entrenched in the thought of the structuralists (Levi-Strauss 1963), from logos and eros to the yin and yang of the Tao, the Shiva-Shakti of the tantric traditions or the anima and animus of Carl Jung.

In times when the patriarchal excesses of modernity seem to be bringing us closer and closer to planetary collapse, psychedelic and plant medicines seem to be potentially powerful tools and allies in our quest to shake off the grip of those systems from our individual and collective consciousness. This is an essential step toward a more conscious paradigm of integrated and mature masculine-feminine synergy and a better integration between rational and erotic medicine. It is the first step in the quintessential alchemical formula for growth: *solve et coagula* (dissolve and recoagulate).

The erotic dimensions of madness, transpersonal states, or psychic suffering are too meaningful to be reduced to pathological neurochemical imbalances, or to be fully grasped by the lens of psychiatric logos. A better integration of logos and eros would allow for nonordinary experiences to be integrated into our ontological and epistemological frames as legitimate, diverse ways of experiencing the world. Without ignoring the possibility of organic pathology in some cases, psychosis, neuroses, depression, or anxiety could all regain their depoliticized dimensions as manifestations of structural violence, of systemic oppression, of social and ecological imbalance, and of repressed dissent. We could recover the transgressive potential of widespread psychic suffering as an agent of deep transformational change for individuals and society.

Moreover, while psychiatric logos tends to disenfranchise patients, psychiatric eros empowers. The passivity that is implicit in psychiatric settings, where the patient is rendered a consumer of psychiatric drugs, is one of the main issues that stand in the way of recovery. Under the crushing weight of a life-changing diagnosis, many patients forfeit their sense of agency and responsibility toward their own healing. Asclepian medicine, on the other hand, "enlists desire in aid of healing" (Morris 2007, 434). It forces the patient to be an active participant in and co-creator of his own healing process, to dig deep into the root causes of affliction, and do the hard, personal (and sometimes social) work that is necessary to overcome them. It can also inspire people to be more involved in the restructuring and reimagining of the social and cultural mechanisms that have played a part in their suffering. Eros puts the power back in the hands of the person and encourages them to explore ways to not only heal, but to transform and grow.

Psychiatric eros, in its diverse incarnations as *mad pride* activism, neurodiversity advocacy, nonpathologizing extra-therapeutic spaces, and the current resurgence and globalization of psychedelic medicines can tap into the core of what is ailing us. It can help us challenge the efforts of psychiatric power in order to individualize mental illness, while inspiring us to co-create stronger communities, healthier societies, and harmonious environments. As Morris writes, a better paradigm will be one where:

> Hippocratic medicine will focus on the objective cellular biology of disease, while Asclepian medicine will focus on intersubjective desire and on the individual, social, and cultural aspects of illness. . . . An Asclepian medicine suited to an era skeptical of Greek gods might reinterpret eros as a power that invokes desire (as distinct from knowledge), that credits intersubjective experience (as distinct from objective data), and that values bodily presence (as distinct from meaning). This interpretation of eros embraces recent innovations in narrative medicine and in mindful practice. It extends to the growing concern for spirituality in medicine. It includes an interest in therapeutic approaches that focus on prevention and on healing, from complementary and alternative medicine to holistic health, wellness programs, and Navajo ceremonies. (2007, 434)

Psychedelic plant medicines like ayahuasca are erotic in the sense that they elicit fully embodied experiences. They are often holistic, acting simultaneously on the body and psyche in its original sense of mind-spirit. In many indigenous languages, the local name for *ayahuasca* translates to "the purge," evoking its powerful emetic properties and the centrality that its effects on the body play in their medical systems. Purging can happen through vomiting or defecating, but it can also manifest as uncontrollable shaking and tremoring, yawning, or crying. Although an infallible way to reconnect with our body, purging is not confined to the physiological realm. Purging also entails the liberation of emotional content or the release from hexes and spells that have been cast on the person in cultures where witchcraft and sorcery are integral to their ontologies.

Furthermore, ayahuasca is erotic in the sense that it plays an important role in maintaining the hygiene of our social ecology. It oftentimes prompts us to examine our relationships with ourselves, our families, friends, community, and environment and thus allows us to become better embodied in our collective social bodies and our local and global ecosystems. Healthier relationships, healthier communities, and healthier environments mean healthier individuals; this is the essence of preventive medicine.

This is, I feel, precisely the kind of medicine that is most urgently needed right now. It is the kind of medicine that can simultaneously address individual affliction and institutionalized madness as a whole. It is the kind of medicine that empowers the resurgence of the repressed torrential forces of the feminine. Eros unbound seems to be essential as we strive to stop Western civilization from running itself off the cliff, and taking everyone else with it. It isn't only about washing away the excesses of psychological patriarchy and the institutions and enterprises it has spawned, including biological psychiatry. It is also about reframing our notions of normalcy and sanity and shifting our psychiatric gaze away from the individual and toward the structural violence that is creating epidemics of mental affliction in our societies. Perhaps more than anything, medical eros affords us the opportunity to imagine what a new-paradigm health care system could look like in a more harmonious and balanced society.

# 22

# Cognitive Dispossession

## Ecofeminism, Entheogens, and Neuroqueering Drug Policy

### Nadia Erlam

The sense of interconnectedness and critical awareness that psychedelic experiences seem to produce has been said to have subversive implications, helpful in challenging hegemonic values and lifestyles as well as political structures (Riley, Thompson, and Griffin 2010). Despite this, Corbin (2006) notes the lack of analysis and discussion of power relationships in various psychedelic projects. Woodward's (2015) work describes a concern with the lack of gender equality and feminist discourse. And women in another study report low levels of gender equality in psychedelic communities, and tell how men ignored this dynamic while enjoying their gendered privileges (Gelfer 2012). Girl (2007) notes the almost absolute omission of women in the history of psychedelic discovery.

## Intersectional Necessity in Psychedelia

Many credited as psychedelic explorers are overwhelmingly white American or European men despite psychedelic use being a global phenomenon (Harvey 2011). Indeed, much psychedelic literature is "unaccountable to colonialism and the politics of location in a global capitalist system" (Corbin 2006, 245). This is why feminist critical awareness and more inclusivity is needed in these communities as well as in related analysis. As is becoming clear, despite an endogenous reputation of these communities as progressive, even (r)evolutionary, rampant inequality still persists.

For inequalities to permeate countercultural communities is not at all uncommon (Conway 2011), and that only adds to the absolute necessity of applying these ideas in practice. Having a psychedelic community and an academia that do not adequately (beyond formally) reflect feminist teachings is profoundly ironic, when so much of psychedelic philosophy echoes these pedagogies. For example, *identity destabilization* is at the heart of much feminist theory as well as psychedelic experience. Identity destabilization is a recognition of the fluidity of categories we often take for granted, whereby new visions and insights allow for new imaginaries and new relationships with regards to identity (Anzaldúa 1987).

If entheogenic theory and research is not coming from an intersectional standpoint, challenging inequalities and/or helping the most marginalized, then I would argue that there is limited scope in this work. The community must become more feminist and realize that inequality is systemic. It must also realize that it takes consistent critical efforts and reflexivity to begin to perceive one's own privileges and conditioning in order to make attempts to mindfully challenge them if we are to allow for these spaces to become more inclusive, accessible, and truly transformative.

## Conceptualizing Gender Variance

A common discourse within the psychedelic community focuses on psychedelics as deconditioning agents that are increasingly being viewed as valuable mechanisms for exploring consciousness (Beiner 2015;

Papaspyrou 2015). *Neurodivergence* refers to mental states and processes that operate in ways that diverge from the dominant norm (Walker 2014). The neurodivergent states that the use of psychedelics gives people access to often defy simplistic binary notions of reality and ask us to question these concepts.

Euro-American culture places bifurcation into two oppositional gender types: the feminine and the masculine. As I will illustrate below, these are commonly used to typify reality in a way that devalues vulnerable groups and states of consciousness. We have inherited and taken part in a history steeped in power dynamics that are often organized according to dichotomous notions that have to be examined in order to be exposed and transcended. That is indeed what psychedelics and feminism imply: a reality that recognizes and moves beyond such dichotomies and acknowledges usually unseen power dynamics at play.

This chapter celebrates a gender variant perspective in relation to gendering reality, observing human diversity when it comes to gender, sex, and how that correlates to the mind. In such queer approaches it is seen that "biology produces sex and gender diversity in processes that are nonlinear, chaotic, dynamic, and indeterminate. This paradigm undermines the determinism of sociobiology and evolutionary psychology, offering rich resources for feminist and trans analysis. Heteronormative and sexist assumptions in biological science have hidden animal sex and gender variance" (Lane 2009, 147).

It is in this sense that we need to understand *the feminine,* and the impact that a process of feminization has had in terms of our perceptions of reality, and consequently, of our understanding and legislating against certain parts of the mind and psychedelics.

## Feminist Revelations

Feminist analysis allows us to assert critiques over normalized beliefs. More specifically, these feminisms can be a tool for understanding how hegemonic structures are served and thus inequalities perpetuated. Many beliefs that we hold are structured by ideologies that are built into and through our cultural norms. Feminist analysis helps us to map these out and challenge conventionally accepted assumptions (Hemmings 2011). Ecofeminism can help us question privileged and devalued forms of taxonomy by elucidating the structuring of categories in modern discursive interactions, which inevitably perform a selective process of what is considered historically important—or not (Shortall 2014).

Gender describes a power relationship that is based upon an asymmetrical, unbalanced, and socially constructed binary: "women" and "men." Without a gender-informed (feminist) analysis, the gendered binarisms through which we categorize reality would remain largely unseen.

Ecofeminism argues that these gendered metaphors have been extended to other perceived dichotomies (able/disabled, human/nature, colonizer/colonized, civilized/uncivilized, cis/queer, sane/insane) and in effect delineate who and what is valued (the masculine) and who and what is devalued (the feminine). Plumwood (1993) understands this as the *master model,* and she notes that this process of binary categorization feminizes the secondary group, which by default means that they are devalued and dehumanized. In other words, the second of these two identities (disabled, nature, colonized, women, queers, and insane) are stigmatized and exploitable because of their feminization. Put another way: this is *the feminine.* This is not to imply that feminized categories are of equivalence (woman equals colonized, queer equals insane), but to illustrate that there is a link in terms of a powerful and gendered "logic of domination" that is operating in dichotomous conceptualization in Euro-American society.

For example, we can see how the colonized have been feminized by looking at texts such as *Colonial Masculinity: The 'Manly Englishman' and the 'Effeminate Bengali'* by Sinha (1995). Here Sinha details how the British Empire used processes of feminization/emasculation in India to contribute to their colonial project and racist policies at the expense of the local Indian population.

Shuttleworth, Wedgwood, and Wilson's (2012) article "The Dilemma of Disabled Masculinity" highlights how disability is feminized, reviewing how notions of masculinity (the masculine) are in conflict with the identity of disability (the feminine). Similarly, with regard to the mind, the *rational* mind has been valued and masculinized in our culture while *divergent* states and minds have been feminized and therefore devalued. We can see clearly and consistently that secondary categories are devalued because they have been feminized, set in opposition to the valued masculinized characteristics.

Ecofeminist theorists such as Anzaldúa (1987) and Keating (2008) also believe that inequalities are *enabled* by binary thinking (Anzaldúa was also known to have taken mushrooms, which undoubtedly influenced her theories). If we position our lives and our political environments according to this reductive outlook, "we assume that there is only one right way to think, act, theorize, or self-define" (Keating 2008, 65). Anzaldúa argues that binary culture is actively violent and oppressive in that it is unable to account for the complexity of the subject, limiting epistemological and ontological development (Keating 2008). Despite this, Western hegemonic discourse continues to instill the standard of oppositional binary concepts. Unless we question this, we will find ourselves unable to deal with the complexities of contradiction and paradox (Keating 2012), a primary essence of the world around us.

## Drug Policy Processes and Hegemonic Discourse

Lazar (2005) notes that discourse structures how we relate to the world, producing and maintaining ontological conditions; hegemonic discourse is that which dominates in a given society, producing and reproducing prevailing cultural and categorical assumptions (Béland 2009). Politicians and scientists are often seen as stipulating neutrality in areas such as drug policy (Friend 2014), however, feminist discourse analysis dislodges this assumption by noting the historical and social undercurrents of certain policy processes, such as how history has been "tied to militarism, capitalism, colonialism, and male supremacy" (Haraway 1988, 581), thus exposing the asymmetric power relationships at play.

Assumptions around identities are evident in policy practices such as policy framing. Policy framing refers to the agenda that policy actors reveal by their specific selection of particular aspects of an issue (Daviter 2011). This can be seen in various metaphors and policy narratives that are used by actors to garner public support for their position on a perceived problem (Stone 1989). With regard to drug policies, solely negative and pathologizing metaphors have been used to describe psychedelic substances and their users as *evil*, and mentally unsound, which then subsequently shapes policy (Tupper 2012). It is common for policy actors to select particular parts of a narrative in order to present it in a narrow manner that supports their agenda. When actors select the notion of psychedelics invoking seemingly evil and immoral qualities, the whole debate is set within these parameters.

There is also a colonial trajectory that accompanies the criminalization of drugs. In the mainstream discourse on drugs, little is mentioned, for example, of the positive effects of khat, an African plant remedy, "in sustaining communities through stressful situations, such as exile, war or social deprivation" (Klein 2014, 141). Ignoring the motivations and cultural contexts underpinning substance use across the world leads to inadequate and biased international policy responses that disregard subaltern knowledge, and further, allows the exportation of a simplistic Euro-American view on drugs and the mental states they give access to. *White solipsism* is a neologism coined by Adrienne Rich (1979), and it describes a *white perspective* and a narrow interpretation of reality that ignores racially marginalized perspectives. As much feminist analysis highlights, modern discursive interactions selectively privilege what is considered *historically significant* (Shortall 2014). This damaging and reductive ontology can be seen from anthropologists who observed communities who used psychedelics during the nineteenth century. They typified the communities that used these substances as "savage" and "uncivilized." (Hunter 2015). The usage of the civilized/uncivilized dichotomy is common toward indigenous psychedelic users by so-called neutral observers (Maroukis 2012), and, in line with Plumwood's master model, it automatically delineates them and their associated cosmology to secondary status.

We can start to see how colonial and racist perspectives have influenced drug discourse and policy by racially associating psychedelic usage and by portraying it as being *devilish*. Indeed, Tupper (2012) argues that the primary reason *why* drug policy has legislated against entheogens so harshly has been *because* of this racialized association. For example, peyote use by Native Americans was considered "a crime not less heinous than that of eating human flesh" (Montagne 1988, 419), while Native Americans experienced peyote as divine (Feeney 2014). There are many ways in which imperialism remains active and influential, such as through the abovementioned techniques of dehumanization and repression of indigenous forms of knowledge. Epistemological historiography carries coloniality in the guise of *modernity* and rationalizes violence through the devaluing of certain human beings and mental landscapes while privileging others (Joseph 2015).

In continuing with the theme of coloniality, psychedelics were typified as uncivilized because they were seen as threatening *the liberal mind*, or in other words, "rational" beliefs, notions of the mind that are steeped in gendered and colonial legacy (Gilbert 1999). Psychedelics were seen to embody the other half of that binary: the irrational, pathological, feminized, and fragmented mind (Moore 2008). The fact that information on the healing potential of psychedelics in communities across the world that use them day-to-day has been largely absent from hegemonic discourse and that these substances are still *actively stigmatized* is, at the very least, illustrative of a persistent colonial discourse that puts these communities and their related knowledge at great risk.

It further represents a major disservice to all who entheogens could help. Anzaldúa (1987), like many ecofeminists, actively invokes these ignored narratives, and she often revalues shamanic and indigenous knowledge in her pedagogies (Vásquez 2005). *Shamanism* here refers to spiritualism outside mainstream religions, often invariably condemned and ignored in mainstream narratives (Keating 2008; Williams 2013). By revaluing neglected discourses that often critique colonial and globally persistent epistemologies, we can gain unique perspectives that help to challenge the dominant paradigms.

Through the abovementioned mainstream narratives that cast psychedelic practices, substances, and the mental landscapes they provide access to as uncivilized, insane, and morally wrong (Tupper 2008), we can start to see how responses and policy in regard to psychedelics, users, and related neurodivergent states are primarily determined according to how these substances and users are categorized and *othered*. According to Anzaldúa (1987), policy actors recreate white solipsistic presumptuous ideational patterns. This helps to explain the racialized impact of drug policy and why psychedelics are so stigmatized.

## Policy Implications

In light of this history, what is emerging is how the policy framing of socially stigmatized drugs in a pathological light is illustrative of a prohibitionist discourse from the nineteenth century (Hunter 2015, 135). Feeney and Labate (2014), Bhabha (1994), and Friend (2014), call into question the Misuse of Drugs Act 1971 (MDA), and other policies that homogenize notions of health and in so doing pathologize any subversive mental landscapes (Joseph 2015). What is a divergent mental landscape and what constitutes *the appropriate mind* is drastically varied across the world (Gilbert 1999). Yet policies such as these delineate what mental states are *wrong* and export them across the globe. This means that subaltern voices on different approaches and therapeutic practices (that can hold a more nuanced and positive outlook on divergent insight) are "already superseded by the Euro-American scientific worldview" (Hunter 2015, 136). One must only compare the legal responses to the Christian ceremonial use of alcohol, the Native American use of peyote, the West African usage of khat, and the Rastafarian usage of cannabis to see a clear example of the racialized distinction between *civilized* and *uncivilized* interpretation of different substances, spiritual activity, and mental states.

Mental health and drug policies are operating according to a narrow understanding of the human mind, which has led to the severe mistreatment of neurodivergent states as a way to paternalistically prevent people from accessing parts of their own minds. Indeed, these notions have often been used to oppress certain groups disproportionately, such as women of color, the elderly, and other people who have experienced categorical inequality (Foucault 1965; Castrodale 2014; Joseph 2015). As is becoming clear, drug policies such as the Misuse of Drugs Act prescribe an imperialist, limited, and white solipsistic way of being (human) and of interpreting reality.

## Cognitive Dispossession and Transcending Paradox

For those of us who inhabit the spaces between the cracks, the neuro-queers who wander outside a prescribed notion of "cognitive normalcy," we know things are not that simple. We often find ourselves inhabiting the paradoxes, a space Anzaldúa refers to as the *borderlands*; somewhere between those mental sates that are considered "sane" and "insane." Thankfully, these states are often "painful yet also potentially transformational spaces where opposites converge, conflict, and transmute" (Keating 2009, 10). Indeed, some communities believe that what the Western world would consider as perceived *disabilities* in this reality can prove to be a source of great learning and a way through to the unconscious. According to the Hmong people, epilepsy and autism are viewed as an indication of spiritual and healing power (Fadiman 2012). The Itako in Japan consider those with visual impairments as being able to see into different and informing realities because of their lack of vision in this one (Williams 2013).

This complexity can be seen in the results of psychedelic research itself, which go against hegemonic and gendered binary frameworks for understanding the mind. Despite a wholly negative stereotype of divergent mental landscapes such as psychosis and dissociation, psychedelic researchers have found that often long-term healing happens *because* of the ability of psychedelics to invoke intense, seemingly psychotic and/or dissociative experiences (Shortall 2014). This reflects a more holistic understanding of mental health whereby such experiences have "heralded a positive breakthrough in working through repression" (Shortall 2014, 195). Such experiences can be incredibly difficult, terrifying perhaps, but can often help facilitate a *schema breakdown,* and for many, enduring through these experiences has proven to be transformative (Ruane 2015). Of course, this process is not recommendable for everyone, especially not without an experienced guide. Yet policies illegalizing psychedelics with the highest penalty mean that this is not an easy option for those who may greatly benefit from this process.

In light of neurocognitive multifacetedness and its heterogeneous nature, I propose that the homogenization of drug-control approaches is not adequate or sophisticated enough to sincerely address harm management in the interests of the public. Rather than naming all types of neurodivergent states as forms of mental *illness,* we ought to interpret them more holistically. Considered outside of a pathologizing paradigm, dissociative and psychotic experiences often arise as a reasonable response to traumatic events, which is why experts in this field—such as Longden, Madill, and Waterman (2011)—believe that neurodivergence can be experienced as informative, transformative, and extremely positive as a result.

Instead, policy responses and prevailing discourse indicate that these people need to be *fixed* or *civilized* (Friend 2014); a position that becomes "permeable to eugenic thinking and civilizing, regulating projects as it seeks to fix that which is represented as abnormal through systems of inspection, taxonomization, and the application of treatments to erase difference" (Joseph 2015, 13). Therefore, Weil (1998) proposes that drug policy is a form of epistemic *violence*, especially if it is not formulated according to evidence-based harm reduction. As such it limits our cognitive liberty, our freedom to explore our minds and consciousness, which could be seen as essential for our maturation process (Walsh 2010; Bernauer and Rasmussen 1988).

Considering these interpretations on the policy discourse and its conceptual limitations, contradictions, and selective use of evidence it becomes evident that such policies deprive the public from accessing and becoming acquainted with *non-neuro-typical* states, and block access to the potentially therapeutic experiences of such environments. This amounts to epistemic violence and cognitive dispossession, with real material consequences. Insights from feminist disability studies, queer theory, and psychedelic philosophy have informed the positions in this essay, and as theoretical systems they support in-depth exploration and understanding of how we conceptualize the world through gendered, colonial, dichotomous, and oppositional forms of taxonomy, which value or devalue aspects of our reality.

The utility of feminist analysis and the critical reflections it provokes is of fundamental value in psychedelic community discourse as well as within the institutions that produce the relevant policies and drug-related research. Without such input, these important revelations with regard to policies and assumptions in research and behaviors cannot be perceived. Thus the most vulnerable people, whom psychedelics can benefit, may continually be excluded and denied legal and safe access to the help that they may need and that psychedelics can provide.

# 23

# Psychedelics, Self-Creation, and Article 8 of the European Convention on Human Rights

## A Feminist Perspective

### Charlotte Walsh

In 2015, the United Kingdom All Party Parliamentary Group for Drug Policy Reform—an informal, yet high profile and authoritative group of parliamentarians—stated that "the European Convention on Human Rights (ECHR), in particular Article 8, could be invoked in support of the argument that possession or purchase (or cultivation of drugs for personal use) (particularly in small quantities) do not injure other people's rights either directly or indirectly and therefore should not be criminalised" (APPG 2015, 7). Addressing the question of whether or not the system of global prohibition—as enshrined within the United Nations Drug Conventions—strangles the hope of such progressive reform at birth, they concluded that domestic drug laws need to "reflect the supremacy of human rights conventions" (APPG 2015, 21).

This chapter explores the promise of—and potential barriers to—a test case being brought on such grounds. One prospective obstacle to change, and worth engaging with at the outset, is this issue being framed in such a way as to trivialize it, thereby rendering it easy to dismiss. So, for instance, the *Express* responded to this proposal with the headline: "Taking Drugs Is a HUMAN RIGHT, MPs Say—and Junkies Could Use Euro Laws to Avoid Jail" (Parfitt 2015).

What this chapter hopes to elucidate is that narrowing the focus in this way is a disingenuous tactic. This is not about our right to drugs— the importance of which people may agree or disagree on—but rather the seminal issue of our freedom and the extent to which it is acceptable for the state to impinge upon it.

Article 8 provides a right to respect for privacy, which has happily (and justly) been read broadly by the courts, encompassing the idea that people should have the freedom to develop their own unique identity (*Connors v. U.K.* 2005). The central claim here is that the criminal-ization of (in particular, psychedelic) drugs, interferes with this right to self-creation, as these substances can be pivotal to enhancing our potential to exist in the world in a meaningful way. Feminist theory is deployed in making this assertion. This theory is rooted in a view of the drug war as patriarchal, with human rights potentially acting as a countervailing force, enabling universal respect for freedom. Parallels are drawn with the gay rights movement, with the extraordinary legal progress made in that sphere largely scaffolded on human rights. Differentiating factors—along with the criticisms that drawing such analogies inevitably attracts—are also explored. The limitations of the human rights' approach are engaged with, including a feminist critique of the wisdom (or otherwise) of relying on legal reform to effect societal change, along with an excavation of underground alternatives. However, ultimately it is argued that the dream of a shift in the legal paradigm ought not to be abandoned.

## Human Rights and Drug Prohibition

It seems apposite to open with a consideration of the general principles underpinning human rights protections, directing our minds to what they are designed to achieve, and for whom: "[they] signify the core set of rights which relate to all persons, without exception, because they are all human beings and which underpin our social, legal, moral and political relationships" (Amatrudo and Blake 2015, 1). Human rights are normative, embodying a vision of how those who ascribe to them believe the world *should* be. One of the fundamental roles of such provisions is to patrol the boundaries between the state and the individual, guarding against unreasonable, arbitrary interference with the latter by the former. Thus, human rights can be seen to be rooted in classic liberalism, with its foundation stone of necessary limits on state power (Mill 1865). This is particularly apposite when considering the *negative* dimension of human rights, the right to be left alone. They have evolved to also incorporate a *positive* component, involving the state having responsibilities to ensure conditions are ripe such that freedoms can flourish. While there is no bright line between the two, it is the former that is of most relevance here.

Instruments of human rights provide a lens through which our laws can be viewed, interrogating whether they comply with ethical standards or, conversely, if the legislature has stepped beyond its acceptable remit: they can thus offer a challenge to state power (Mikalsen 2015). Indeed, it is a legal necessity that the processes of criminalization are scrutinized in this way: the ECHR was ratified by the United Kingdom in 1951, and the Human Rights Act 1998 enshrined the freedoms guaranteed therein into domestic law, such that primary legislation *must* be read and given effect to in a manner that is compatible with Convention rights, so far as is possible (s. 3[1]). Where it is deemed impossible to resolve a conflict between the two, the higher courts may grant a declaration of incompatibility (ss. 4 and 5), whereby the relevant minister may, by order, amend the legislation to remove it (s. 10) (Richardson 2015). Through such processes, human rights have had an enormous influence both in amending—and helping to shape—criminal law (Ashworth 2009).

However, the application of human rights in the realm of drug law has been less propitious. Domestic prohibition of (some) drugs is rooted in an international matrix, which has been shown repeatedly—and on manifold fronts—to result in egregious human rights violations (Transform 2016). While the focus here is narrower, homing in on a particular breach on the home front, that ought not to obscure this broader context. Indeed, the deeply stigmatizing effect of the global War on Drugs (Mena and Hobbs 2010)—along with our perceived international obligations—can be convincingly argued to be inextricably bound up with a notable reticence to accord rights to drug users in the United Kingdom.

What is being argued here is that *the very existence*—rather than a particular application—of the drug prohibitions unjustifiably breaches ECHR rights. Recognition of this fact by the courts would necessitate repeal of the relevant legislation: namely, the Misuse of Drugs Act 1971 (MDA), recently joined by the Psychoactive Substances Act 2016 (PSA). While the scope of these two pieces of legislation is (extremely) broad, the concern here is with the criminalization of psychedelics, in line with the properties of those substances, the author's interest, and the parameters of this book. In tandem with human rights laws, a quest for freedom is often at the heart of the ingestion of these molecules.

What is espoused here is a protest variant of human rights, consciously deploying them to pursue social transformation (Douzinas 2000). The law usually changes—whether through judicial interpretation or through legislation—as society evolves. However, taking psychedelics is a minority pursuit, and there is unlikely to be a mass social movement pushing for legal reform in this realm anytime soon. That is why the human rights' approach is so useful: it only takes one person to successfully argue in court that their rights are being breached by the drug laws to potentially precipitate legislative shifts. Furthermore, the language of human rights provides a potent way of framing the issue, thus constituting an important tool for activists. As Transform—the leading U.K. charity campaigning for drug policy reform—has made clear: "[t]he arguments for the personal freedom of consenting adults to use nonmedical psychoactive substances are intellectually strong. The principle underpinning most modern law making is that consenting adults should be free to engage in whatever behavior they wish, as long as it does not harm others, and that risky personal behavior or self-harm, while a legitimate concern of government, should generally not be the concern of criminal law" (Transform 2014, 118).

Stirring feminist theory into this mix, the traditionally combative approach to drug policy has been analyzed as arising out of a system dominated by male power: "[t]he War on Drugs bears all the hallmarks of the patriarchy. . . . By means of propaganda and force, [it] has reshaped peoples' perception of reality and diverted economic and psychic resources away from constructive solutions to social problems" (Luff 1992, 7). Thus, what is needed is to *re*-reshape people's perception of reality: human rights—and the psychedelics themselves—may play an important role here. While feminism has come in different waves, manifested in diverse styles, underpinning them all is a call for nondiscrimination. This fits in well with the human rights paradigm, which is universalist at its core: the aim being equal protection of rights for all.

Importantly, in a pluralist, liberal democracy, equality is not (or should not be) grounded in sameness: people should have the space to be different, yet equal, and to have their rights respected regardless. As a critical addendum to such feminist analysis, it is, of course, crucial to avoid gender essentialism. To wit, it is not the case that patriarchal mind-sets and structures are the sole preserve or creation of men—or, indeed, of "masculine" traits, whatever that means—any more than it is true that a new approach to drug policy must be "feminized" to be progressive. It is hoped that psychedelic consciousness blasts us beyond such artificial divisions.

## The Right to Self-Creation

Previously, human rights-based challenges to the U.K. drug laws have been brought using Article 9, which protects the right to freedom of religion (*Taylor* 2001; *Aziz* 2012). These were unsuccessful, so—in line with the APPG recommendation—a change of strategy seems apt, moving on to fresh legal territory, where arguments have not been closed down by the courts. It is also the case that, even were a plea for religious exemption from prohibition to be successful, it would only apply to that specific religious group. The reasoning here is all-encompassing, reflecting a wider shift from external to internal ethical approaches to living. Article 9 also protects freedom of thought, and this author has previously argued that psychedelic prohibitions breach this right and should be challenged accordingly (Walsh 2016).

Although this belief is still vehemently held, the claim that we should have control over our own consciousness and that drug prohibition represents a censorship of our cognitive liberty is perhaps too radical for the courts at this time. The difference is really one of framing, as, in actuality, the clusters of rights that are protected within the ECHR are all interwoven. There is a clear overlap, for instance, between what we have the freedom to think and who we have the privacy to become, engaging Articles 9 and 8, respectively. There have, in fact, already been (unsuccessful) attempts to deploy Article 8 in this forum, but these have been calls for therapeutic exemptions from prohibition (*Quayle* 2005; *Altham* 2006). Again, the approach suggested here hopefully takes us beyond any such restricted categories.

Article 8 holds particular promise given that the contours of the right to privacy have been read expansively. In the first of her two important texts on the relationship between human rights and identity—which offer an excellent overview of the relevant European case law—Marshall comments: "[r]ecently it has been argued that there seem to be two contradictory rationales to privacy. The first entails privacy as seclusion or intimacy, which is often spatially defined. The second privacy is freedom of action, self-determination and autonomy. It is argued that the two strands can be united in perceiving privacy as protecting the free development of one's personality" (2009, 52).

Both these external and internal dimensions of privacy can be seen to be breached in manifold ways by drug legislation. Without diminishing the importance of the former—alongside full acknowledgment that the two dimensions are inextricably entwined—the focus here is on how the drug laws threaten the latter. In her later book, Marshall looks at whether internal privacy is important so that we can discover who we "truly" are, or rather is it necessary in order to leave us space to create who we wish to become? She advocates for the latter, arguing that the essentialist notion that we have a "true" self that merely requires excavating is a spurious—and indeed limiting—notion: "self-creation is a version of human freedom in which persons are free if they can become something they are not yet, different to, more than, possibly better than, what they are now" (Marshall 2014, 217).

While this existentialist notion of the human becoming is thoroughly endorsed—marrying well, as it does, with the practice of using psychedelics to help transform oneself—it is also interesting that these same tools, in freeing the human mind from the strictures of the default mode network, the grooves it typically treads, the sense of being a particular ego, located in a given point in space-time, can lead to a sense of boundlessness and inner peace that feels as though it were always there to be discovered. Or, as the title of one of the neuroscientific publications on this subject so succinctly puts it, "finding the self by losing the self" (Lebedev et al. 2015). Identity formation may thus be simultaneously an unearthing and a moving toward, discovering the authentic self within while building your own avatar, imagining oneself in to being.

Even if one takes the view—as this author somewhat reluctantly does—that we are, in fact, determined, we still need to create ourselves (even if we were never going to materialize in any other way, as a particular biological organism enmeshed in a given environment) (Harris 2012). And, of course, we are all many different selves that shift dependent upon who we are with, and where we are located in the time and space coordinates of our journey. As Whitman famously said, "I contain multitudes" (Whitman 1997, 39). This is perhaps never more apparent than during the psychedelic experience where the paradox of not existing as a distinct identity while simultaneously embodying the entire universe is often keenly felt.

As noted, our modern-day concept of human rights was seeded in the ground of classic liberalism, most famously espoused by the nineteenth-century philosopher (and early feminist) John Stuart Mill, who argued that true freedom necessitated "liberty of tastes and pursuits; of framing the plan of our life to suit our own character; of doing as we like, subject to such consequences as may follow: without impediment from our fellow creatures, so long as what we do does not harm them, even though they should think our conduct foolish, perverse, or wrong" (Mill 1865, chapter 1, pages 9–10). He famously advocated "experiments in living" (chapter 3, page 1),* which many psychonauts would claim to be engaged with in a rather literal manner, using their own bodies as mystical chemistry sets. Accordingly, Article 8 protects our right to construct a narrative of our own choosing, to spin our own yarn: "[w]e have a finite amount of time in which to live our own life, at least on this earth in the material form we now experience and are conscious of. In living this life, we seek to live in ways that make sense to us, that give our lives value and meaning, and a sense of our own personal identity" (Marshall 2014, 6–7).

Again, there is both an internal and an external dimension to this, with inner exploration being necessary in order for us to know what we value, which paths we thereby wish to follow out in the world.

True freedom of self-authorship "involves discovering new ways of understanding ourselves and each other, refusing to accept the dominant culture's characterization of our practices and desires, and redefining them from within resistant cultures" (Marshall 2014, 243). How does this ideal translate into legal practice? When it comes to psychedelics, not only are users' rights not protected, but their activities are criminalized: "Law can be used as an enabling tool, by changing the social conditions to enable people to make their own choices or as a

---

*In Mill's book, each new chapter begins with page 1.

restricting tool, preventing certain choices and ways of life through legal prohibitions or bans" (Marshall 2009, 6–7). The current situation is especially problematic when one considers the close alignment between what is supposedly protected by Article 8 and the psychedelic experience, which often goes to the core of our inner beings. Although drug taking is frequently demonized and trivialized, many psychedelic users conceptualize themselves as being on a deep philosophical and spiritual quest, exploring what it means to be human and how best to live in this world. A successful test case has the potential to heal this rift.

## A Qualified Right

In bringing any such case, it's important to remember that, while it is contended here that Article 8 is inarguably breached by psychedelic prohibitions—and thereby engaged—this is not an absolute right. In other words, it can legitimately be interfered with in certain circumstances, and these will inevitably be relied upon in defending against any such challenge. These qualifiers are contained within Article 8(2), which reads: "[t]here shall be no interference by a public authority with the exercise of this right except such as is in accordance with the law and is necessary in a democratic society in the interests of national security, public safety or the economic well-being of the country, for the prevention of disorder or crime, for the protection of health or morals, or for the protection of the rights and freedoms of others."

Unfortunately, in previous cases where drug prohibition has been challenged on human rights grounds, the qualifiers (whether in Article 8(2), or their equivalents in relation to other articles) have been judged to apply in an exceptionally cursory fashion, often simply through reference to the existent system of prohibition (*Taylor* 2001; *Aziz* 2012). Such an approach is unacceptably circular, with the courts avoiding the rigorous process of legislative scrutiny they should be engaged with. Consequently, they neglect their constitutional role: namely, to ensure that legislation does not unjustifiably transgress the rights of citizens.

Working systematically through the relevant criteria in Article 8(2)—as the courts must if adhering to due process—that the interference created by psychedelic prohibition is both "by a public authority" and in "accordance with the law" is beyond dispute, given the existence of both the MDA and the PSA. However, such intercession must also be shown to be "necessary in a democratic society": viz, a proportionate response in pursuit of a legitimate aim. In relation to the MDA, the stated aim is the control of "drugs which are being or appear . . . likely to be misused and of which the misuse is having or appears . . . capable of having harmful effects sufficient to constitute a social problem" (s. 1[2]). This is (theoretically) unproblematic from a liberal perspective, although the reality of the legislation in operation is far more controversial (Nutt 2012).

While there has not yet been time to assess the PSA in practice, even on paper its stated ambitions are alarming: namely, to control substances that have a psychoactive effect, with no reference made to consequences, other than that their ingestion "affects the person's mental functioning or emotional state" (s. 2 [2]). As such, the very aims of the PSA appear to be in unjustifiable conflict with Article 8, with there being little that is more private than our inner states. To ensure proportionality, the burden of proof is on the state to show there is a pressing social problem caused by psychedelics and that prohibition is both the most effective and least intrusive way of dealing with it, relying on facts, not fears. It would prove very difficult to make this claim convincingly, given that the drug prohibition laws, global and domestic, have been shown time and again to be iatrogenic, creating more problems than they solve, both for individuals and wider society (Transform 2016; Transform 2014). This is true when speaking broadly of controlled drugs and becomes ever more so when one focuses in on psychedelics.

The incursions into the right to privacy that occur as a result of the prohibitive approach must also be justified with reference to one of the grounds specified in Article 8(2), most likely "the prevention of disorder or crime" or "for the protection of health or morals." This reference to "morals" in the qualifiers is deeply problematic from a liberal perspective. Article 8 is deontological, enshrining the value of privacy as a normative good. Thus, it should only be interfered with for consequentialist, empirically proven reasons, rather than through incorporating (potentially) opposing values by reference to "morals"—a slippery concept, vague enough that it can distort unrecognizably, depending upon which reality tunnel it is viewed through.

To square this circle, any recourse to a threat to "morals" should be grounded in proof of a particular *harm*, lest the qualifier itself become immoral, mired in irrational fears and prejudices. Of the potentially relevant harms listed, while the use of certain drugs can feasibly be linked with crime, this is not the case with the psychedelics. Health harms associated with them are also minimal (Nutt, King, and Phillips 2010).

Although it would be disingenuous to deny the potential for *any* harm—be that physical or psychological—such risk needs to be contextualized. Most people live lives we might judge as physically, emotionally, and indeed, spiritually unhealthy. That, however, is their business, even accepting that there are, undeniably, consequences for broader society. We do not float around in hermetically sealed bubbles, and the state in its various guises—as funded by the taxpayer—is often called upon to mop up the mess from unwise choices that have been made. However, that does not mean that those choices ought not still be respected (or, at the very least, tolerated). There are necessary limits on what the state should be trying to achieve—certainly through the blunt tool of criminal law—with paternalistic intervention being unacceptable from a liberal perspective. Furthermore, the fact that both crime and health issues are much more strongly associated with a substance that is not prohibited—namely alcohol—evidences that this approach does not constitute the least intrusive measure available, as required when making justifiable inroads into human rights.

A proportionate response might entail, rather, education and interventions rooted in harm reduction. The current discrepancy of approach violates Article 14 of the ECHR, which protects against discrimination in protection of rights. Our system of law should be principled, not arbitrary, and it is no more acceptable to discriminate against users of certain drugs and not others because that is customary, than it is, for instance, to discriminate against women on similar grounds.

Human rights start to eat themselves where the law only truly respects them when they append to individuals deemed to be exercising their autonomy in an acceptable way. When thereby narrowed—whether manifested through outright denial that a particular right is engaged, through trigger-happy recourse to the qualifiers, or indeed, through criminalization—true freedom is corroded. This state of affairs tends to be "justified" with vague reference to the protection of society, with "[t]he problematic mutation of the notion of the community toward a closed and rigid community reaffirming its own authenticity" (Gozdecka 2015, 310). This fatal flaw with the operation of human rights in practice is elaborated upon by Ukri Soirila: "No room is available in this framework for the singular, unique existence of absolute difference, the individual in the state of becoming. It is not possible for the singular being to challenge and try to escape the norms of the dominant majority" (2015, 354).

The tendency to view Article 8 as embodying the tension between the individual and the collective—with the former represented in the right itself, the latter in its qualifier—is unnecessarily divisive. As is rendered apparent by the psychedelic experience, such dichotomies between self and other are false. Furthermore, we need autonomous, self-realized individuals to help society to progress. Or, perhaps it is such progression that is railed against, with those invested in the current situation recognizing what is truly at stake here, the conflict actually between the individual and the state, with protection of society a mere fig leaf. As Charles Eisenstein so astutely puts it:

> In fact, the prohibitionists are correct. The legalization of cannabis, LSD, MDMA, psilocybin mushrooms, ayahuasca, and the other psychedelics would indeed mean the end of society *as we know it.*

The threat that conservative political forces have identified is real. If these were just innocuous bourgeois play-things, "experiences" that one could consume on weekends to make life-as-usual a little more tolerable, then the guardians of the status quo would have little reason to prohibit them. They recognize, if only unconsciously, the revolutionary social and political potential these substances carry. Psychedelics can bestow expanded consciousness, perceptions, and ways of being that are incompatible with those that undergird our society. (Eisenstein 2016, 4)

## Stigmatization and Coming Out

These difficulties in psychedelic users being recognized as rights bearers are fueled by—and recursively fuel—stigmatization. Such stigmatization can have deep psychological effects, perhaps leading to a (often subconscious) sense of shame among users (Holland 2016). This—along with fear of criminalization and all its attendant side effects—can render it less likely that rights will even be sought. Recognition of this trap has been the spur to a number of calls for psychedelic users to "come out." For example, in 2015, the U.K. Psychedelic Society promoted a National Psychedelic Coming Out Day, while in 2016 the online psychedelic magazine *Psymposia* ran a series of pieces on the advantages and risks of "Coming out of the Psychedelic Closet."

Such an approach draws valuable lessons from gay rights campaigns: although a successful test case is technically only reliant on proving an unjustifiable breach of the rights of a single individual, pragmatically any fight for psychedelic users' rights in the courts is more likely to succeed when undergirded by something of a shift in broader public attitudes.

A coming-out movement may help to prompt this, revealing "the vast spectrum of doctors, lawyers, scientists, writers, and politicians who encompass the category of psychedelic people" (Devenot 2016a). As with being gay—and unlike "race"—psychedelic use is not (necessarily!)

apparent without speaking about it. There is much to be gained from bringing in the personal rather than relying on abstract arguments. It is substantially harder to make false claims about psychedelic users when one is standing in front of you as living disproof of them (Miller 2016).

In her work, Neşe Devenot (2016a; 2016b) elucidates these parallels with the gay rights movement, seeing psychedelic prohibition as being similarly both a social justice issue and one of identity politics. She charts comparable stories of oppression, of criminalization, of potential imprisonment for nonviolent offences that cause no harm to others, of losing one's job (and potentially children). These are all risks that were previously faced by those who are gay and which remain the case for psychedelic users (which, is, of course, why coming out is so unpalatable to many).

Encouragingly, the evolution from homosexuality being criminal- ized through to same-sex marriage being recognized and celebrated has been premised on a rights-based discourse (see, for instance, *Dudgeon v. the United Kingdom*) as have many other extraordinary transformative movements (Solnit 2016). However, as Devenot interro- gates, drawing this analogy has proven controversial for some. At times this antagonism arises because drug use is seen as chosen, sexuality as a given. Whether either of those statements are true—and their converse false—is debatable in both directions. The answer doubtless varies between individuals, with both nature and nurture exerting differing influences on sexual and drug preferences (Whisman 2012).

Regardless, rights should not only come into operation to protect a status that is viewed as "fixed," and Article 8 is certainly not restricted in this way in theory. However, in practice "[w]hen aspects of a person's identity are viewed as the result of choice, and then viewed as 'unrea- sonable,' there is correspondingly less respect and accommodation given to them, if they are not in line with the majority's viewpoint" (Marshall 2014, 66–67). From a deterministic perspective, at root *nothing* is freely chosen, but that does not mean that we should not have the right to choose, and to have those choices respected.

There is also the potential differentiation of triviality, with psychedelic use—unlike sexuality—perhaps unlikely to be seen (from the outside) as core to that person's identity. However, this is just a reminder that we need to listen to what people tell us is important to them, rather than impose our own priorities upon them. I might find religious belief unfathomable, superstitious nonsense that should have long since been swept away by the power of reason, whereas you might find it accords your life meaning, and anchor your existence around it, which you should be free to do. Finally, psychedelic users perhaps attract limited sympathy for their cause owing to the fact that, while they undeniably represent a cultural minority, they are *not* generally oppressed—even in relation to their psychedelic use that, as often as not, goes undiscovered. Thus they may be dismissed as a privileged group "appropriating legitimate struggles in service of hedonistic recreation" (Devenot 2016a).

In response, it needs to be remembered that this is not a competition where only those who are the most subjugated can legitimately fight for their rights. Indeed, such an impoverished interpretation "risk[s] reinforcing the very foundations of inequality and discrimination that resulted in the problem to begin with" (Devenot 2016b). We want a world where *everybody's* rights are respected and should be helping each other toward that ideal. After all, "[p]sychedelic users and sexual minorities are both involved in the same struggle to transform the body politic on the topic of body politics" (Teafaerie 2016). And lest we forget, gay rights have now been legally embedded (at least in the West), while psychedelic use remains mired in stigmatization, in criminalization.

## Is Law the Answer?

Some would argue that it is naive to expect this situation to change through the courts. Indeed, this is a common feminist critique of the rights-based approach, with Carol Smart warning that we must avoid being seduced by the "siren call of the law" (2002, 160). The fundament of this position is that problems that are themselves systemic cannot be solved through the very same systems.

The law "constitutes a kind of institutionalized and formalized site of power struggles" (Smart 2002, 138) with the game rigged. If human rights are brought into existence by the powerful through language— and can thereby mean whatever they want them to mean—this renders them effectively meaningless. The problem is that we are trying to use these freedoms as a shield to protect us from the criminal law and yet similar prejudices may pervade those who draft prohibitive enactments and those responsible for upholding human rights. Smart also argues against using the law to effect change for deeper reasons, seeing law in general—not just the drug laws—as iatrogenic. By relying on it, she says, "The idea that law is the means to resolve social problems gains strength and the idea that the lawyers and the quasi-lawyers are the technocrats of an unfolding Utopia becomes taken for granted" (2002, 161).

Such an analysis calls for activism over legal formalism, to birth "an alternative reality to the version which is manifested in legal discourse" (Smart 2002, 160). The potential relevance of this critique to the psychedelic movement is apparent, where there is a strong drive for prohibition to be replaced not by compulsory, top-down, legal regulation, but, rather, by grassroots, user-generated models of best practice, voluntarily ascribed to, such as those promoted by the International Center for Ethnobotanical Education Research and Service. This mistrust of traditional legal processes is perhaps particularly warranted given the political climate in the United Kingdom at the moment. It consists of an ever more authoritarian drug policy heralded by the passage of the PSA, along with the incumbent Conservative government's plans to withdraw from the ECHR, doubtless rendered ever more likely to materialize given the recent vote to leave the EU, and with Theresa May—one of the champions of abandonment of the ECHR—having become prime minister.

Accordingly, rather than waiting for change from above, many have adopted the Confucian model of "acting as if." In harmony with our earlier discussion regarding the fluidity of identity, the Chinese philosopher was skeptical of the existence of a "true" self that could be discovered. Rather, he viewed being human as a process, with his advice thereby stating that we should act "as if" we were the best version of ourselves, an ancient precursor of the adage to "fake it till you make it" (Puett and Gross-Loh 2016, chapter 3).

In a similar vein, large swathes of people around the world are acting "as if" the drug laws have already been reformed, whether that be, for instance, through simply taking psychedelics, selling them online over the dark web (Martin 2014), or setting up cannabis clubs (Transform 2015). In relation to the latter, beginnings rooted in an exploitation of legal loopholes are evolving as these collectives move toward a firmer legal footing (having, effectively, faked it until they made it). Relatedly, many of the underground cannabis growers in the United States have pushed their heads through the topsoil, helping to transmogrify a once criminalized activity into a legitimate (and booming) industry (Pardo 2014).

As an important aside, this latter development potently demonstrates that the international drug conventions are nowhere near as constrictive of domestic legal transformation as might previously have been assumed. Or, at least, they have lost much of their power and "moral" authority in the wake of these evolutions in the land of their progenitors (Thoumi 2014). What these living examples reveal is that differing approaches are not mutually exclusive. Combining insubordination and activism with legal change helps to stabilize new paradigms that have emerged organically. In a similar fashion, there will likely be activist groups behind the bringing of any test case.

This was so with the 2015 challenge brought before the Supreme Court of Mexico by the activist group SMART, protesting prohibitions on personally producing and possessing cannabis on the grounds that they violate the rights contained in Article 1 of that country's constitution, largely analogous to Article 8 (Supreme Court of Mexico 2015). The plaintiffs' argument that such criminalization creates undue restrictions on the fundamental right to personal identity, self-image, free development of personality, self-determination, and individual freedom—all in relation to the principle of human dignity—was accepted by the highest court in that land, and, importantly, not deemed to be outweighed by the existence of the qualifiers to Article 1, equivalent to those found in Article 8(2).

Their submission is worth reading in full as it is a tour de force, a scathing attack on prohibition from multifarious angles. It mirrors many of the arguments articulated herein—ranging from an ideological perspective, rooted in human rights and legal philosophy—through to pragmatic concerns, namely, that the current approach is not efficacious, and is, indeed, harmful.*

While the Supreme Court was of the opinion that the prohibitions in question pursued necessary aims, given the relatively low levels of harm from cannabis, they ruled that these could best be achieved through alternative, less intrusive measures—such as education and harm reduction—that did not impinge on human rights. Hearteningly, there was no need for recourse to therapeutic or religious use here, with the court accepting that prohibition of *recreational* use of cannabis is unconstitutional on rights-based grounds. Predictably, this decision was reported in a way that somewhat narrowed and trivialized the issue. For instance, the headline of the *Washington Post* declared: "Mexico's Supreme Court Rules that Smoking Pot is a Fundamental Human Right" (Ingraham 2015).

To summarize this essay, instruments of human rights (along with psychedelics themselves) are proven tools that can free us from heteronomy into autonomy. It has been argued herein that a test case should be brought, challenging psychedelic prohibitions on human rights grounds, specifically the Article 8 right to privacy contained within the ECHR,

---

*An English translation is available on Scribd's documents collection under the title "Mexico's Supreme Court Ruling on Cannabis—English Translation."

encompassing our freedom to self-creation. Although human rights challenges to prohibition have been unsuccessful in the past, this is no reason to give up hope. All that is actually needed is for the courts to follow the enshrined rules in a principled manner. The judiciary must be brave in holding the legislature to account, scrutinizing psychedelic prohibition rigorously through the prism of human rights.

When they do this, the justification for such a system will collapse. Although it might seem ambitious to expect the courts to declare our drug laws incompatible with human rights, it is actually no more than their duty. This duty is to make certain that the lawmakers do not over-step their boundaries, ensuring that we live in a society where rights are respected, even in those realms where this is most controversial. Indeed, it is how judges rule in these contentious areas that serves as a valuable gauge of the extent to which democratic states have collapsed into majoritarian rule, or not. The Supreme Court of Mexico—a nation that has suffered unimaginably as a result of drug prohibition—is lead-ing the way here, and hopefully we will follow in its footsteps. The law should be used as a force for good rather than as a system of oppression, empowering rather than constraining us, and enabling us to flourish to our highest potential.

# Weaving Our Way
# Back Home

The genesis of this book was the intention to give space to stories, perspectives, and opinions concerning the feminine principle and altered states of consciousness, as well as to give a platform to the voices of women in the psychedelic community. There is a sense of urgency that can be perceived in these essays. This sense of urgency stems from the need to spread those perspectives that, until now, have been brewing at the edges of the edge, within the psychedelic scene and yet at its margins. These perspectives have also been prevalent but obscured in other scenes and disciplines that share certain commonalities with the psychedelic scene and yet, until now, they remained in the periphery of those disciplines as well.

There is a need to reclaim women's heritage in the millennia-old practice of shamanic techniques to induce altered states for the healing of oneself, the community, and the environment. There is a seed of awareness that in addition to women, those individuals who did not have a clear binary identity were often shamans and healers and that rituals could be spaces wherein gender identities were deconstructed and liberated from fixed rules and convention. This allows for a greater variety of expression in gender, sexuality, morality, spirituality, and humanity.

These essays consistently call for the legitimization of a new cultural paradigm in which uncertainty, paradox, nonduality, divine intervention, and embodied intuition are embraced. Here they enjoy their rightful place next to the need to measure, control, compute, and institutionalize. This is a new cultural paradigm whereby a balance is reestablished between the mind, the heart, and the body, between the tangible and the ineffable. There is a need and a necessity to co-create a society where women feel empowered to function according to those principles and qualities inherent to their being, supported and inspired by the practice of altered states.

This book expresses the knowing that through a revived connection with our embodied selves, alongside the capacity for wider perception engendered through altered states of consciousness, we can find our way toward the remembering of our visceral connection to Earth as a living being. Only then may we hope for a more responsible use of resources, securing not only our own survival but also the survival of all ecosystems. We do this in large part by the rediscovery of humanity's role in the stewardship of this planet and its many species. Psychedelic culture already contains the seeds for this transformation as long as the old patriarchal patterns, which might still persist within it, can be uncovered, acknowledged, and dismantled. Psychedelic states can service the restoration of the feminine into our psyches and consequently into our culture. In fact, it is in these states that we often find the vision of the new paradigm and the courage and inspiration to manifest it. For the evolutionary task ahead, we will need all of us, women and men, the old and the young, collaborating and synergizing, painfully working through the remnants of outdated societal norms and expectations, weaving our way back into the heart and back into the Earth herself.

# Contributors

**Cameron Adams**, Ph.D., completed his Ph.D. in environmental and ecological anthropology in 2004 with his study of highland Maya ethnophysiology and cognitive metaphor. He has studied psychedelic communities online since 2009 and has focused on psychedelic phenomenology, healing with psychedelics, and the relationship between psychedelics and conspiracy theories. Cameron is a cofounder and director of Breaking Convention: Multidisciplinary Conference on Psychedelic Consciousness.

**Adam Aronovich** lives and works in the Peruvian Amazon rain forest where he is conducting fieldwork for his doctoral dissertation. After studying psychology and cognitive science at Ben Gurion University in Israel he went on to study medical anthropology and global health on the graduate level in a joint program between the Universitat Rovira i Virgili in Tarragona and the Universitat de Barcelona, both in Catalonia. He also obtained a diploma in traditional Mexican medicine from the University of Morelos, Mexico. He is interested in the socio-ecological dimensions of mental health and the potential role that ayahuasca and other psychedelic medicines play in the emergence of holistic and interdependent epistemological frameworks.

**Chiara Baldini** is an independent researcher from Florence, Italy. Her focus is the evolution of the ecstatic cult in the West, particularly in ancient Greece and Rome. She wrote "Dionysus Returns: Contemporary Tuscan Trancers and Euripides's *The Bacchae*" featured in *The Local Scenes and Global Culture of Psytrance* and coauthored "Dancing at the Crossroads of Consciousness: Techno-Mysticism, Visionary Arts and Portugal's Boom Festival" for the Brill *Handbook of New Religions and Cultural Production*. In 2010, 2012, 2014, and 2018 she coproduced Boom Festival's cultural area: Liminal Village. In 2015 and 2016 she inaugurated and cocurated the program of ConTent, the new cultural area at the Fusion Festival in Germany.

**Alana Bliss** has been exploring solutions to ecological and social issues, holistic wellness, and conscious birth for more than ten years. A permaculture teacher, home birth doula, and cofounder of the Fruition Center for Holistic Ecology in Costa Rica, she incorporates holistic wellness and permaculture in designing supportive relationships between humans and nature. Alana has had three empowering water home births and is raising her sons with an ecological and feminine awareness. She recently moved back to Minneapolis, Minnesota, to support her youngest son's journey with his special needs. There, she and her partner have started a business designing and implementing permaculture systems.

**Max Dashu** founded the Suppressed Histories Archives in 1970 to document global women's history. Over the years she has built an immense collection of images from which she has created 130 slideshows on female cultural heritages with attention to the patterns of conquest, female spheres of power, matricultures, medicine women, shamans, and witches. In 2016, Dashu published *Witches and Pagans: Women in European Folk Religion, 700–1100.* The work is the first volume of a sixteen-part series exploring two thousand years of women's history. The next volume, with a working title of *Pythias, Melissae, and Pharmakides,* will focus on Greece.

**Timothy Davis** graduated with a degree in philosophy and religion from the University of Kent in Canterbury, England, where he was president of the UKC Psychedelics Society from 2014 to 2017. He is currently training in psychoanalytic thought with the SITE for Contemporary Psychoanalysis, a training organization and a member of the Council for Psychoanalysis and Jungian Analysis College (CPJAC) of the United Kingdom Council for Psychotherapy (UKCP). As well, he is studying the social psychology of cults and social movements as part of his training as a psychoanalytic psychotherapist. Timothy is a unit manager for TTK Welfare in the United Kingdom, a mental health first-aid instructor, and a volunteer sitter for Kosmicare, a harm-reduction program at Portugal's Boom Festival.

**Nadia Erlam** studied issues of gender, policy, and inequality on the graduate level at the London School of Economics, and currently explores how these aspects intersect with psychedelic philosophy in her academic work. She was previously the head of inclusion and diversity at the Psychedelic Society, which she ran for more than two years. Her graduate school dissertation "Cognitive Dispossession: Entheogens,

Ecofeminism, and Neuroqueering Drug Policy" won the Breaking Convention 2017 Social Science Research Award. A condensed version has been presented at a number of events and conferences, most recently at the Theorising the Drug War Conference at the University of Essex in England.

**Stuart Griggs** is an artist of the imaginal. He works with interior narrative, symbol, and intention as a way of portraying the numinous visually. His work is an exploration into the nexus of drawing and digital art, synthesizing the two approaches into an idiosyncratic visual language. It is a journey into the creative process that immerses and probes into the psychic pool of collective archetypes. Multidimensional spaces and symbols weave together to explore and manifest the primordial and the transpersonal, resonating with a profound sense of awareness of our unity and interconnection. He has exhibited artwork and custom installation design worldwide.

**Kathleen (Kat) Harrison** is an ethnobotanist who loves to explore the relationship between plants, mushrooms, and human beings—particularly in the realms that are often hidden: cultural beliefs, personification of species, rituals of healing and initiation, vision-seeking modalities, and artistic creations that illustrate the plant-human relationship. Kat founded Botanical Dimensions (BD) in 1985, with her then-husband Terence McKenna. Kat has been the president and project director for BD throughout its history and continues to actively manage new and ongoing projects. She teaches courses in Hawaii, Northern California, and the Peruvian Amazon.

**Martina Hoffmann** is an artist who paints portals into inner and other worlds. She uses a visual language that is inspired by the realms of the imagination, shamanic journeys, and the dream state, which she believes to be indigenous to us all. Her great interest lies in creating awareness of our global oneness and universal interconnectedness. She has spoken on this subject and, as well, has taught painting workshops worldwide, together with her late husband, the fantastic realist Robert Venosa. She keeps a home and studio in the United States as well as in France. In France, her work is represented in the permanent collection of Naia Museum.

**Shonagh Home** is a shamanic therapist, teacher, author, and poet. Her specialized private sessions and retreats assist clients in breaking chronic, self-defeating patterns in order to move into empowered personal sovereignty. She is an international public speaker on the subject of visionary shamanic-spirit medicine, a voice for stewardship of the honeybees, and an expert on traditional foods. She is author of *Ix Chel Wisdom: 7 Teachings from the Mayan Sacred Feminine; Love and Spirit Medicine; Poetic Whispers from the Green Realms;* and *Honeybee Wisdom: A Modern Melissa Speaks.*

**Patricia 'Iolana**, Ph.D., is a writer, interfaith activist/educator, independent researcher, and an ordained pagan and interfaith minister. She holds a Ph.D. in literature, theology, and the arts. Her primary research focuses upon personal experiences with the Goddess, and she approaches this from a post-Jungian psychodynamic methodology called depth thealogy. Her publications include *Literature of the Sacred Feminine: Great Mother Archetypes and the Re-emergence of the Goddess in Western Traditions; Goddess Thealogy: An International Journal for the Study of the Divine Feminine; Goddess 2.0: Advancing a New Path Forward; Spaces of Spirituality;* and *Goddesses in Myth, History, and Culture.*

**Maria Christine Kvilhaug** is a Norwegian author and translator of Old Norse who writes in the English language. She was born in Oslo in 1975 and studied the history of religions, history, philosophy, and Old Norse philology (the study and interpretation of ancient languages) at the University of Oslo at the graduate level. She has written both fiction and nonfiction centering on the pre-Christian culture of Scandinavia, better known as the Viking Age. She has published with VDM Verlag, Whyte Tracks, and Createspace. Her most recent books are *The Poetic Edda: Six Cosmology Poems,* and *The Trickster and the Thundergod: Thor and Loki in Old Norse Myths.*

**Anna Luke** is a novelist and nonfiction writer. She was educated at Oxford University and the Royal Academy of Dramatic Arts, and earned a master's degree in creative writing at Birkbeck College, University of London. Her fiction, published as Anna Hope, includes the novels *Wake* and *The Ballroom.* Her books have been translated into twenty languages. She has been short-listed for New Writer of the Year at the National Book Awards and for the Prix Femina prize. She won the 2018 Grand Prix des Lectrices Elle and the 2018 Prix Charles Brisset—the latter an award from the French Psychiatric Association for best novel. She was recently a visiting fellow at the University of Essex where she lectured on Rebecca Solnit and the politics of uncertainty.

**David Luke**, Ph.D., completed his Ph.D. on the psychology of luck in 2007 and is now senior lecturer in psychology at the University of Greenwich, London, where he teaches an undergraduate course, the Psychology of Exceptional Human Experience. He is also guest lecturer in transpersonal psychology and consciousness studies at the University of Northampton in England. David is a cofounder and director of Breaking Convention, the biennial multidisciplinary conference on psychedelic consciousness.

**Christa Mackinnon** has been working internationally for twenty-five years as a psychologist, therapist, university lecturer, and trainer. In addition to her conventional qualifications she studied with Buddhist teachers in Asia, apprenticed with indigenous shamans in South America, and trained with international contemporary shamanic teachers. She is the author of three books, among them the 2012 groundbreaking publication *Shamanism and Spirituality in Therapeutic Practice* in which she combines contemporary therapeutic with ancient shamanic approaches.

**Caroline Manière** allows "the medicine women" to come to her, and through her to the world, to transmit their message, their wisdom, their knowledge, their experience, their power, their brilliance, and their vibration. They remind her of our connection with the Great Spirit and with Mother Earth. She paints on a copper foil surface because she loves its light, which illuminates these women and provides them with respect, sacredness, and majesty. Caroline listens to her heart and lets herself be guided. When she paints she listens to shamanic drumming, *icaros,* Amerindian Native songs, mantras, and other sounds of the world soul.

**Eleonora Molnar** is a health care systems planner, relational somatic psychotherapist, and an independent researcher with interests in public and primary health, ethics, policy reform, ecopsychology and consciousness studies. Eleonora's passion for women's roles and perspectives in the area of cognitive liberty led her to organize the Women's Visionary Congress salon at Simon Fraser University in Vancouver, British Columbia.

**Annie Oak** is the founder of the Women's Visionary Council (WVC), a nonprofit organization that produces the Women's Visionary Congress and other gatherings in the United States and Canada that presents the work of scholars, healers, activists, and artists who investigate nonordinary forms of consciousness. Annie is also the creator of the Full Circle Tea House, a mobile tea service that offers a place of rest, hydration, and integration. She is the coeditor of the *Manual of Psychedelic Support,* a guide to setting up and running compassionate care services for people who have challenging drug experiences at music festivals and other gatherings.

**Lorna Olivia O'Dowd**, Ph.D., is a psychotherapist and postdoctoral research fellow, specializing in psychosis, trauma, and gendered power relationships. She has published widely on adoption and fostering, non-normative family relationships, origin stories, and cults. She is interested in using visual research methods—photography, art, and film—to tell life stories. She has a master's degree in counseling and psychotherapy and a Ph.D. in psychology.

**Omolewa** is a loving mother, holistic massage therapist, doula, mid-wives' assistant, placenta alchemist, and urban gardener. A massage therapist of thirteen years, she has shared her gift of healing touch and Earth medicine with women, men, children, and elders in her community. Through this healing work she has cultivated her ancestral and spiritual gifts as womb worker, keeper of ancient plant medicine, sacred ceremonies, and women's blood mysteries.

**Maria Papaspyrou** is an accredited integrative psychotherapist and systemic family constellations facilitator. Her research interests have focused on the interface between entheogenic experiences and psychotherapy as well as the intersections between the archetypal feminine and altered states of consciousness. She has given talks and published articles on the sacramental and healing properties of entheogens supporting their reintroduction in psychotherapy. She is the cofounder of Club Imaginal, a lecture series in Brighton, England, and has developed T.R.I.P.P. network, a U.K.-wide psychedelic psychotherapy integration database.

**Jessica Perlstein** is a visionary artist based in San Francisco. Through her work, she has been able to deliver her messages of interconnectedness with everything in nature, and the ambition to inspire by living life as an example of being all that we can be. She carries a strong message of taking action toward respecting a thriving planet and the resulting reality we can create when we choose to be aware of our symbiotic relationship with nature.

**Tim Read**, MBBS, is a medical doctor and consultant psychiatrist based in London. He has trained with the Institute of Group Analysis (IGA) in psychoanalytic therapy and also trained in holotropic breathwork with the renowned transpersonal psychiatrist Stanislav Grof. He is a cofounder of the Institute of Transpersonal and Archetypal Studies (ITAS). Tim is also cofounder and commissioning editor of Muswell Hill Press. His book *Walking Shadows: Archetype and Psyche in Crisis and Growth* was published in 2014.

**Carl A. P. Ruck** is best known for his work with other scholars in mythology and religion on the sacred role of entheogens (a word that he coined), or psychoactive plants, as used in religious and shamanistic rituals. His focus has been on the use of entheogens in classical Western culture as well as their historical influence on modern Western religions. He currently teaches a mythology class at Boston University. He is the coauthor, together with Albert Hofmann and Gordon Wasson, of the seminal book *The Road to Eleusis: Unveiling the Secret of the Mysteries.*

**Amanda Sage** is an artist driven to reveal art's critical role in spiritual transformation. A celebrated visionary artist, she is a citizen of the world, exhibiting in galleries, art fairs, and festivals as well as lecturing and teaching worldwide at places such as the Chapel of Sacred Mirrors in New York, Paradise One in Australia, and the Vienna Academy of Visionary Art in Austria. She is passionate about artistic social experiments such as the Werkstätten und Kulturhaus (WUK) in Vienna, Burning Man, and bridging worlds for creative flourishing. When not traveling she can be found in her studios in Los Angeles and Colorado.

**Autumn Skye's** paintings gracefully weave together refined realism, iconic imagery, profound symbolism, and subtle geometries. She offers up her artwork as a mirror, both an intimate personal reflection and a grand archetypical revelation. Within these visions each viewer may recognize their own sacred heart and cosmic divinity. And, through this recognition, viewers may remember the innate grace that dwells within. Living on the beautiful Sunshine Coast of British Columbia, she considers herself immensely blessed and strives to support others through creative empowerment and the perpetuation of inspiration.

**Heidi Taillefer** was born, lives, and works in Montreal. Considered a self-taught artist, she nevertheless attended weekly art classes as a child before hitting upon her own unique style of art for which she is recognized today. She worked for fifteen years as a commercial illustrator while pursuing her fine-art career, each of which complemented each other professionally. Her work is an original creative fusion of classical figurative painting, surrealism, contemporary realism, and mythology, combined with popular figurative traditions ranging from Victorian romanticism to science fiction.

**Charlotte Walsh** is a lecturer in law at Leicester Law School, England, where she runs a course on criminology that is largely concerned with drug policy. The focus of her research is on the interface between psychedelics and the law, viewed from a liberal, human-rights-based perspective. She has published widely on this subject—in journals and edited collections—and also has been a regular speaker at psychedelic conferences. She is a member of the legal advisory committee of the International Center for Ethonobotanical Education Research and Service (ICEERS) and is on the steering committee of the Ayahuasca Defense Fund.

**Hannah Faith Yata** is a half Japanese, half American magical surrealist painter. She currently lives and works with her husband and fellow artist, Jean Pierre Arboleda, in Pennsylvania. Yata was born in 1989 in Douglasville, Georgia. She grew up in the southern United States and studied art at the University of Georgia. Upon graduation in 2012, she moved to New York City and began to exhibit internationally. Yata's work was commissioned by renowned rapper/musician B.o.B for album covers including *Psycadelik Thoughtz* and the series of mixtapes entitled *The Elements*. Her most recent solo exhibition was in 2016 at Corey Helford Gallery in Los Angeles.

# Bibliography

This bibliography encompasses works cited in the chapters as well as sources that comprised background research not specifically cited.

Adams, Cameron. "Cultural Variation in the Apparent Jungian Archetype of the Feminine in Psychedelic Personification." In *Proceedings of Daimonic Imagination: Uncanny Intelligence,* edited by Angela Voss and William Rowlandson. New Castle upon Tyne, U.K.: Cambridge Scholars Publishing, 2013.

———. "Healing and its Discontents: Reflections on Identity and Altered States of Consciousness by People Who Use Psychedelics as Medicine." Paper presented at Plants and Consciousness, the 32nd Annual Conference of the Society for the Anthropology of Consciousness, Boulder, Colo., February 9–12, 2012.

———. "Preliminary Findings of an Anthropological Investigation of Psychedelic Healing." Paper presented at Breaking Convention: A Multidisciplinary Conference on Psychedelic Consciousness, Canterbury, England, April 1–3, 2011.

Adams, Cameron, David King, and Anna Waldstein. "Being High and Being Healed: Reflections on Identity and Altered States of Consciousness by People Who Use Cannabis, Magic Mushrooms and other Psychedelics as Medicine." Paper presented at the 22nd Annual Conference of the European Society for Social Drug Research, Aarhus, Denmark, September 22–24, 2011.

All Party Parliamentary Group for Drug Policy Reform (APPG). *Guidance on Drug Policy: Interpreting the UN Drug Conventions.* London: APPG, 2015.

Alper, Kenneth R., Howarf F. Lotsof, and Charles D. Kaplan. "The Ibogaine Medical Subculture." *Journal of Ethnopharmacology* 115, no. 1 (2008): 9–24.

Amatrudo, Anthony, and Leslie William Blake. *Human Rights and the Criminal Justice System*. Abingdon, U.K.: Routledge, 2015.

Anzaldúa, Gloria. *Borderlands/La Frontera, the New Mestiza*. San Francisco: Aunt Lute Books, 1987.

Apawo Phiri, Isabel. *Women, Presbyterianism, and Patriarchy: Religious Experience of Chewa Women in Central Malawi*. Blantyre, Malawi: Kachere, 2000.

Arendt, Hannah. *The Life of the Mind*. New York: Harcourt, 1978.

Arieli, A., and S. Aychen. "Mental Disease Related to Belief in Being Possessed by the 'Zar' Spirit." *Harefuah* 126, no. 11 (1996): 636–42.

Aristotle. *The Metaphysics*. London: Penguin Classics, 1998.

Arvigo, Rosita. "Ix Chel: Maya Goddess of Medicine, Weaving and Childbirth." The Official Site of Dr. Dr. Rosita Arvigo, DN. Accessed August 10, 2016.

Ashworth, Andrew. *Principles of Criminal Law*. Oxford: Oxford University Press, 2009.

Ask Dr. Sears. "How to Reduce Pain during Childbirth." Accessed January 5, 2017.

Ayahuasca Community Awareness Canada. "Guillermo Arevalo Sexual Abuse Open Letter: Baris Betsa, Anaconda Cosmica, La Nueva Luz Cosmica Ayahuasca Centers." 2013. Reddit.

Ayahuasca Foundation. "Retreats." Accessed January 14, 2017.

Azevedo, Paulo Verlaine, Leonardo Caixeta, Laura Helena Silveir Andrade, and Isabel A. Bordin. "Attention Deficit/Hyperactivity Disorder Symptoms in Indigenous Children from the Brazilian Amazon." *Arquivos de Neuro-Psiquiatria* 68 (2010): 541–44.

Bacigalupo, Ana Mariella. *Shamans of the Foye Tree: Gender, Power, and Healing among Chilean Mapuche*. Austin, Tex.: University of Texas Press, 2007.

Baldini, Chiara. "Dionysus Returns: Contemporary Tuscan Trancers and Euripides's The Bacchae." In *The Local Scenes and Global Culture of Psytrance*, 170–85. London and New York: Routledge, 2010.

———. "The Politics of Ecstasy: The Case of the Bacchanalia Affair in Ancient Rome." In *Neurotransmissions: Essays on Psychedelics from Breaking Convention*, edited by Dave King, David Luke, Ben Sessa, Cameron Adams, and Aimee Tollan. London: Strange Attractor, 2015.

Baring, Anne. *The Dream of the Cosmos: A Quest for the Soul*. Dorset, England: Archive Publishing, 2013.

Beauchamp, Tom, and James F. Childress. *Principles of Biomedical Ethics*. Oxford: Oxford University Press, 2001.

Becker, Ernest. *The Denial of Death*. London: Souvenir Press, 2011.

Beiner, Alexander. "Psychedelic Mindfulness: Can Meditation Be Used in Conjunction with Psychedelics to Increase Self-awareness?" In *Neurotransmissions: Essays on Psychedelics from Breaking Convention*. London: Strange Attractor, 2015.

Béland, Daniel. "Gender, Ideational Analysis, and Social Policy." *Social Politics* 16, no. 4 (2009): 558–81.

Bennett, Jane. *Vibrant Matter: A Political Ecology of Things*. Durham, N.C.: Duke University Press, 2009.

Bernauer, James, and David Rasmussen. *The Final Foucault*. Cambridge, Mass.: MIT Press, 1988.

Bhabha, Homi K. *The Location of Culture*. Abingdon, U.K.: Routledge, 1994.

Bieberman, Lisa. *Session Games People Play: A Manual for the Use of LSD*. Cambridge, Mass.: Psychedelic Information Center, 1967.

Blackledge, Catherine. *The Story of V: A Natural History of Female Sexuality*. London: Weidenfield and Nicholson, 2003.

Bøgh, Birgitte. "In Life and Death: Choice and Conversion in the Cult of Dionysos." In vol. 16 of *Conversion and Initiation in Antiquity: Shifting Realities Creating Change (Early Christianity in the Context of Antiquity)*, edited by Birgitte Bøgh, 25–46. Bern, Switzerland: Peter Lang, 2014.

Bolen, Jean Shinoda. *Crossing to Avalon: A Woman's Midlife Pilgrimage*. New York: Harper Collins, 1994.

Bremmer, Jan. "Greek Maenadism Reconsidered." In vol. 55 of *Zeitschrift für Papyrologie und Epigraphik,* 267–86. Bonn, Germany: Dr. Rudolf Habelt, 1984.

———. "A Macedonian Maenad in Posidippus." In vol. 155 of *Zeitschrift für Papyrologie und Epigraphik,* 37–40. Bonn, Germany: Dr. Rudolf Habelt, 2006.

Brown, Ray. A. "Angels and Elves, Archetypes and Aliens: Anomalous Encounter Experiences Viewed through a Depth Psychological Lens." Ph.D. diss., Pacifica Graduate Institute, Santa Barbara, Calif., 2008.

Buck, Adriaan de. *The Egyptian Coffin Texts 1: Texts of Spells 1–75*. Volume 34.

Chicago: Oriental Institute Publications at the University of Chicago Press, 1935.

Buckley, Sarah J. "Hormones in Labour & Birth—How Your Body Helps You." BellyBelly website. Updated December 8, 2014.

Bugge, Sophus. *SÆMUNDAR EDDA HINS FRÓDA—Norrøn Fornkvædi-Islandsk Samling av Folkelige Oldtidsdigte om Nordens Guder og Heroer.* Rev. ed. Oslo: Universitetsforlaget, 1965. First edition published in 1867.

Burkert, Walter. *Ancient Mystery Cults.* Cambridge, Mass., and London: Harvard University Press, 1987.

Butler, Judith. *Bodies That Matter: On the Discursive Limits of Sex.* Abingdon, U.K.: Routledge, 1993.

———. *Gender Trouble: Feminism and the Subversion of Identity.* New York and Abingdon, U.K.: Routledge, 1990.

———. *Gender Trouble: Feminism and the Subversion of Identity.* New York: Taylor & Francis, 2006.

Byock, Jesse L. *The Saga of King Hrolf Kraki.* Harmondsworth, U.K.: Penguin, 1998.

Campbell, Joseph, Bill Moyers, and Betty Sue Flowers. *The Power of Myth.* New York: Anchor Books, 1991.

Cancer Research U.K. website. "New Study Suggests Alcohol Promotes Breast Tumour Growth." May 3, 2007.

Carey, Caroline. "The Embodied Shamanic Journey." *Sesame Journal* 19 (Spring 2014).

Carhart-Harris, Robin L., Mark Bolstridge, James Rucker, Camilla M. J. Day, David Erritzoe, Mendel Kaelen, Michael Bloomfield, James A. Rickard, Ben Forbes, Amanda Fielding, David Taylor, Steve Pilling, Valerie H. Curran, and David J. Nutt. "Psilocybin with Psychological Support for Treatment-Resistant Depression: An Open-Label Feasibility Study." *Lancet Psychiatry* 3, no. 7 (July 2016): 619–27.

Cartwright, Samuel. A. "Diseases and Peculiarities of the Negro Race." In *De Bow's Review (XI)* (1851), edited by J. D. B. De Bow. Accessed January 19, 2018 at PBS website. *Africans in America* series. Historical Document in Resource Bank."

Casimiro, Jesuita Natalia Pineda. "Dona Julia Julieta Casimiro." *BOMB Magazine* website (Winter 2007).

Casimiro, Julieta. "Julieta Casimiro." (Interview) By Joanna Harcourt-Smith. *Future Primitive* podcast. (December 10, 2010).

Castrodale, Mark Anthony. "Mad Matters: A Critical Reader in Canadian Mad Studies." *Scandinavian Journal of Disability Research* 17, no. 3 (2014): 284–86.

Cheater, Angela P. "The Role and Position of Women in Pre-Colonial Zimbabwe." *Zambezia* 13, no. 2 (1986): 65–79.

Christ, Carol P. "A New Definition of Patriarchy: Control of Women's Sexuality, Private Property, and War." *Feminist Theology* 24, no. 3 (2016): 214–25.

Cohen, Bruce M. Z. "Passive-Aggressive: Māori Resistance and the Continuance of Colonial Psychiatry in Aotearoa New Zealand." *Disability and the Global South* 1, no. 2 (2014): 319–39.

Conway, Janet. "Analyzing Hegemonic Masculinities in the Anti-Globalization Movement(s)." *International Feminist Journal of Politics* 13, no. 2 (2011): 225–30.

Corbin, Michelle. "Facing Our Dragons: Spiritual Activism, Psychedelic Mysticism and the Pursuit of Opposition." *Human Architecture: Journal of the Sociology of Self-Knowledge* 4, no. 3 (2006): 239–47.

Curott, Phyllis. *Book of Shadows: A Modern Woman's Journey into the Wisdom of Witchcraft and the Magic of the Goddess.* New York: Broadway Books, 1998.

Czaplicka, Maria Antonina. *Aboriginal Siberia: A Study in Social Anthropology.* Oxford: Clarendon Press, 1914.

Dashu, Max. "A Gallery of Toxic and Pornified 'Goddesses.'" *Velada,* blog by Max Dashu. April 24, 2011a.

———. "A Non-definition of Shaman." 2011b. *Velada,* blog by Max Dashu.

———. "The Nyabingi Oracles." *Suppressed Histories.* 2007.

———. "Pomo Dreamers and Doctors." *Source Memory.* 2010a.

———. "Shaman, Samaan, S'aman." *Source Memory.* 2010b.

———. *Witches and Pagans: Women in European Folk Religion, 700–1100.* Richmond, Calif.: Veleda Press, 2016.

———. "Woman Shaman: The Ancients." *Suppressed Histories.* 2013.

Daviter, Falk. *Policy Framing in the European Union.* New York: Palgrave MacMillan, 2011.

Deikman, Arthur J. *The Wrong Way Home: Uncovering the Patterns of Cult Behavior in American Society.* Boston: Beacon Press, 1994.

Delcourt, Marie. *Hermaphrodite: Myths and Rites of the Bisexual Figure in*

*Classical Antiquity* London: Studio Books, 1961 (translated from the French 1956 edition).

Deleuze, Gilles. *A Thousand Plateaus: Capitalism and Schizophrenia.* Minneapolis, Minn.: University of Minnesota Press, 1987.

Derrida, Jacques, and David Wills. "The Animal That Therefore I Am (More to Follow)." *Critical Inquiry* 28, no. 2 (Winter 2002): 369–418.

Devenot, Neşe. "Psychedelics and Identity Politics." *Psymposia* (2016a).

———. "Psychedelics and Identity Politics: Final Thoughts." *Psymposia* (2016b).

Devereux, Georges. *Baubo, la vulve mythique.* Paris: Édition Payot, 2011 (originally published in 1983).

Diószegi, Vilmos. *Tracing Shamans in Siberia: The Story of an Ethnographical Research Expedition.* Oosterhout, the Netherlands: Anthropological Publications, 1968.

Dobkin de Rios, Marlene. *Hallucinogens: Cross-Cultural Perspectives.* Long Grove, Ill.: Waveland Press, 1990.

———. "Twenty-Five Years of Hallucinogenic Studies in Cross-Cultural Perspective." *Anthropology of Consciousness* 4, no. 1 (1993): 1–8.

Dodds, Eric R. Introduction to *The Bacchae,* by Euripides, xi–lvi. Oxford: Oxford University Press, 1960.

———. *The Greeks and the Irrational.* Berkeley and Los Angeles: University of California Press, 2004. (Originally published in 1951.)

Douzinas, Costas. *The End of Human Rights: Critical Legal Thought at the Turn of the Century.* Oxford: Hart Publishing, 2000.

Echevarría, Nicolás. *Maria Sabina: Mujer Espiritu (Spirit Woman).* 1979. Youtube video translated by Max Dashu. Accessed November 13, 2017. No longer available.

Eggen, Erik. *Snorre Sturluson: Den yngre Edda.* Oslo, Norway: Det Norske Samlaget, 1978.

Ehrenreich, Barbara. *Dancing in the Streets: A History of Collective Joy.* New York: Metropolitan Books, 2007.

Eisenstein, Charles, "Psychedelics and Systems Change." *MAPS Bulletin* XXV1, no. 1 (2016): 4–6.

Eisler, Riane. *The Chalice and the Blade: Our History, Our Future.* New York: HarperCollins, 2011.

Eliade, Mircea. *Shamanism: Archaic Techniques of Ecstasy,* Princeton, N.J.:

Princeton University Press, 1964, 1972. Both editions are cited in various chapters of this book.

———. *Zalmoxis: The Vanishing God: Comparative Studies in the Religion and Folklore of Dacia and Eastern Europe.* Chicago: University of Chicago Press, 1972 (translated from the French edition of 1970).

Elton, Oliver. *Saxo Grammaticus: The Danish Histoy Books I–IX.* London: Norroena Society, 1905.

Enright, Michael. *Lady with a Mead Cup: Ritual, Prophecy and Lordship in the European Warband from La Téne to the Viking Age.* Great Britain: Four Courts Press, 1996.

Erickson, Susan N. "'Twirling Their Long Sleeves, They Dance Again and Again': Jade Plaque Sleeve Dancers of the Western Han Dynasty." *Ars Orientalis* 24 (1994).

Eskeland, Severin. *Eiriks saga rauða/Soga om Eirik Raude: Gamalnorsk Grunntekst og Nynorsk umsetjing Gamalnorske Bokverk 2.* Oslo, Norway: Samlaget, 1907.

Estés, Clarissa Pinkola. *Women Who Run with the Wolves: Contacting the Power of the Wild Woman.* London: Rider, 1992.

Estrada, Álvaro. *Vida de Maria Sabina: La sabia de los hongos.* Mexico: Siglo XXI Editores, 1977.

———. *María Sabina: Her Life and Chants.* Translated by H. Munn. Santa Barbara, Calif.: Ross-Erikson, 1981.

Euripides. *The Bacchae.* Translated and with an introduction by William Arrowsmith. Chicago: University of Chicago Press, 1994.

———. *The Bacchae of Euripides.* Translated by Gilbert Murray. London: George Allen, 1906.

Evans, Arthur. *The God of Ecstasy: Sex Roles and the Madness of Dionysos.* New York: St. Martin's Press, 1988.

Fadiman, Anne. *The Spirit Catches You and You Fall Down: A Hmong Child, Her American Doctors, and the Collision of Two Cultures.* New York: Overseas Editions, 2012.

Feeney, Kevin. "Peyote, Race, and Equal Protection in the United States." In *Prohibition, Religious Freedom, and Human Rights: Regulating Traditional Drug Use,* edited by Beatriz Caiuby Labate and Clancy Cavnar. London: Springer, 2014.

Feeney, Kevin, and Beatriz Caiuby Labate. "The Expansion of Brazilian Ayahuasca Religions: Law, Culture and Locality." In *Prohibition, Religious*

*Freedom, and Human Rights: Regulating Traditional Drug Use*, edited by Beatriz Caiuby Labate and Clancy Cavnar. London: Springer, 2014.

Fernandez, James W. *Bwiti: An Ethnography of the Religious Imagination in Africa*. Princeton, N.J.: Princeton University Press, 1982.

Fotiou, Evgenia. "Encounters with Sorcery: An Ethnographers Account." *Anthropology and Humanism* 35, no. 2 (2010): 193–202.

———. "From Medicine Men to Day Trippers: Shamanic Tourism in Iquitos, Peru." Ph.D. diss., University of Wisconsin–Madison, Madison, Wisc., 2010. Available on the Núcleo de Estudos Interdisciplinares sobre Psicoativos website.

Foucault, Michele. *El nacimiento de la clínica: una arqueología de la mirada médica* [The Birth of the Clinic: An Archaeology of Medical Perception]. Madrid, Spain: Siglo XXI, 2007.

———. *Madness and Civilization*. New York: Vintage Books, 1965.

Frazer, James George. *The Golden Bough: A Study in Magic and Religion*. New York: Simon & Shuster, 1996.

Friend, John M. "The Biopolitics of Policy-Making: Medical Activism in the Century of the Brain." *New Political Science* 36, no. 1 (2014): 32–51.

Fry, Jane, and Robert Bogdan. *Being Different: The Autobiography of Jane Fry*. London: John Wiley and Sons, 1974.

Geertz, Clifford. "Religion as a Cultural System." In *Anthropological Approaches to the Study of Religion,* edited by Michael Banton, 1–46. New York: Praeger, 1966.

Gelfer, Joseph. "Entheogenic Spirituality and Gender in Australia." *Paranthropology: Journal of Anthropological Approaches to the Paranormal* 3, no. 3 (2012): 22–33.

Geoffrey, Martin, and Ann Williams. *Domesday Book: A Complete Translation*. London: Penguin Classics, 2003.

Gershman, Carl. "Psychiatric Abuse in the Soviet Union." *Society* 21, no. 5 (July–August 1984): 54–59.

Gieser, Suzanne. *The Innermost Kernel: Depth Psychology and Quantum Physics. Wolfgang Pauli's Dialogue with C. G. Jung*. New York: Springer, 2005.

Gilbert, Jane. "Responding to Mental Distress in the Third World: Cultural Imperialism or the Struggle for Synthesis?" *Development in Practice* 9, no. 3 (1999): 287–95.

Gilmore, David. *Manhood in the Making: Cultural Concepts of Masculinity*. New Haven, Conn.: Yale University Press, 1990.

Goldenberg, Naomi R. *Resurrecting the Body*. New York: Crossroad, 1993.

Goody, Jack. "Inheritance, Property and Marriage in Africa and Eurasia." *Sociology* 3 (1969): 55–76.

Goody, Jack, and Joan Buckley. "Inheritance and Women's Labour in Africa." *Africa: Journal of the International African Institute* 4, no. 2 (1973): 108–21.

Gozdecka, Dorota A. "Identity, Subjectivity and the Access to the Community of Rights." *Social Identities* 21, no. 4 (2015): 305–11.

Grant, Bridget F., Patricia S. Chou, Tulshi D. Saha, Roger P. Pickering, Bradley T. Kerridge, W. June Ruan, Boji Huang, Jeesun Jung, Haitao Zhang, Amy Fan, and Deborah S. Hasin. "Prevalence of 12-Month Alcohol Use, High-Risk Drinking, and DSM-IV Alcohol Use Disorder in the United States, 2001–2002 to 2012–2013: Results from the National Epidemiologic Survey on Alcohol and Related Conditions." *JAMA Psychiatry* 74, no. 9 (2017): 911–23.

Gregor, Thomas. *Anxious Pleasure: The Sexual Lives of Amazonian Peoples*. Chicago: University of Chicago Press, 1985.

Griffiths, Jay. *Pip Pip: A Sideways Look at Time*. London: Penguin, 2000.

Griffiths, Roland R., Matthew W. Johnson, William A. Richards, Brian D. Richards, Una McCann, and Robert Jesse. "Psilocybin Occasioned Mystical-Type Experiences: Immediate and Persisting Dose-Related Effects." *Psychopharmacology (Berl)* 218, no. 4 (2011): 649–65.

Griffiths, Roland R., William A. Richards, Una McCann, and Robert Jesse. "Psilocybin Can Occasion Mystical-Type Experiences Having Substantial and Sustained Personal Meaning and Spiritual Significance." *Psychopharmacology (Berl)* 187, no. 3 (2006): 268–83.

Grob, Charles S., Alicia L. Danforth, Gurpreet S. Chopra, Marycie Hagerty, Charles R. McKay, Adam L. Halberstadt, and George R. Greer. "Pilot Study of Psilocybin Treatment for Anxiety in Patients with Advanced-Stage Cancer." *Archives of General Psychiatry* 68, no. 1 (2011): 71–78.

Grof, Stanislav. *Beyond the Brain: Birth, Death and Transcendence in Psychotherapy*. Albany: State University of New York Press, 1985.

———. "The Great Awakening: Psychology, Philosophy, and Spirituality in LSD Psychotherapy." In *Higher Wisdom: Eminent Elders Explore the Continuing Impact of Psychedelics,* edited by Roger Walsh and Charles Grob. Albany: State University of New York Press, 2005.

———. *When the Impossible Happens: Adventures in Non-Ordinary Realities*. Boulder, Colo.: Sounds True, 2006.

Gutmann, Matthew C. "Trafficking in Men: The Anthropology of Masculinity." *Annual Review of Anthropology* 26 (1997): 385–409.

Haden, Mark, Brian Emerson, and Kenneth W. Tupper. "A Public-Health-Based Vision for the Management and Regulation of Psychedelics." *Journal of Psychoactive Drugs* 48, no. 4 (2016): 243–52.

Haft, Nina Otis. "Initiation into Ecstasy: An Interview with Hiah Park—Korean Mudang." *Global Shamanic Healing Arts. Hiah Park. Korean Shamane.* (1992).

Halpern, John H., Andrea R. Sherwood, James I. Hudson, Deborah Yurgelun-Todd, and Harrison G. Pope. "Psychological and Cognitive Effects of Long-Term Peyote Use among Native Americans." *Biological Psychiatry* 58, no. 8 (2005): 624–31.

Haraway, Donna. "Situated Knowledges: The Science Question in Feminism and the Privilege of Partial Perspective." *Feminist Studies* 14, no. 3 (1988): 575–99.

———. *When Species Meet.* Posthumanities vol. 3. Minneapolis: University of Minnesota Press, 2007.

Harner, Michael J. *Hallucingens and Shamanism.* Oxford: Oxford University Press, 1973.

Harris, Marvin. *Culture People Nature: An Introduction to General Anthropology.* 7th ed. New York: Longman, 1997.

Harris, Sam. *Free Will.* New York: The Free Press, 2012.

Harrison, Jane Ellen. *Prolegomena to the Study of Greek Religion.* Princeton, N.J.: Princeton University Press, 1991. (Originally published in 1903.)

———. *Themis: A Study of the Social Origins of Greek Religion.* Cambridge, U.K.: Cambridge University Press, 2010. (Originally published in 1912.)

Harvey, Graham. *Contemporary Paganism: Religions of the Earth from Druids and Witches to Heathens and Ecofeminists.* New York: New York University Press, 2011.

Hays, Terence E. "'Myths of Matriarchy' and the Sacred Flute Complex of the Papua New Gunnea Highlands." In *Myths of Matriarchy Reconsidered,* edited by Deborah Gewertz, 98–120. Sydney, Australia: University of Sydney, 1988.

Heick, William, and Gordon Mueller. *Pomo Shaman.* (1953 Film). Available at the American Indian Film Gallery, University of Arizona. Accessed November 13, 2017.

Hemmings, Clare. *Why Stories Matter: The Political Grammar of Feminist Theory.* Durham, N.C.: Duke University Press, 2011.

Henderson, Jefferey. *The Maculate Muse: Obscene Language in Attic Comedy.* New Haven, Conn.: Yale University Press, 1975.

Henrichs, Albert. "Changing Dionysiac Identities." In *Jewish and Christian Self-Definition*, edited by Ben Meyer and E. P. Sanders. Philadelphia: Fortress Press, 1982.

Herdt, Gilbert, ed. *Third Sex, Third Gender: Beyond Sexual Dimorphism in Culture and History.* Cambridge, Mass.: Zone Books, 1996.

Hill, Gareth S. *Masculine and Feminine: The Natural Flow of Opposites in the Psyche.* Boulder, Colo.: Shambhala Publications, 1992.

Hillman, D. C. A. *The Chemical Muse: Drug Use and the Roots of Western Civilization.* New York: St. Martin's Press, 2008.

Holland, Julie. "Out Yourself." *Psymposia.* May 25, 2016.

Hollander, Lee M. *The Poetic Edda.* Austin: University of Texas Press, 1962.

Holmes, Oliver Wendall. "Autocrat of the Breakfast Table." *The Atlantic Monthly* 2, (November 1858): 496–506.

Home, Shonagh. *Love and Spirit Medicine.* New York: Turning Stone Press, 2013.

hooks, bell. *The Will to Change: Men, Masculinity, and Love.* New York: Atria Books, 2003.

Hreinson, Viðar, ed. *The Complete Sagas of the Icelanders.* Vols. I–V. Reykjavik, Iceland: Leifur Eiríkson, 1997.

Humphrey, Caroline. *Marx Went Away—But Karl Stayed Behind.* Ann Arbor: University of Michigan Press, 1998.

Hunter, Jack. "Beyond Castandeda: A Brief History of Psychedelics in Anthropology." In *Neurotransmissions: Essays on Psychedelics from Breaking Convention,* edited by Dave King, David Luke, Ben Sessa, Cameron Adams, and Aimee Tollan. London: Strange Attractor, 2015.

Ingraham, Christopher. "Mexico's Supreme Court Rules that Smoking Pot Is a Fundamental Human Right." *Washington Post,* November 5, 2015.

Irigaray, Luce. *This Sex Which Is Not One.* Ithaca, N.Y.: Cornell University Press, 1985.

Jacobson, Esther. *The Deer Goddess of Ancient Siberia: A Study in the Ecology of Belief.* Leiden, the Netherlands: Brill, 1993.

Jónsson, Finnur, ed. *EDDA Snorra Sturlusonar.* Reykjavik, Iceland: Mál og Menning, 1907.

Joseph, Ameil J. "The Necessity of an Attention to Eurocentrism and Colonial Technologies: An Addition to Critical Mental Health Literature." *Disability & Society* 1, no. 21 (2015): 1021–41.

Jung, Carl Gustav. *The Archetypes and the Collective Unconscious.* 2nd ed. Abingdon, U.K.: Routledge, 1968.

———. *Memories, Dreams, Reflections.* London: Flamingo, 1983.

———. *Memories, Dreams, Reflections.* London: Fontana Press, 1995.

Jung, Carl Gustav, and Wolfgang Ernst Pauli. *The Interpretation of Nature and the Psyche.* New York: Pantheon Books, 1955.

Kapferer, Bruce. *A Celebration of Demons.* Bloomington: Indiana University Press, 1983.

Keating, AnaLouise. *The Gloria Anzaldúa Reader.* Durham, N.C.: Duke University Press, 2009.

———. "'I'm a Citizen of the Universe': Gloria Anzaldúa's Spiritual Activism as Catalyst for Social Change." *Feminist Studies* 34, no. 1/2 (2008): 53–69.

———. "Speculative Realism, Visionary Pragmatism, and Poet-Shamanic Aesthetics in Gloria Anzaldúa—and Beyond." *Women's Studies Quarterly* 40, no. 3/4 (2012): 51–69.

Keats, John. *The Complete Poetical Works and Letters of John Keats.* Boston: Houghton Mifflin, 1899.

Kerényi, Karl. *Dionysos: Archetypal Image of Indestructible Life.* Princeton, N.J.: Princeton University Press, 1996.

Kesler, L. K. "Altar'd [*sic*] States of Consciousness: Ritual Intoxication in the Boeotian Kabeirion and the Athenian Anthesteria Festival." Honors thesis, Emory University, Atlanta, Ga., 2012.

Kidd, Sue Monk. *The Dance of the Dissident Daughter: A Woman's Journey from Christian Tradition to the Sacred Feminine.* 10th ann. ed. San Francisco: Harper One, 2007.

Klapp, Edzard. "Raven's Bread and Other Manifestations of Fly Agaric in Classical and Biblical Literature." In *Entheogens and the Development of Culture: The Anthropology and Neurobiology of Ecstatic Experience,* edited by John A. Rush, 333–42. Berkeley: Atlantic Books, 2013.

Klein, Axel. "Framing the Chew: Narratives of Development, Drugs and Danger with Regard to Khat." In *Prohibition, Religious Freedom, and Human Rights: Regulating Traditional Drug Use,* edited by Beatriz Caiuby Labate and Clancy Cavnar. London: Springer, 2014.

Kofman, Sarah. "Beyond Aporia?" In *Post-Structuralist Classics,* edited by Andrew Benjamin, 7–45. Abingdon, U.K.: Routledge, 1988.

Kraemer, Ross Shepard. "Ecstasy and Possession: the Attraction of Women to the

Cult of Dionysus." *Harvard Theological Review* 72, no. 1/2 (1979): 55–80.

———. *Her Share of the Blessings: Women's Religions among Pagans, Jews and Christians in the Greco-Roman World*. Oxford: Oxford University Press, 1992.

Kvilhaug, Maria. *The Maiden with the Mead—A Goddess of Initiation Rituals in Old Norse Myths?* Oslo, Norway: University of Oslo, 2004.

———. *The Seed of Yggdrasill*. Helsinge, Denmark: Whyte Tracks Publishers, 2013.

———, trans. "Oddrunargrátr" and "Vǫluspá" by Sophus Bugge, 1867 in *Norroen fornkvaedi: islandsk samling af folkelige oltidsdigte om nordens guder og heroer, almindelig kaldet Saemundar Edda hins fróda, Medforfatter/ Bidragsyter*. Christiania, Noway: P. T. Malling, 1867.

Lane, Riki. "Trans as Bodily Becoming: Rethinking the Biological as Diversity, Not Dichotomy." *Hypatia* 24, no. 3 (2009): 136–57.

Lazar, Michelle M. "Performing State Fatherhood: The Remaking of Hegemony." In *Feminist Critical Discourse Analysis: Gender, Power and Ideology in Discourse,* edited by Michelle M. Lazar. Basingstroke, U.K.: Palgrave Macmillan, 2005.

Lebedev, Alexander V., Martin Lövdén, Gidon Rosenthal, Amanda Feilding, David J. Nutt, and Robin L. Carhart-Harris. "Finding the Self by Losing the Self: Neural Correlates of Ego Dissolution under Psilocybin." *Human Brain Mapping* 36, no. 8 (2015): 3137–53.

Lévi-Strauss, Claude. *Structural Anthropology*. New York: Basic Books, 1963.

Lewis, I. M., *Ecstatic Religion: Anthropological Study of Spirit Possession and Shamanism*. London: Penguin, 1971.

Loftsdóttir, Kristin. "Never Forgetting? Gender and Racial-Ethnic Identity during Fieldwork." *Social Anthropology* 10, no. 3 (2002): 303–17.

Longden, Eleanor, Anna Madill, Mitch G. Waterman. "Dissociation, Trauma, and the Role of Lived Experience: Toward a New Conceptualization of Voice Hearing." *Psychological Bulletin* 138, no. 1 (2011): 28–76.

Longwe, Sara Hlupekile. "Education for Women's Empowerment or Schooling for Women's Subordination?" In *Gender, Education, and Training,* edited by Caroline Sweetman, 19–26. Oxford: Oxfam, 1998.

Luff, Ellen. "The Drug War and Patriarchy." *Off Our Backs* 22, no. 6 (1992): 7, 15.

Mackinnon, Christa. *Shamanism and Spirituality in Therapeutic Practice*. London: Jessica Kingsley Publishers, 2012.

Maroukis, Thomas C. *The Peyote Road: Religious Freedom and the Native American Church*. Norman: University of Oklahoma Press, 2012.

Marshall, Jill. *Human Rights Law and Personal Identity*. Abingdon, U.K.: Routledge, 2014.

———. *Personal Freedom through Human Rights Law?: Autonomy, Identity and Integrity under the European Convention on Human Rights*. Leiden, the Netherlands: Martinus Nijhoff Publishers, 2009.

Martin, James. *Drugs on the Dark Net: How Cryptomarkets are Transforming the Global Trade in Illicit Drugs*. Basingstoke, U.K.: Palgrave Macmillan, 2014.

Martínez-Hernáez, Angel. *What's behind the Symptom? On Psychiatric Observation and Anthropological Understanding*. Amsterdam: Harwood Academic, 2000.

Maslow, Abram Harold. *The Psychology of Science: A Reconnaissance*. New York: Harper and Row, 1966.

McKenna, Terence. *Dreaming Awake at the End of Time*. 1998 video. Uploaded to Youtube on September 17, 2012, by nndmtube.

———. *The Human Future*. 2010 video. Uploaded to vimeo on July 23, 2010 by Mimetic Mind.

McKenna, Terence, and Riane Eisler. *Man and Woman at the End of History*. Terence McKenna Archive. 1988 video. Uploaded to Youtube on August 4, 2012, by Deus Ex McKenna.

McKenna, Terence, and L. Hagerty, producer. "The Importance of Psychedelics." *Number 117; Psychedelic Salon* podcast. November 29, 2007.

Meade, Margaret. *Sex and Temperament in Three Primitive Societies*. New York: William Morrow, 1963.

Medco Health Solutions. "America's State of Mind: A Report by Medco." 2011. World Health Organization website.

Mena, Fernanda, and Richard Hobbs. "Narcophobia: Drugs Prohibition and the Generation of Human Rights Abuses." *Trends in Organised Crime* 13 (2010): 60–74.

Merchant, Carolyn. *The Death of Nature: Women, Ecology and the Scientific Revolution*. New York: HarperCollins, 1990.

Mikalsen, Roar. *To End a War: A Short History of Human Rights, The Rule of Law, and How Drug Prohibition Violates the Bill of Rights*. Scotts Valley, Calif.: CreateSpace, 2015.

Mill, John Stuart. *On Liberty*. London: Longman, Rees, Orme, Brown, Green, and Longman, 1865.

Miller, Daniel. "Why I Came Out of the Psychedelic Closet." April 15, 2016. *Psymposia*.

"Misuse of Drugs Act (1971)." The National Archives on Behalf of Her Majesty's Government website.

Montagne, Michael. "The Metaphorical Nature of Drugs and Drug Taking." *Social Science & Medicine* 16, no. 4 (1988): 417–24.

Moore, David. "Erasing Pleasure from Public Discourse on Illicit Drugs: On the Creation and Reproduction of an Absence." *International Journal of Drug Policy* 19, no. 5 (2008): 353–58.

Moore, Henrietta L. *A Passion for Difference: Essays in Anthropology and Gender*. Bloomington: Indiana University Press, 1994.

Morris, David B. "Un-Forgetting Asclepius: An Erotics of Illness." *New Literary History* 38, no. 3 (2007): 419–41.

Mountain Girl [Carolyn Garcia]. *The Primo Plant: Growing Sinsemilla Marijuana*. Berkeley: Leaves of Grass/Wingbow Press, 1977.

Muller, R. T. "The Heart Is a Drum Machine: Drumming as Therapy." *Psychology Today,* 2015.

Multidisciplinary Association for Psychedelic Studies. "Statement Regarding the Ethnobotanical Stewardship Council (ESC)." Accessed on February 2, 2017.

Murphy, Yolanda, and Robert F. Murphy. *Women of the Forest*. New York: Columbia University Press, 1985.

Mylonas, George Emmanuel. *Eleusis and the Eleusinian Mysteries*. Princeton, N.J.: Princeton University Press, 1961.

Narby, Jeremy. *The Cosmic Serpent: DNA and the Origins of Knowledge*. London: Phoenix, 1998.

National Museum of Denmark, "A Seeress from Fyrkat?" The Viking Age Shortcut/Religion, Magic, Death and Rituals. Accessed November 1, 2016.

NeuroscienceNews. "Magic Mushrooms' Effects Illuminated in Brain Imaging Studies." January 23, 2012.

Nichols, David E. "When Will Medicinal Magic Mushrooms Be Legalized?" *Reset.me*. June 17, 2014.

Nietzsche, Friedrich Wilhelm. *The Birth of Tragedy*. Oxford: Oxford University Press, 2000.

Nikhilananda, Swami, trans. *The Gospel of Sri Ramakrishna*. New York: Ramakrishna-Vivekananda Center, 1942.

Noble, Vicky. *The Double Goddess: Women Sharing Power*. Rochester, Vt.: Bear & Co., 2003.

Nordin, Andreas. *Jordanes: Getica: Om goternas ursprung och bedrifter*. Stockholm, Sweden: Atlantis, 1997.

Nowhere Girl. "Remembering Miss Ramstein: Feminism and LSD." *DoseNation*. September 21, 2007.

Nutt, David J. *Drugs without the Hot Air*. Cambridge: UIT Cambridge Ltd., 2012.

Nutt, David J., Leslie A. King, and Lawrence D. Phillips. "Drug Harms in the UK: A Multicriteria Decision Analysis." *Lancet* 376, issue 9752 (November 6–12, 2010): 1558–65.

Nuttall, Zelia. *The Fundamental Principles of Old and New World Civilizations: A Comparative Research Based on a Study of the Ancient Mexican Religious, Sociological and Calendrical Systems*. Cambridge, Mass.: Peabody Museum, 1901.

Oak, Annie. "Do Not Depend on Others to Keep You Safe: Knowledge Is Power in Visionary Ceremonies." *Women's Visionary Council*. January 21, 2015.

O'Mara, Peggy. *Mothering Magazine's Having a Baby, Naturally*. New York: Atria Books, 2003.

Ortner, Sherry B. "Is Female to Male as Nature Is to Culture?" In *Woman, Culture and Society*, edited by Michelle Zimbalist Rosaldo and Louise Lamphere, 67–87. Stanford, Calif.: Stanford University Press, 1974.

Osmond, Humphry. "A Review of the Clinical Effects of Psychotomimetic Agents." *Annals of the New York Academy of Sciences* 66, no. 3 (1957): 418–34.

Otto, Rudolph. *The Idea of the Holy*. Oxford: Oxford University Press, 1958.

Otto, Walter. *Dionysos: Myth and Cult*. Bloomington: Indiana University Press, 1965.

Palmer, Cynthia, and Michael Horowitz. *Sisters of the Extreme: Women Writing on the Drug Experience*. Rochester, Vt.: Park Street Press, 2000.

Pálsson, Hermann, and Paul Edwards. *Seven Viking Romances*. London: Penguin, 1985.

Papaspyrou, Maria. "On Integrating Numinous Experiences: A Case Study." *The Journal of Transpersonal Psychology* 7, no. 1 (2015): 54–64.

———. "In Search of the Philosopher's Stone." In *Neurotransmissions: Essays on Psychedelics from Breaking Convention,* edited by Dave King, David Luke, Ben Sessa, Cameron Adams, and Aimee Tollan. London: Strange Attractor, 2015.

Pardo, Bryce. "Cannabis Policy Reforms in the Americas: A Comparative Analysis of Colorado, Washington, and Uruguay." *International Journal of Drug Policy* 25 (2014): 727–35.

Parfitt, Tom. "Taking Drugs is a HUMAN RIGHT, MPs say—and Junkies Could Use Euro Laws to Avoid Jail." *Express,* August 19, 2015.

Peluso, Daniela. "Ayahuasca's Attractions and Distractions; Examining Sexual Seduction in Shaman-Participant Interactions." In *Ayahuasca Shamanism in the Amazon and Beyond,* edited by Beatriz Caiuby Labate and Clancy Cavnar. Oxford: Oxford University Press, 2014.

———. "Global Ayahuasca: An Entrepreneurial Ecosystem." In *The World Ayahuasca Diaspora: Reinventions and Controversies,* edited by Beatriz Caiuby Labate, Clancy Cavnar, and Alex K. Gearin. Abingdon, U.K.: Routledge, 2016.

Peschal, Keewaydinoquay. *The Miswedo in Anishinaabeg Life.* Verona, Italy: Stamperia Valdonega, 1984.

Petri, Giovanni, Paul Expert, F. Turkheimer, Robin L. Carhart-Harris, David J. Nutt, Peter J. Hellyer, and Francesco Vaccarino. "Homological Scaffolds of Brain Functional Networks." *Journal of the Royal Society Interface* 11, no. 101 (2014).

Philipps, Dave. "F.D.A. Agrees to New Trials for MDMA as Relief for PTSD Patients." *New York Times,* November 30, 2016.

Plato. *Meno and Other Dialogues.* Oxford: Oxford World's Classics, 2009.

———. *Phaedrus.* Translated with an introduction and commentary by R. Hackforth. Cambridge: Cambridge University Press, 1952.

Plumwood, Val. *Feminism and the Mastery of Nature.* Abingdon, U.K.: Routledge, 1993.

Plutarch. *On the Bravery of Women.* In vol. 3 of *Moralia.* Cambridge, Mass.: Loeb Classical Library, 1931. Accessed July 13, 2017 on Bill Thayer's website.

Puett, Michael, and Christine Gross-Loh. *The Path: What Chinese Philosophers Can Teach Us about the Good Life.* New York: Viking Penguin, 2016.

Putumayo, Antonio. "An Open Letter in Support of the Cofán People and against the Activities of Alberto José Varela." August 1, 2015.

Redmond, Layne. *When the Drummers Were Women*. New York: Three Rivers Press, 1997.

Regueiro, Javier. *Ayahuasca—Soul Medicine of the Amazon Jungle: A Comprehensive and Practical Guide*. Bloomington, Ind.: iUniverse, 2014.

Rich, Adrienne. *On Lies, Secrets, and Silence: Selected Prose 1966–1978*. New York: W. W. Norton, 1979.

Richardson, James. *Archbold: Criminal Pleading, Evidence and Practice 2016*. London: Sweet and Maxwell, 2015.

Rigoglioso, Marguerite. *Virgin Mother Goddesses of Antiquity*. New York: Palgrave Macmillan, 2010.

Riley, S., J. Thompson, and C. Griffin. "Turn On, Tune In, but Don't Drop Out: The Impact of Neo-Liberalism on Magic Mushroom Users' (In)ability to Imagine Collectivist Social Worlds." *International Journal of Drug Policy* 21 (2010): 445–51.

Ritter, M. "Ancient Wine Cellar Unearthed in Israel Shows Canaanites Enjoyed a Sophisticated Drink." Associated Press. November 22, 2013.

Rives, James B. *Tacitus, Cornelius Germania*. Oxford: Clarendon Press, 1999.

Robinson, Britany. "'It Was Crazy Sh*t': Ayahuasca, Vomiting and My Search for a Spiritual Experience." *Salon*. February 15, 2015.

Rose, Jacqueline. "Who Do You Think You Are?" *London Review of Books* 38, no. 9 (2016): 3–13.

Ross, Lily Kay. "I Survived Sexual Abuse in the Amazon and Victim Blame at Home." *Lily Kay Ross* blog. January 18, 2017.

Roth, Gabrielle. *Sweat Your Prayers: Movement as a Spiritual Practice*. New York: Tarcher/Putman, Penguin, 1999.

Rothenberg, Jerome, ed., and Alvaro Estrada, text and commentary. *Maria Sabina: Selections (Poets for the Millennium)*. Berkeley: University of California Press, 2003.

Ruane, Deirdre. "The Mystical Is Political: Festival Crowds, Peer Harm-Reduction and the Sociology of the Psychedelic Experience." In *Neurotransmissions: Essays On Psychedelics from Breaking Convention*, edited by Dave King, David Luke, Ben Sessa, Cameron Adams, and Aimee Tollan. London: Strange Attractor, 2015.

Ruck, Carl A. P. "Aristophanes' Parody of Socrates as a Pothead and the Spartan Warrior Cult of the Wolf." In *Seeking the Sacred with Psychoactive Sacraments: Chemical Paths to Spirituality and God*. Vol. 1, *History and*

*Practices,* edited by J. Harold Ellens, 75–91. Santa Barbara, Calif.: ABC-CLIO, 2014.

———. "The Cave of Euripides." In *Time and Mind: the Journal of Archeology, Consciousness and Culture.* Abingdon, U.K.: Routledge, 2015a.

———. "The Great God Sabazios and the Crab Dance in Athens." In *The Stone Mushrooms of Thrace.* (Bilingual ed., English and Greek), 193–220. Alexandroupoli, Greece: EKATAIOS, 2012.

———. *The Great Gods of Samothrace and the Cult of the Little People.* Berkeley: Regent Press, 2015b.

———. "Mushrooms and Philosophers: On Aristophanes and the Necromancy of Socrates." *Helios* 8, no. 2 (1981): 1–28.

———. "The Offerings from the Hyperboreans." *Journal of Ethnopharmacology* 8 (1983): 177–207.

———. "On the Sacred Names of Iamos and Ion: Ethnobotanical Referents in the Hero's Parentage." *Classical Journal* 71, no. 3 (1976): 235–52.

———. *Sacred Mushrooms of the Goddess: Secrets of Eleusis.* Berkeley: Ronin Publishing, 2006.

———. "The Wild and the Cultivated: Wine in Euripides' Bacchae." In *Persephone's Quest: Entheogens and the Origins of Religion,* 179–225. New Haven and London: Yale University Press, 1982.

Rudd, Rose A., Noah Aleshire, Jon E. Zibbell, and Matthew Gladden. "Increases in Drug and Opioid Overdose Deaths—United States, 2000–2014." CDC website. January 1, 2016.

Rush, Brian, et al. "Statement Critiquing the Ethnobotanical Stewardship Council (ESC)." December 22, 2014.

Rymland, Lizabeth. *Strange Evolutionary Flowers.* New York: Spuyten Duyvil, 2006.

Saint Louis, Catherine. "A Balm When You're Expecting: Sometimes Pot Does the Trick." *New York Times,* February 20, 2017.

Schmid, Janine Tatjana, Henrik Jungaberle, and Rolf Verres. "Subjective Theories about (Self) Treatment with Ayahuasca." *Anthropology of Consciousness* 21, no. 2 (2010): 188–204.

Schultes, Richard Evans, Albert Hofmann, and Christian Ratsch. *Plants of the Gods: Their Sacred, Healing, and Hallucinogenic Powers.* Rochester, Vt.: Healing Arts Press, 1979.

Schwarcz, Ben. "Finding Our Rhythm—Discovering Connection: The Magic of Drumming Therapy." Tapping Coach website. October 17, 2014.

Seidler, Victor J. *Rediscovering Masculinity: Reason, Language, and Sexuality.* Abingdon, U.K.: Routledge, 1989.

Serbonich, Andrea. "The Experience: I Took Ayahuasca in the Amazon." *Sakara.* February 26, 2016.

"Shamanism in Siberia." *Wikipedia.* Accessed November 16, 2017.

Sheldrake, Rupert. *The Presence of the Past: Morphic Resonance and the Habits of Nature.* London: Icon Books, 2011.

Short, April M. "A Feminist on a Mission to Introduce Women to Ayahuasca, the 'Cosmic Spirit.'" *Alternet.* March 11, 2016.

Shortall, Sarah. "Psychedelic Drugs and the Problem of Experience." *Past & Present* 222, no. 9 (2014): 187–206.

Shulgin, Alexander, and Ann Shulgin. *Pihkal: A Chemical Love Story.* Berkeley: Transform, 1991.

———. *Tihkal: The Continuation.* Berkeley: Transform, 1997.

Shuttleworth, Russell, Nikki Wedgwood, and Nathan J. Wilson. "The Dilemma of Disabled Masculinity." *Men and Masculinities* 15, no. 2 (2012): 174–94.

Sinha, Mrinalini. *Colonial Masculinity: The "Manly Englishman" and the "Effeminate Bengali" in the Late Nineteenth Century.* Manchester, U.K.: Manchester University Press, 1995.

Smart, Carol. *Sociology of Law and Crime: Feminism and the Power of Law.* Abingdon, U.K.: Routledge, 2002.

Soirila, Ukri. "Smothered to (Un)death: on Identity and the European Court of Human Rights as an Administrator of Human Life." *Social Identities* 21, no. 4 (2015): 345–58.

Solnit, Rebecca. *Hope in the Dark: Untold Histories, Wild Possibilities.* Edingburgh: Canongate Books, 2016.

———. *Men Explain Things To Me.* London: Granta Books, 2014.

Starbird, Margaret. *The Goddess in the Gospels: Reclaiming the Sacred Feminine.* Rochester, Vt.: Bear & Company, 1998.

Starhawk. *The Spiral Dance: A Rebirth of the Ancient Religion of the Great Goddess.* San Francisco: Harper & Row, 1979.

Stevenson, Betsey, and Justin Wolfers. "The Paradox of Declining Female Happiness." *American Economic Journal: Economic Policy* 1, no. 2 (2009): 190–225.

Stone, Deborah A. "Causal Stories and the Formation of Policy Agendas." *Political Science Quarterly* 104 (1989): 281–300.

Strassman, Rick. *DMT: The Spirit Molecule*. Rochester, Vt.: Park Street Press, 2001.

Stuart, George Arthur. *Chinese Materia Medica: Vegetable Kingdom*. Taipei, Taiwan: Southern Materials Center, 1987.

Sturluson, Snorri. "Ynglinga saga 4" in *Sturluson, Snorri: Ynglinga saga 4, Heimskringla, Norges kongesagaer*. Translated by Anne Holtsmark and Didrik Arup Seip. Oslo: Gyldendal Norsk Forlag A/S, 1979.

Sullivan, Lynne P. "Those Men in the Mounds: Gender, Politics, and Mortuary Practices in Late Prehistoric Eastern Tennessee." In *Archaeological Studies of Gender in the Southeastern United States,* edited by Jane. M. Eastman and Christopher. B. Rodning, 1–126. Gainesville: University Press of Florida, 2001.

Teafaerie. "Coming Out in Solidarity." *Psymposia*. June 21, 2016.

Tedlock, Barbara. *The Woman in the Shaman's Body*. New York: Bantam Books, 2005.

Thoumi, Francisco E. "Marijuana in the United States and the International Drug Control Regime: Why What Is Promoted Abroad Is Not Applied at Home." *Crime, Law, Social Change* 61 (2014): 273–85.

Transform Drug Policy Foundation. *The Alternative World Drug Report: Counting the Costs of the War on Drugs*. Bristol, England: Transform Drug Policy Foundation, 2016.

———. *Cannabis Social Clubs in Spain: Legalization without Commercialization*. Bristol, England: Transform Drug Policy Foundation, 2015.

———. *Ending the War on Drugs: How to Win the Global Drug Policy Debate*. Bristol, England: Transform Drug Policy Foundation, 2014.

Treu, Tommaso. "Astronomy Talk. The Remaining 95 Percent: Insights from Gravitational Lensing." Video available at W. M. Keck Observatory website. Accessed August 7, 2017.

Tucker, John, ed. *Sagas of the Icelanders*. New York: Garland Publishers, 1989.

Tupper, Kenneth W. "Ayahuasca Healing beyond the Amazon: The Globalization of a Traditional Indigenous Entheogenic Practice." *Global Networks* 9, no. 1 (2008): 117–36.

———. "Psychoactive Substances and the English Language: Drugs, Discourses, and Public Policy." *Contemporary Drug Problems* 39, no. 3 (2012): 461–92.

Vásquez, Edith M. "La Gloriosa Travesura de la Musa Que Cruza/The

Misbehaving Glory(a) of the Border-Crossing Muse: Transgression in Anzaldúa's Children's Stories." In *EntreMundos/Among Worlds, New Perspectives on Gloria Anzaldúa,* edited by AnaLouise Keating. New York: Palgrave Macmillan, 2005.

Vaughan-Lee, Llewellyn. *The Return of the Feminine & the World Soul: A Collection of Writings and Transcribed Talks.* Inverness, Calif.: Golden Sufi Center, 2013.

Versnel, Henk S. "The Roman Festival for Bona Dea and the Greek Thesmophoria." In *Inconsistencies in Greek and Roman Religion,* vol. 2, *Transition and Reversal in Myth and Ritual,* 229–88. Leiden, the Netherlands: Brill, 1993.

Vulliamy, Ed. "Ciudad Juarez Is All Our Futures. This Is the Inevitable War of Capitalism Gone Mad." *Guardian.* June 20, 2011.

Walker, Nick. "Neurodiversity: Some Basic Terms & Definitions." Neurocosmopolitanism website. September 27, 2014.

Walsh, Charlotte. "Drugs and Human Rights: Private Palliatives, Sacramental Freedoms and Cognitive Liberty." *The International Journal of Human Rights* 14, no. 3 (2010): 425–41.

———. "Psychedelics and Cognitive Liberty: Reimagining Drug Policy through the Prism of Human Rights." *International Journal of Drug Policy* 29 (2016): 80–87.

Walsh, Roger. *The World of Shamanism: New Views of an Ancient Tradition.* Woodbury, Minn.; Llewellyn Worldwide, 2007.

Wasson, R. Gordon. "The Miskwedo of the Ahnishinaubeg." *Entheos: The Journal of Psychedelic Spirituality* 1, no. 2 (2001): 3–12.

Wasson, R. Gordon, Albert Hofmann, and Carl A. P. Ruck. *The Road to Eleusis: Unveiling the Secret of the Mysteries.* New York: Harcourt Brace Jovanovich, 1978.

Wasson, R. Gordon, Stella Kramrisch, Jonathan Ott, and Carl A. P. Ruck, *Persephone's Quest: Entheogens and the Origins of Religion.* New Haven, Conn.: Yale University Press, 1992.

Weber, Max. *The Sociology of Religion.* Boston: Beacon Press, 1993.

Webster, Peter, Daniel M. Perrine, and Carl A. P. Ruck. "Mixing the Kykeon." *Eleusis: Journal of Psychoactive Plants and Compounds.* New Series 4 (2000): 55–86.

Weil, Andrew. *The Natural Mind: An Investigation of Drugs and the Higher Consciousness.* Boston: Houghton Mifflin, 1998.

Whisman, Vera. *Queer by Choice: Lesbians, Gay Men, and the Politics of Identity.* Abingdon, U.K.: Routledge, 2012.

Whitman, Walt. *Leaves of Grass.* New York: Bantam Classics, 1997.

Wieland, Christina. *The Undead Mother: Psychoanalytic Explorations of Masculinity, Femininity and Matricide.* London: Karnac, 2002.

Williams, Mike. *The Shaman's Spirit, Discovering the Wisdom of Nature, Power Animals, Sacred Places and Rituals.* London: Watkins Publishing Limited, 2013.

Wilmer, Dona. "Reinhabiting the Divine Feminine." *Ayahuasca Association.* Accessed January 14, 2017.

Winbladh, Marie-Louise. *The Bearded Goddess: Androgynes, Goddesses, and Monsters in Ancient Cyprus.* Nicosia, Cyprus: Armida Publications, 2012.

Women's Visionary Council website. "Home/Who We Are." Accessed November 12, 2018.

Woodman, Marion, and Elinor Dickson. *Dancing in the Flames: The Dark Goddess in the Transformation of Consciousness.* Boston: Shambhala, 1997.

Woodward, Lynne. "Zoe Helen on Cosmic Sister, Psychedelics, and Feminism." *UTNE Reader.* June 4, 2015.

Zyga, Lisa. "Quantum Mysticism: Gone but Not Forgotten." Phys.Org website. June 8, 2009.

# Index

Page numbers in *italics* preceded by *pl.* indicate color insert plate numbers.